S0-ADN-314

Stewardshift

Stewardshift

An *Economia* for Congregational Change

Bob Sitze

Morehouse Publishing
NEW YORK

Copyright © 2016 by Bob Sitze

All rights reserved. No part of this book may be reproduced, stored in a retrieval system, or transmitted in any form or by any means, electronic or mechanical, including photocopying, recording, or otherwise, without the written permission of the publisher.

Unless otherwise noted, the Scripture quotations contained herein are from the New Revised Standard Version Bible, copyright © 1989 by the Division of Christian Education of the National Council of Churches of Christ in the U.S.A. Used by permission. All rights reserved.

Scripture quotations marked (CEV) are from the Contemporary English Version Copyright © 1991, 1992, 1995 by American Bible Society, Used by Permission.

Scripture quotations marked (KJV) are from The Authorized (King James) Version. Rights in the Authorized Version in the United Kingdom are vested in the Crown. Reproduced by permission of the Crown's patentee, Cambridge University Press.

Morehouse Publishing, 19 East 34th Street, New York, NY 10016

Morehouse Publishing is an imprint of Church Publishing Incorporated.

www.churchpublishing.org

Cover design by Jennifer Kopec / 2 Pug Design

Typeset by Rose Design

Library of Congress Cataloging-in-Publication Data

Sitze, Bob.
Stewardshift : an economia for congregational change / Bob Sitze.
  pages cm
Includes bibliographical references.
 ISBN 978-0-8192-3191-8 (pbk.)—ISBN 978-0-8192-3192-5 (ebook) 1. Christian stewardship. 2. Christian giving. I. Title.
BV772.S58 2016
248'.6—dc23
            2015030332

Printed in the United States of America

*To Betty Nyhus (+), whose cherished mentoring first compelled
me to seek the inner core and power of stewardship.
(Her legacy continues—the work is not yet done.)*

Contents

Preface

I 've had this book in mind probably since I was a teenager. Not its writing or its outcomes, but its content, "stewardship." My parents taught me well in matters of gratitude, generosity, simple living, environmental care, and charity. From their example, I learned about tithing and love of the natural world. From their congregational leadership, I learned about the intricacies of church life, including their understanding of the ministry of pastors. I chose a church vocation because of my parents' stewardship of stewardship.

When I started my career as a parochial day school teacher, though, I first encountered what seemed to be inconsistencies, or at least weaknesses, in some of the practices and doctrines around "stewardship." (I remember wondering out loud in a budget meeting why my salary and benefits were transparent to congregation members but their salaries and budgets remained private, out of sight, none of the church's business!) I was uneasy with the interpretations of stewardship texts that just didn't make sense to me.[1]

I got the feeling that stewardship theology and practice had been cemented in place over the centuries, best not questioned or tinkered with.

Early in my work as a freelance curriculum writer, I was asked to write a Sunday school course for sixth graders on the care of creation. As part of my research, I spent a day with staff members of the Sierra Club. What emerged from that series of conversations was the overwhelming realization that these "secular" folks had for decades been using stewardship precepts as the philosophical underpinnings of their work! They understood the varied dimensions of stewardship attitudes, behaviors, and identities without relying on scriptural proofs. And they were pushing at the boundaries of stewardship wisdom. (For example, long before neurobiologists zeroed in on the fact, Sierra Club folks were already aware that fear of death—and by extension, growing older—likely drives the economic and environmental cancer of materialism.[2])

As I grew into the later stages of my career—denominational executive, resource producer, leadership consultant—I began to see that much of the church's practice and philosophy of stewardship seemed to be bound into tight, formulaic constructs and time-honored—perhaps even time-worn?—language. The same Scripture verses and stories appeared over and over again, the same conclusions drawn from their interpretation. The voices of other, possibly helpful passages seemed muted. I noticed how difficult it seemed to be, almost universally, for church leaders to find enthusiasm for stewardship ministries—locked into "annual pledge drives" and "time/talent/treasure" verbiage. As I looked closer, a nagging possibility grew stronger: Something was missing, something wasn't working. Denominational and congregational leaders seemed to be pushing uphill an ecclesiastical stone that was vaguely disturbing or perhaps even dangerous. And their hard work didn't seem to move that metaphorical load very far uphill.

When I began working in stewardship ministries in the national offices of my home denomination, my colleagues and I explored an essential question: How could stewardship ministry in congregations become vital, exciting, and energizing? We read widely and listened carefully to leading scholars and thinkers, encountering new strands of thought about Scripture, philanthropy, and generosity. We delved into research findings, and we tried to reframe our approaches to congregations—new methods, new language—so that they matched with realities in the pews and on the ground. We went about our stewardship leadership with emotional and intellectual honesty. We could sense a shift in the ways our denomination was beginning to approach stewardship. It felt like we—and stewardship leaders in other denominations—were onto something new; stewardship could draw together the disparate elements of congregational life into realistic, reliable, and effective practices and identities.

The ecclesiastical history of the ensuing years proved us overly optimistic. With the onset of an all-encompassing "discipleship" theology and practice in Protestant Christianity, stewardship seemed to lose its strength as a primary organizing principle for congregational life. Its precepts and practices were subsumed into "marks of discipleship" and other newly minted themes and programs. Even though newer forms of stewardship theology and practice held their ground, it was apparent that stewardship was a subset of discipleship and not the other way around. Discipleship became the preeminent organizing principle underlying mature faith and congregational vitality.

One final note about the personal history that underlies the writing of this book: Early in my career, convinced that I didn't have competence in matters of daily life Christianity, I dropped out of professional church work for a period of time. During those years I worked in the world outside of church culture, living out this newfound conviction about God's way of getting work done: In their homes, relationships, and vocations, the people of God labor to bring God's will to bear on the world. The church's role is to gather the people in, equip them, and send them out.

By the time I came back to professional church work, I had also learned one other important lesson: God's people probably know more about stewardship than church leaders assume. Those of us who claim to teach lay-people about stewardship-related matters—generosity, money management, care of creation—might admit how little we know about God's revelation outside of Scripture and humble ourselves to learn about stewardship wisdom from our supposed students.

My life journey has brought me to this book: a conversation that I hope brings you a fresh look at stewardship wisdom in the Scriptures and in the world outside the church. Why do this? For the good of congregations and the ultimate goal we share: to fulfill God's holy will for the world God loves so dearly.

This book is about "shifts" that might be important for stewardship theology as it's taught and practiced in congregations. If you're a stewardship professional, it might seem like I'm raining on your parade. I get that. But I also understand what Anne Lamott says in *Help, Thanks, Wow* (her delightful witness about her experience of prayer): "If you want to know only what you already know, you're dying."[3]

Let me be direct: It feels to me that stewardship ministry in congregations is stuck in neutral, perhaps most noticeably among younger generations or newer Christians. And it's becoming more and more obvious that, out there in the world outside the church, stewardship-related wisdom and enterprises are growing in number and influence.

Whether you're a stewardship professional or a congregational leader trying to make sense of the rapid changes in church life, you probably can't afford only to keep trying harder to persuade others about what you already know. The time may be coming when your congregation or your denomination devolves into the kind of desperation (about money and members) that will keep you from thinking and acting with clarity, focus, and hope. This anxiety, when it's left to grow or fester, produces opposite states of mind that can paralyze you into fighting, fleeing, or freezing—not especially fruitful frameworks for ministry.

I believe that the shifts proposed here—looking at Scripture with fresh eyes and finding actionable wisdom among secular stewardship-related enterprises—will enliven congregations. Deep love for the church, decades of participation and leadership in lively congregations, and hope for the continuing renewal of the church—these undergird all the "shifting" language and invitations in this book. I'm welcoming you into a different way of looking at this conceptual and practical pillar of the sanctified life. (Remember that wonderful definition of stewardship that says it all? "Stewardship is everything you do after you say 'I believe.'")

I'm writing this book after about a decade of focused research. Reading, interviewing, attending seminars, observing, and asking questions, inside and outside the church. I've collected together what I've learned so that you can put into practice what you read here. I'll be operating on hunches as well, sharing my intuition based on experiences with congregations and their leaders over several decades. Still, I could be wrong.[4]

I have sensed God's leading toward the writing of this book. I commend it to your reading so that your stewardship will be hopeful and joyful. Stewardship is always about joyful living, and so also is this book!

As Anne Lamott so aptly states:

> If I were going to begin practicing the presence of God for the first time today, it would help to begin by admitting the three most terrible truths of our existence: That we are so ruined, and so loved, and in charge of so little."[5]

May God's loving presence continue to guide your stewardship ministry!

Notes

1. Some of the interpretations of Jesus's parable about The Dishonest Manager (Luke 16) come to mind here, especially those that overlook the role of this specific kind of steward within Jesus's economic context. For one interpretation that rings true, see William Herzog's *Parables as Subversive Speech: Jesus as Pedagogue of the Oppressed* (Louisville, KY: Westminster/John Knox Press, 1994), chapter 13.

2. For a thorough treatment of this and other connected subjects—mortality salience, terror management, self-esteem, and acquisitiveness—see chapter 8, "Lethal Consumption: Death-Denying Materialism," by Sheldon Solomon, Jeff Greenberg, and Thomas A. Pysczynski in *Psychology and Consumer Culture: The Struggle for a Good Life in a Materialistic World*, ed. Tim Kasser and Allen D. Kanner (Washington, DC: American Psychological Association, 2004).

3. Anne Lamott, *Help, Thanks, Wow* (New York: Riverhead Books, 2012), 86.

4. Prefacing his book's wide-ranging explanation of the functions of the human brain, experimental neurobiologist V. S. Ramachandran defends hunch-following as part of the necessary foundation for all of scientific inquiry. V.S. Ramachandran, *The Tell-Tale Brain: A Neuroscientist's Quest for What Makes Us Human* (New York: W.W. Norton, 2011), xvii .

5. Lamott, *Help, Thanks, Wow*, 27.

First Things First: Introduction

Before you and I get into the heart of this book, I'd like to spread a little ink on some introductory matters—things that might be important foundations for what follows. Each of the subjects in this chapter will help you understand better what I'm proposing in the remainder of the book. Taken together, these ideas will help draw you into the spirit behind my writing and the benefits I hope you can derive from your reading.

Summarizing Stewardship

The term "stewardship" is like a really good sponge: It absorbs a lot of meaning wherever it's placed. For now, let's agree that this word—however defined, clarified, illustrated, or interpreted—has these characteristics:

- Stewardship is a set of beliefs. Your beliefs center on God, not yourself: God's nature, God's will, God's gifts, God's presence.
- Stewardship describes practices or behaviors. Your beliefs compel actions, reactions to God's gifts, and obedience to God's commands.
- Stewardship becomes an identity. Over time, your actions become habits which, in turn, layer themselves over the core of your being: a servant of God.

When you come to the point of integrating beliefs, actions, and identity into your sense of self, "stewardship" describes a way of life that is satisfying and joyful. In the chapters that follow, I invite you to consider the underlying hypothesis that motivates my writing: More than any other current stream of ecclesiological thought, stewardship theology and practice have a strong possibility of rejuvenating the faith lives of believers and the congregations they form.

Stewardshifting Continues

The basic qualities of stewardship have been part of spiritual and economic thought for eons. The shape of stewardship, though, shifted during the past two millennia.

This New Testament biblical concept originated in a first-century BCE Greek economic role—the *economos* (manager) who carried out the *economia* (plan) of a frequently absent estate-owner. Paul adapted that idea into a description of God's dominion, and the Christ-like life.[1]

As the Church melded into civic society, the biblical concept of stewardship receded into the background for several centuries. Its secular form reemerged in the Middle Ages within an Anglo-Saxon etymology—the *stigwaerden* whose castle-responsibilities were more humble and earthy. Biblical stewardship once again gained meaning and usefulness by the middle of the nineteenth century, when the practical applications of stewardship theology found new utility within the fervor of the Church's missionary zeal.

Describing "Shifts"

This is a book that describes possible shifts—gentle movements that form the basis for something new in the theology and practice of stewardship. Shifting implies both voluntary, purposed endeavors (redefining a theological term) and involuntary movements (the trembling of an earthquake). Depending on circumstances and context, you could be both a shifter and the one who is shifted. You might participate in the shifting—actively or passively—or choose somehow to avoid the entire process or outcomes. The end results of any shifting are perceptible changes, whatever their scale or scope.[2]

The objects or locations of a shifting can be large or small—the safety of passenger ships in the North Atlantic or the arrangement of chairs on the deck of the Titanic. Shifting can take place suddenly or over eons—topographic changes caused by cloudbursts or those produced by the gradual upswelling of tectonic plates.

Small shifts occurring at the right point in time and space can trigger ripples of change, in what neuroscientist V. S. Ramachandran calls "phase transitions"—points in any system where a single shift brings about immediate, measurable change. Phase transitions occur in social systems (such as the Church), economics, and politics.[3]

For example, consider how the movement of a single stone on just the right slope at the optimum time of day can precipitate the collapse of an entire hillside in a landslide. Seemingly small changes in thought—sometimes called "paradigm shifts"—can signal the development of new products, relationships, or outcomes.

In this book, you'll encounter several variations of "shifting." In some cases, shifting will refer to a changed position, way of thinking, or viewpoint about stewardship, resulting in the possible displacement of one pattern of thought by another. This kind of shifting could imply a need for continuing change over time.

Shifting can also refer to the kind of back-and-forth movement that results in a more settled, secure, or comfortable position. Think how shifting your posture while seated in a chair helps you take advantage of the relationship you and that chair have established! Or consider how a bird will settle deeper into her nest, adjusting her weight and vantage point to keep her eggs warm and her safety assured. That variety of shifting may not yield anything new. A change in your position, thought, or action may not result in condemnation of the old in favor of the new. Instead, you might gain perspective about stewardship theology and practices you've held for a long time. As a result of your reading of this book, you might become even more assured about your views. A stewardshift will still take place!

Why not use *reformation*, *revolution*, *modernization*, *transformation*, or more impressive descriptions of wholesale change? These words describe disruptions of an entire landscape of behavior and thought. Those kinds of shifts are sometimes valued because they're large-scale, drastic, cleansing, and quick—even though they're sometimes violent. In that mindset, present frameworks of thought are presumed inadequate at best and problematic at worst, requiring their complete elimination.

These kinds of upheaval have dotted the history of the Church—and may still be occurring in some places. But the bombast that can accompany directives for top-to-bottom change can also create negative reactions and other unintended consequences. Throughout these chapters, I'm opting instead for a quieter, more manageable and sustainable approach to change. This seems to me to be a more useful methodology for invigorating congregations.

This Book in Three Paragraphs

1. *Stewardshift* offers theoretical, practical, and perhaps radical propositions that might help you ensure the vitality of your stewardship ministries. The book suggests two major shifts in thinking and practice:

2. A reexamination of traditional scriptural bases for stewardship theology and practice—using more accurate interpretations of familiar passages and relevant Scriptures that might have been overlooked.

3. Exposition of extensive extrascriptural (secular) stewardship wisdom, as it is practiced outside of ecclesiological settings, with an eye to their possible benefits for congregational stewardship ministries.

Why Does This Matter?

In my estimation, the stewardship theology and practice that has resided in the church over the past two hundred years is not going to last much longer. Four reasons come to mind:

- The Scriptures' original focus on stewardship has been narrowed to only a few categories.
- After all these decades of emphasis, those understandings still don't seem to captivate the imagination of God's people or compel their lifestyle decisions.
- In many places throughout the Church, leaders are unaware of secular stewardship wisdom. This contrasts remarkably with the broad-based understandings of congregation members, who encounter stewardship in many forms and many places in their daily lives.
- The generation(s) for whom time-honored stewardship theology was useful will soon be supplanted by younger age cohorts—who work with secular understandings of stewardship every day.

To put this bluntly: As it presently stands, the subject of biblical stewardship may become as arcane—or out-of-touch—as any biblical interpretation that denies the findings of contemporary wisdom or science. The Church cannot maintain its relevance or vitality in the face of diminished attention.

On the other hand, a theology that shifts—deeper into Scripture and the secular world—can offer God's people the broadest possibilities for purposed living. Just as the original *economos* found meaning in a variety of roles, so can God's people today respond to God's calling in the variety of their roles, both inside and outside the institutional Church. As it proclaims a richer body of wisdom about life, the Church will remain central to people's lives of faith. Equipped by their congregations to live out their part of God's plan, Christians will hold dear these gatherings for worship and service. And they will see to it that their congregations are supported financially. The church will grow stronger as an institution that's valuable to its constituents.

Then What?

When stewardship is more broadly and deeply understood and practiced in your congregation, it might:

- Provide you a tangible, well-known conceptual basis for restructuring or repurposing your congregation.

- Integrate the revealed stewardship wisdom of Scripture with Spirit-led stewardship revelations in contemporary culture.
- Gather congregation members around their already known and valued affinities, expertise, or areas of interest.
- Provide more avenues for involving members in the life of your congregation, because their secular knowledge and skills are honored and put to use. Members' vocations might serve as a focus for congregational programs.
- Provoke rigorous discovery and discussion about the place of Scripture in a life of stewardship.
- Encourage imagination about newer forms and styles of missional identity.
- Strengthen the foundations for writing case statements—concise presentations about the effect of members' financial contributions on the congregation's ministries.

Why Now?

This may be an especially good time to rethink stewardship ministry in congregations. Considering some of the ongoing metrics of congregational ill-health, that statement may seem counterintuitive or even Pollyannish, but it holds the nugget of an ongoing truth: Just as God's Spirit first moved over the formless void of a universe yet to be fully created, so can the Spirit work today. That work could take advantage of these convergences:

- The continuing importance of stewardship in the secular world brings increased attention to its application in the Church.
- People in our culture, sensing the gradual dismantling of their lives, want something to hang onto. "You're God's stewards" could fill that need.
- Our previous approaches to stewardship seem ready for a fresh look.

It's probably arrogant to think of ourselves or our times as unique in all of human history—social and media critic Eugeny Morozov calls this historical amnesia "epochalism." He further skewers this faulty mindset as "rupture talk," a frame of mind in which we think of our times and our actions as a complete break from the path of history, as though we live at the dawning of a completely new era.[4]

A better approach? To admit our difficulties, humbly releasing ourselves into the grasp of God's power to change and renew the Church once again.

Anosognosia Writ Large

Humbly admitting difficulties might be tough for any of us. Neurobiology provides an analogy that might be helpful. One of the more fascinating brain dysfunctions discovered by neuroscientists is a condition called *anosognosia*. Most readily observed in situations where limb function is impaired or missing, the condition might also play a part in other neurobiological disabilities. Those who live with this deficit of self-awareness are unaware of their disabilities. In an attempt to match their supposed well-being to what is clinically observable, these individuals deny outright any possibility of a problem. When presented with the facts, they rationalize, confabulate, and repress what is obvious to others. And even if they admit to those facts, they deny having negative emotions about their incapacity or infirmity.[5]

It seems possible that organizations—collections of brains—can also refuse to admit disabilities or dysfunctions readily apparent to any objective observer. And yes, churches might also suffer from an ecclesiastical form of anosognosia. (For example, no matter how dour their faces or how inattentive they are to visitors, most congregations rate themselves as "friendly and welcoming.")

I bring up this matter here because the end results of this syndrome probably don't bode well for churches that persist in institutional denial. Papering over difficulties might seem like a way to restore harmony or to retain a good self-concept, but objective truth eventually catches up with us.

In the Church's historical attempts to make stewardship a lively and attractive way of thinking, we may have skipped over or diluted some important truths, perhaps disregarding what isn't working all that well. Our intentions may have been good—to invite people into generosity toward the Church. But the end result of our self-delusions about dysfunctional stewardship could be an invisible erosion of stewardship's relevance to daily life.

Even though anosognosia may be prevalent, don't approach your congregation as though it is only a collection of truth-deniers! The more important—and restorative—part of your congregation's self-image is grateful honesty about its capabilities, assets (useful gifts), proven strengths, and values. Because of needs-based planning processes, you might be more highly aware of your incapacities than your assets. To keep you from falling into "ain't it awful" thinking, I've included several reminders in this book about "asset-based planning and thinking," a proven, pragmatic way to approach change.[6]

Stewardship Speaks Two Languages

It's important that stewardship theology and practice get communicated accurately and effectively. Depending on your experiences in life, you may have noticed that the language of the Church is not always the language of daily life. The Scriptures certainly reflect down-to-earth matters—especially as expressed in newer translations and paraphrases. But sometimes that gritty style of communication has gotten lost in the centuries-old interpretations and teachings of the Church.

Because of stewardship's secular roots, the linguistic conventions of stewardship theology and practice should logically correspond to the realities that God's people find throughout their lives. But somewhere along the path of its etymology, the original language of stewardship was coopted by the language of the Church. This may have contributed to the difference between the Church's use of "stewardship" language and that term's use in the world outside of the Church. That variance may add to the tension congregation members feel as they try to place the Church's teachings about stewardship inside their experience in other areas of life.

Those of us who are stewardship leaders in the Church face a dilemma: Do we attempt to speak about stewardship in purely ecclesiastical language, or do we incorporate secular vocabularies—and the concepts they carry—into the life of the Church? The dichotomy may be false, but in too many places the tension between the Church's use of stewardship language and that of the secular world may be perpetually weighted toward only ecclesiastical formulations. We may even operate as though congregation members did not know or value another stewardship vocabulary.

Although these two languages of stewardship are complementary, each requires some interpretation or translation in order to be fully useful. Thus it stands to reason that stewardship leaders can communicate more effectively when they are conversant in both spiritual and secular stewardship vocabularies.

A Linguistic Example

Let me illustrate this two-language idea by examining how we may depend on metaphors to carry the freight of spiritual thinking, including stewardship. Metaphors are extremely valuable in matters of faith. The Scriptures are full of rich metaphors, similes, and analogies. (The words of the prophets and psalmists, and Jesus's parables are prime examples.) Why this form of communication? The depth of spiritual truths probably outruns the capacities of our brains to find words. Metaphors fill that gap, even though ineffability continues to accompany our encounters with God.

Extensive use of metaphors may also create a problem. Whether in matters of faith or other areas of human endeavor, metaphor-enriched language is among the most neurobiologically complex forms of discourse. This means that our metaphor-rich spiritual conversations—including stewardship theology—may require forms of communication that are difficult for many people! So it's possible that members not adept at constructing or using metaphoric language in their daily lives may feel somewhat ill-at-ease or put-off when it seems that sacred truths are couched mostly in metaphors. In my thinking, this situation calls for a shift away from resorting on metaphor-saturated language as we attempt to invite God's people into a life of stewardship. We can employ fewer metaphors that are unique to church-based situations. We can adapt the stewardship-related language in the secular world for our uses.[7]

Changing the Questions

Let's look at another communications-related matter: the quality of our questions. A familiar communications axiom goes something like this, "Change the questions and you get different answers." What lies behind the statement is the invitation to reframe, refocus, or reorder communications. Questions provide an immediate structure for a conversation or other discourse. They engage a variety of brain processes, functions, and structures—e.g., emotion, memory, motivation, or imagination. Questions also gently nudge aside other thoughts as your brain attends more closely to the necessity of responding. Without the framing function of questions, much of human discourse would be a jumble of statements whose order or flow would be indiscernible.

Questions comprise a core expertise in many professions. For example, the work of philosophers rests on the construction and deployment of chains of connected questions. Therapists, counselors, financial advisors, and medical personnel begin their visits with carefully selected probes.[8]

Theology could also be considered as the collected history of answers to life's deepest questions. In their foundational work on the neurobiology of religion, University of Pennsylvania professors Andrew Newberg, Vince Rause and Eugene d'Aquili note that "the deepest origins of religion are based in mystical experience" as well as the embedded questions that follow.[9]

As a body of knowledge and practice that encompasses much of human agency, biblical and secular stewardship also rests on life-connected questions—and workable answers. Some examples: The returning owner in Jesus's parables asks "Can you give an account of what you've done while I've been gone?" Natural historians probe the problem, "How can the environment continue to sustain itself in the light of human activity?" Financial planners form their client relationships with a process of inquiry that begins with "What are the most important goals for your life?"

Single-minded pursuit of answers is one way to approach questions about life's mysteries. But if the questions remain the same, their answers will likely stay inside a small catalog of thought. New technologies arise from "Aha!" moments made possible by imaginative questions. "What if?" lies at the heart of most of these inquiries. Most fortunately for continuing human endeavor, answers to new questions seem to breed more questions.

Where am I going with this? Any shifting of stewardship also requires new questions. This approach is both more honest—who among us really has *all* the answers?—and more interesting. So, instead of asking only "Why don't more church members tithe?" we might also wonder, "What already practiced forms of generosity in today's world resemble the tithe?" Alongside questions about greed and selfishness, we might ask about the strength of virtues like gratitude and generosity. And we might start all explorations of Scripture with the necessary question, "What did the first hearers or readers of these words think they meant?"

Getting Personal about You

I suspect that by your reading of this book you're acknowledging your hope for a more viable stewardship ministry in your congregation. (Maybe in the rest of your life, too?) It may also be true that you harbor some questions about your failure as a stewardship leader (e.g., contributions lagging behind expenses, pledge drives coming up short, the stewardship committee attracting few willing leaders). Your positive witness as a leader depends on your emotional well-being, so your real or imagined "failure" is perhaps not as important as the development of your skills, knowledge, and wisdom regarding stewardship.[10]

Expertise

One antidote to failure-thinking is to develop expertise. David Ward, associate dean at the School of Theology and Ministry, Indiana Wesleyan University, names "expertise" as a key factor in the flourishing of pastors. Ward is quick to note that this cherished quality in ministry takes time to develop, and that depth is an important ingredient of expertise. He uses the analogy, "You become a reservoir, not a pipe" to describe the gradual and deepening process of turning repeated execution of skills into expertise. (The reservoir holds years of experience and insight; the pipe merely passes along only what it receives.) Resolute determination to persevere may not be as important for your growing expertise as seeking energizing experiences that increase your understanding and wisdom over time.

Another key factor in developing expertise: the "chunking" of skills and knowledge into identifiable blocks of practical wisdom that can fill that reservoir to its depths. When your expertise is reasonably deep, you can sidestep knee-jerk reactivity when new conditions require answers. Instead, your brain can more easily recall and put into practice the experiences that you have aggregated and refined. Here Ward draws on his understanding of learning theory and applied brain science: When you gather practiced skills into larger constructs, your brain can more easily store the information for later retrieval and application. As your skills and knowledge grow over time, the chunks integrate with each other into the "depth" Ward describes. Your reservoir holds useful wisdom![11]

Knowing the People You Serve

Another important anchor for your stewardship leadership: respecting the people of your congregation. Increasingly, they do not behave like the "sheep" that Scripture seems to extol as ideal believers. "Shepherd and sheep" metaphors of the Bible don't seem to square with our contemporary views of human agency, free will, and giftedness.

Because of their day-to-day stewardship-related interactions, many congregation members observe, understand, practice, or yearn for wiser leadership philosophies every day of the week. In their work relationships, they exhibit considerable personal power and expertise. They are not going to be satisfied with a congregation that only tells them what to do.[12]

The members of your congregations base their self-concepts on their roles or expertise in their daily vocations. Some are certainly caught up in workplace webs of dysfunction that rob their spirit of energy; they may consider "work" as a difficult, even stressful matter. But many others prosper in their work lives, some returning to trades and vocations in which heart, hands, and mind combine to yield meaning. Among certain generational cohorts, there seems to be a resurgence of interest in the manual trades. Given the stresses that seem to be embedded in other occupational settings, this trend will likely continue.[13]

How do you exercise your stewardship leadership in a world in which expertise is more widely distributed? Continue to refine your skills in collaborative decision-making and your reliance on asset-based planning. Without giving up your own expertise—scriptural stewardship wisdom that has stood the test of time over centuries—you can maintain your posture as a willing and appreciative learner. You can coach, and you can be coached. You can also shift.

A Matter of Identity

"Identity" is a quick way to characterize all the worthy descriptions of your congregation and yourself. Carried alongside this term are concepts like self-image, sense of purpose, heritage, or personality. Your identity can make you unique, attention-worthy, approachable, or describable. Without those qualities, you or your congregation would be indistinguishable from the generic identity mush of our culture!

Christianity began with a unique identity. Separated soon enough from its Judaic roots, the first believers came together in communities of faith that were radically different. Their actions diverged enough from the general culture to warrant societal disfavor and worse.

Because it stood apart from the general first-century culture, Christianity grew and prospered well before Constantine's edict made this "marginal Jesus movement" into the Western world's dominant religion. In *The Rise of Christianity: How the Obscure, Marginal Jesus Moment Became the Dominant Religious Force in the Western World in a Few Centuries*,[14] sociologist of religion Rodney Stark documents the numerical growth of Christianity through the early centuries. Despite the collapsing influence of secular Roman culture—or perhaps because of it—Christians stayed true to their beliefs and modeled the simplest virtues of the faith. For example, they cared for their sick (in spite of plagues) and did not practice infanticide. In Stark's opinion, the Church prospered first because of its deeds, which made its message believable.

It's critical that you are able to name your personal and congregational identity. Why? Without a distinctive persona, you and your congregation might fade into the woodwork of others' regard, and lose much of your ability to build the relationships that lie at the heart of mission. Lacking uniqueness, you could wallow in the muck of undefined, nonspecific ministries. You could be easily swayed by peer pressure, fads-of-the-month, and cultural currents that are not necessarily all that godly or good. With a distinctive identity firmly in place, you can marshal your unique assets to accomplish the mission to which you are called.

Your identity comes from what you do. When your collected actions or deeds are seen by others, they know who you are, and you're able to use in powerful ways whatever gifts God has provided you.[15]

The basic theses of this book could help you shift your identity in ways that will attract others' attention, interest, and regard. Complementing your core identity—stewards of God's mysteries—secular stewardship wisdom could provide you with additional qualities that help you bear witness to God's love and grace in Jesus Christ.

How to Approach Your Reading

You can extract the most meaning from this book if you complement its straightforward reading with other related activities. Consider these possibilities:

- Mark up this book. Underline or highlight noteworthy ideas, and scribble questions and connector thoughts in the margins. Your thoughts will improve mine!
- Carry the book into the settings of your daily vocation(s). During quiet moments, see how your daily life stewardship intersects with what you're reading.
- Talk with someone about what you read. Along the way or when you've finished your reading, share your discoveries—and disagreements!—with a colleague or friend. As you do so, you'll cement the content of this book into the parts of your brain that motivate you toward action.

Before You Start Reading

Let me restate the strong belief that compels my writing: More than any other current stream of ecclesiological thought, stewardship theology and practice have a strong possibility of rejuvenating the faith lives of believers and the congregations they form. My reasons for this belief are these:

1. Stewardship is already well-known and lived out in the vocations and relationships of congregation members, as well as in the general culture.
2. When their stewardship successes and struggles are validated by the church, members of all ages and levels of spiritual maturity will see their congregations as vital, relevant, and realistic—therefore worth their continuing financial and volunteer support.

3. Stewardship—in sacred/secular union—is implicitly hopeful and joyful, even beautiful! Joy and hope motivate more assuredly and continually than duty or truth alone.

4. Stewardship connects disparate elements of meaning and purpose, calling God's people toward a mature faith.

Perhaps you share my convictions?

Notes

1. In the original Greek, *oikonomia* and *oikonomos*. In this book I use the Latinate derivations simply because they are easier on the eye and brain, perhaps more easily pronounced and connected to the various uses of "economy" in English.

2. The term "shift" originated in Northern European usage—Old Norse, Old Frisian, Dutch, Swedish—as a way of describing the periods of time that successive parties of workmen spent in mines. Gradually the noun morphed into verbs describing the acts of dividing, separating, arranging, or ordering. Old English moved "shift" farther, toward the ideas of classifying and decision-making based on categories. Today, the synonyms of "shift" carry both noun and verb meanings. (The more negative connotations—"shiftless" or "shifty"—don't occur in common usage until the sixteenth century.)

3. V. S. Ramachadran, *The Tell-Tale Brain: A Neuroscientist's Quest for What Makes Us Human* (New York: W. W. Norton, 2011), 13.

4. Eugeny Morozov, *To Save Everything, Click Here: The Folly of Technological Solutionism* (New York: Public Affairs Books, 2013), 36, 44.

5. Ramachadran, *Tell-Tale Brain*, 264ff.

6. A full treatment of the philosophy and practice of this approach—including "asset-mapping"—can be found in Luther K. Snow's inviting and accessible *The Power of Asset-Mapping: How Your Congregation Can Act on Its Gifts* (Herndon, Virginia: The Alban Institute, 2004).

7. As an example, I found these expressions in a recent stewardship essay: first-fruits giving, a gift from God, money as a conduit of gifts, Divine Master, hallmark, body of Christ, and abundant life with God. Marty E. Stevens, "Stewardship: Biblical Perspectives," *The Lutheran Magazine*, September 2014, 14–15.

8. Therapist and brain-science author John Ratey suggests that fellow therapists base their explorations with patients on a new question, "How do you know that?" Replacing "How do you feel?" this more-productive line of inquiry is based on the practices of mindfulness and metacognition. John Ratey, *The User's Guide to the*

Brain: Perception, Attention and the Four Theaters of the Brain (New York: Vintage Books, 2002), 7–8.

9. See Andrew Newberg, Eugene d'Aquili, and Vince Rause, "The Origins of Religion," in *Why God Won't Go Away: Brain Science & the Biology of Belief* (New York: Ballatine Books, 2001).

10. J. R. Briggs, author of *Fail: Finding Hope and Grace in the Midst of Ministry Failure* (Downer's Grove, IL: InterVarsity Press, 2014), notes that faulty notions of "success" can be a major factor in supposed failures, and transparent, listening conversations especially helpful. One encouraging habit among pastors who pull through these times: developing significant relationships with non-Christians. "Pulpit Disappointment: Interview with J.R. Riggs," *Christianity Today*, July/August 2014, 87.

11. From "The Missing Ingredient in Clergy Wellness," a workshop presentation by Dr. David Ward at the September 2013 "Flourishing in Pastoral Ministry" Conference at Indiana Wesleyan University, Marion, IN.

12. Peter Block, *Stewardship: Choosing Service Over Self-Interest* (San Francisco: Berrett-Koehler, 1993), 17–18.

13. For a thoughtful and encouraging treatment of this matter among young adult males, see "The Work of Their Hands" by Jeff Haanen and Chris Horst, in *Christianity Today*, July/August 2014, 66–71.

14. Rodney Stark, *The Rise of Christianity: How the Obscure, Marginal Jesus Moment Became the Dominant Religious Force in the Western World in a Few Centuries* (Princeton, NJ: Princeton University Press, 1996).

15. You can get a handle on your congregation's identity by completing this descriptive sentence fragment, "We're the folks who _____." Fill in the blank with verbs and descriptors that summarize the congregation's signature behaviors. (For example, "We're the folks who make friends easily" or "We're the folks who worship God quietly.") See what patterns emerge, and give your identity a name: What's unique about you, attention-worthy, surprising, or inspiring?

PART I

Scriptural Stewardshifts

Economia: A Short History of Stewardship Theology and Practice

Although there are only a few places where "steward" is used in the New Testament, the impact of these passages has lasted throughout the Church's history. The story of this concept's growth and development comprises the pages of this chapter.[1]

Depending on the translation, there are between eighteen and twenty-three instances in the New Testament where *economia* or *economos* appear. "Steward" can also be translated from a less frequent term, *epitropos*, whose meaning approximates *economos*. Leonard Sweet advocates that both terms be more accurately translated as "trustee," a term he believes is better understood by postmodern minds.[2]

The history of stewardship—an Anglo-Saxon approximation of the original Greek term *economia*—carries with it the notion that God's original and continuing providence runs through all of history. New Testament theologian John Reumann calls this "God's working towards a goal"—which includes, but is not limited to God's continuous line of redemption.[3]

Back to the Beginnings

No Hebrew words capture the Greek terms *economia* or *economos*. There is no exact equivalent for "stewardship" or "steward" in Hebrew. When it appears in the Septuagint, the concept is transliterated from the Greek into Hebrew letters.[4]

Still, some of the stewardship-related themes in the Old Testament connect to New Testament–era understandings of the term:

- God's directive to the first humans—essentially to care for the natural world—lies at the heart of psalms that extol the wonders of nature and the God who creates them.

- Isaiah compared God to an insistent gardener.[5]
- In economic matters, the prophets railed against unjust business practices.[6]
- The tithe was instituted to support the functions of the Old Testament Temple.[7]

In their faithful service to rulers, biblical heroes such as Joseph, Nehemiah, Daniel, and Esther may exemplify some of the characteristics of New Testament stewards, but in a limited way. Joseph comes the closest. He was in charge of Potiphar's entire household and later functioned in the same way while in prison. But when he assumed a steward-like role for the entire country of Egypt, he eventually foreclosed on landowners suffering during the seven years of famine, turning them into landless sharecroppers who were forced to give 20 percent of their crop earnings back to the Pharaoh (Gen. 47:13–26). Nehemiah was only a sometimes wine-steward for King Cyrus. Esther and Daniel behaved like stewards, but undertook their roles primarily within political spheres. Moses was a kind of steward, in the sense that he was constantly serving the will of God.

God's people before Christ lived through a catastrophic history. It was filled with unjust economic systems, captivities, oppressions, and occupations—at the hands of despotic rulers, Babylonians, Persians, the Hasmonean priest-kings, and finally the Romans. That continuous chaotic social order may have precluded the development of an enduring stewardship theology.

Jesus and Stewards

Jesus's view of stewards was shaped by his cultural context. In the decades before Jesus's birth, the ancient Greek role of steward had been corrupted by a socioeconomic system that was enforced by the iron fist of Roman rule. The near oppression of the Temple cult's taxation added to the weight of a dysfunctional economy.[8]

In first-century Palestine, "stewards" were middlemen who prospered in an unjust economic system. Exorbitant interest rates on agricultural loans benefited the wealthy elite, increasing their incomes and adding to their land holdings because of inevitable foreclosures. As agents of these injustices, stewards were despised by the people among whom Jesus ministered.

This is why the parables and other teachings of Jesus that deal with economic matters—for example, the Parable of the Talents in Matthew 25[9]—can be read more accurately as Jesus's exposure of the injustices perpetrated by the haves on the have-nots of his time. This may also be the major reason why "steward" appears only twice in Jesus's narratives, in both cases describing a negative role.[10]

It seems clear that Jesus disapproved of the role of a steward in his semi-monetized society—one harmful to illiterate farmers whose land was being stolen by the super rich. This context also helps explain Jesus's thoughts about money, economics, and even the Temple—all of them connected to a socio-political system that oppressed people who were poor.

Paul and Stewards

The overwhelming majority of our understanding about stewardship comes from Paul. Educated in Greco-Roman cultural traditions—and also schooled as a Pharisee—Paul was familiar with the understanding and practice of stewardship. He was likely to see the steward less as a despicable agent of oppression, and more as an admired functionary in the economic life of Roman society.[11]

He appropriated this secular role into a theological image that emphasized God's ownership of all that exists. He further developed this thought into something useful for understanding a life of faith. For example, Paul thought of himself as a steward "of the mysteries of God" (1 Cor. 4:1–2) and as a "servant" (or minister) of the *economia* of God (Col. 1:25). He understood the matter of trustworthiness in the life of stewards (1 Cor. 4:2). He considered bishops or overseers as stewards (Titus 1:7).

An important side note before we proceed further: Taken together, the relatively small collection of New Testament references to stewards and stewardship does not warrant the consideration of stewardship as a major New Testament theme, not for the Gospel writers or for Paul. *Grace, covenant, love,* or *redemption* are examples of more strongly rooted doctrinal pillars that also extend back into the Old Testament.

The Economy of God

Paul's use of *economia* and *economos* rested on a foundation of long-standing economic, political, and religious constructs. A significant portion of first-century Christians would have been familiar with this knowledge and practice.[12]

At its root, *economia* started with the household (*oikos*), the essential core of economic life in Greco-Roman times. In Greek antiquity, small households and large estates were managed by rules that were carried out largely by a spouse or a trusted slave. In that part of Paul's cultural context, *economia* was essentially the "art and science of household management."

The household could also include small businesses or enterprises. (Recall, for example, Paul's colleagues, Lydia and Priscilla and Aquilla.) By extension, the city/state (*polis*) could benefit from an "economy"—a way of managing larger-scale matters. Thus the term could also apply to the work of military leaders and administrators in civil society. *Economia* also described administrative matters within cults and temples.[13]

In an even broader use of the term, *economia* also referred to the order of things—more literally, "arrangements"—in matters as diverse as writing, history, oration, ethics, architecture, or even one's last will and testament. For example, at the beginning of his Gospel, Luke proposes "an orderly account" of Jesus's life (Luke 1:3). It was a logical extension of these uses of the term to think of the entire universe as being organized, most likely by the gods. It made sense to early Greek philosophers that the order of the natural world was a sign of the original and continuing creation, ordering, and management of the gods. That's why the Stoics thought of Zeus as administrator of the universe.[14]

This train of thought led early Christian writers to think of *economia* in its broadest sense—as it applied to God's ordering, God's will, or God's plan to reconcile the world to God's self. Thus the concept of "God's economy" was derived.

In this book, "God's will" embodies the larger and more encompassing understandings of *economia*, centering on God's desire to save the world through Jesus Christ. In other manifestations, "God's will" can also be seen in Scripture and the creeds—God who creates, redeems, and sanctifies. Echoes of God's will can be seen in the Lord's Prayer. God works continually to combat evil. God's intention is to love and forgive unconditionally. God wants people to live peacefully, purposefully, patiently. This greater plan of God wraps the entire cosmos into continuing purposes and possibilities.

God's *economia* (plan, ordering, arrangement) becomes the guiding principle by which God's people could know God and carry out God's will for the world. In this framework, God is considered as Owner, but also as "administrator" of all that exists.

Thus we can see that God's arrangements extend beyond mere "household rules." (That earlier translation of *economos* is derived from the mistaken notion that *oikos* referred only to a small household, where rules would perhaps be necessary for a spouse or slave.) Because of the term's broad use in the secular world of the New Testament, we cannot confine *economia*—and by derivation, *economos*—to this simple meaning.

The Anglo-Saxon Gloss

The history of stewardship thought and practice did not proceed to our times directly from Greco-Roman or early Christian understandings. Along the way were centuries during which the entire concept was not considered that important. Larger ecclesiological and societal matters pressed for the attention of lay and clergy alike. (Plagues, empire-building, crusades, and enlightenments come to mind as examples.) Mechanisms for funding the Church's ministries were intertwined with the complex relationships between Church and state.

Even the Renaissance's dawning did not reveal any great need or opportunity for Church leaders to take hold of stewardship as an important feature of ecclesiastical life. Never rising to the status of key doctrine or creedal linchpin, stewardship lay dormant in the Church for centuries.[15]

Lest you forget the premise of this book, *economia* still maintained relative importance—or at least interest—in the secular world of Western societies. The underlying fundamentals of stewardship—the ordering and management of civil and economic affairs—remained important to rulers, merchants, and other societal leaders.

During the Middle Ages, *economia* was transplanted into the orderly maintenance and governance of European castle life. As early as the thirteenth century, the term *stigwaerden* appeared in Anglo-Saxon references. Gradually morphing toward its present linguistic form, the stigwaerden became the *stywarden*. The work of this individual was named by his title: warden or keeper of the sty, which was the repository of the ruler's meat supply.

Over time, faithful stywardens were invited to tend to matters in the Great Hall—where management of the castle and its holdings took place. Now "stewards," these individuals became critical components of the economic and (later) political well-being of the castle.

It made sense, then, for the translators of the King James Version to render *economos* as *steward*. Both individuals dealt with the affairs of a larger economic unit. Both were originally of low estate—slave and peasant. Both shouldered responsibilities when owners or rulers were absent. Both carried out their duties within the general framework of the larger plan or wishes of the owner or ruler. And both were highly regarded because of their trustworthiness.

The shift from *economos/economia* to *steward/stewardship* now took on a distinctly Anglo-Saxon character. The subsequent assimilation of "stewardship" into English paved the way for stewardship to undergird the funding of

Church enterprises, especially global missions. Thus, a linguistic gloss took on presumed substance.

A More Recent History

Stewardship came out of hiding in nineteenth-century North America, when two important ecclesiastical matters needed attention. First, the mechanisms for providing sustenance to an increasingly professional clergy were woefully inadequate. Secondly, the emerging passion for sending missionaries to "foreign lands" became a central feature of a stewardship great awakening that swept the United States.[16]

In their reading and study of Scripture, devout lay leaders found solace, encouragement, and strategies for addressing these funding problems. Looking for a term or ideal that could gather together biblical teachings, stories, and concepts in one place, they came upon "stewardship" as a suitable way to express their views about godly living. Some examples: In 1832, Congregational minister Leonard Bacon was preaching sermons about the "the right use of property on Christian principles." The Old School Presbyterians were advocating for "the use and management of talents, time and substance." Chicago businessman Thomas Kane "rediscovered the tithe," and by 1890 had published and distributed millions of pamphlets on tithing.[17]

It was at this juncture in history that stewardship emphases were narrowed. Ideals such as generosity, gratitude, abundance, and tithing became important touchstones for an emerging body of practice that supported stewardship primarily as mission-funding. The presence of these themes in Scripture seemed to warrant gathering them together into a stewardship theology.

Sometimes called "biblical stewardship principles," the majority of these concepts still concentrated on church funding and support. Waxing and waning during subsequent generations of thought, stewardship now became a revised standard version of the original concepts found in Scripture and secular society.

In more recent church history, some theologians and stewardship leaders have attempted to retain the larger scope and meaning of original stewardship theology. Matters such as creation care, parenting, simple living, social justice, supportive relationships, and life purpose are now included in the conversation. The work of Ron Vallet, Robert Wuthnow, Douglas John Hall, Leonard Sweet, Gary Moore, Walter Brueggeman, and Tony Campolo come to mind.

Limiting Side Effects

The outcomes of the gradual shift toward a concentrated, targeted focus for stewardship—the financial sustainability of the Church as locus of ministry—were positive. The reach of religious enterprises into the world would never have happened without this effort. For example, think of hospitals, social service agencies, or relief and development organizations. Congregations and denominations—and their related enterprises—grew and prospered, sustained by the generous financial support of committed members. Another enduring result: For decades, church members have consistently ranked as the most generous donors across all forms of philanthropic giving.

But this contraction of the original concepts may have created unintended consequences as well. Conflating the biblical witness about stewardship with fund-raising may have prohibited the development of a livelier and more realistic concept of the steward's role. When confined only to "giver," the image of the biblical steward might discount other important tasks and functions. In the role of carrying out an absent owner's plan (*economia*), stewards may also have found it necessary to take, receive, plan, borrow, sell, save, reuse, invest, repair, manufacture, or collect. They might have sown, harvested, and learned efficiency, effectiveness, humility, and honesty. Stewards would have been accountable and even shrewd in their dealings. They would need to be wise and careful decision-makers. That's why, when you limit stewardship only to "giving," you may be casting aside other worthwhile activities that could add to your personal and congregational mission.

Other possible side effects ripple out from a narrowed scope of stewardship.

The broader biblical witness for stewardship might have gotten lost. Other scriptural wisdom about God's *economia* could be overlooked. Bible stories and passages could be pressed into service as supposed foundations for "stewardship-as-giving" themes. Other stewardship-related scriptural themes—e.g., forgiving debt, contentment, the perils of riches, purposed living, or inequities in economic systems—might get short-shrift, or be ignored altogether.

The most widespread result of the single-minded application of "stewardship" only to church matters may also be the most damaging: diminished regard for any message with "stewardship" in its title. Repeated references to the same biblical stories and passages can result in a lack of attention among congregation members. Stewardship may not be all that interesting any more.

After "Discipleship"

Presently, stewardship is deemed important because it is included under discipleship's broad umbrella. Nested inside one's self-identity as a disciple, there should also be the smaller identity of "steward." Although discipleship theology and practice are currently pervasive throughout various manifestations of Christianity, that emphasis may also be ready for its own shifting: challenging "disciples" toward the maturity of stewards. Stewardship could be discipleship's "what's next."[18]

Who is the disciple? Like the *economos* (steward), the *mathetes* (learner/disciple) had secular origins that were easily applied to religious relationships. The term predated Jesus by centuries, denoting the followers of philosophers, wandering charismatics, rabbis, and even brigands. Socrates, Homer, Aristotle, Pythagoras, and Plato lived and worked within teacher/learner relationships. Some Old Testament prophets may have had disciples—Elijah or Jeremiah are possible examples. The bandit-terrorist Zealots of Jesus's time followed charismatic leaders.

Even after the teachers had died, their followers continued what they learned, forming fellowships of disciples who carried on the oral or written traditions of the now absent teacher. The personal allegiance and zeal of disciples was transferred to a body of knowledge or set of practices.

The scriptural concept of "disciple" may be as minimally supported as "steward." Although there are 250+ occurrences of "disciple" in the New Testament, the vast majority are found in the Gospels—most commonly in Matthew. Of that number, the preponderance refer specifically to Jesus's followers. The term is very rarely used in the epistles.

"Discipling" seldom occurs and "discipleship" is not found in the Greek New Testament. The uses of *mathetes* are usually literal in nature, and do not present any metaphorical ideals. German Catholic theologian Gerhard Lohfink is clear about the Gospel writers' use of "discipleship": "There is no such thing in the Gospels as abstract discipleship. It is not an idea or a purely inward disposition; it exists only as a concrete, visible, tangible event."[19]

Over the past decade, some writers have begun to ask whether "disciple" should be used to denote the most desirable characteristics of Christians. While acknowledging the deep meanings and applicability of a disciple identity to Christian living, they suggest some difficulties with disciple-focused theology:

- The disciple is always a learner and a follower. Though always true metaphysically, this idea also allows for the possibility of stalled faith development.

- The self-identity of a disciple can lead to false comfort, dependency, or irresponsibility.
- Discipleship rests primarily on the real or imagined presence of the revered leader.
- When that person is absent, the disciples measure the relationship—with their former teacher and other disciples—only by obedience, being faithful students, or diligently following the principles set down by the leader/teacher.

Developmental psychologist Evelyn Eaton Whitehead and her husband, pastoral theologian James, summarize their concerns thusly: "Comfortable as a follower, and grateful for the luxury of having others make the final decision, the disciple may resist new invitations to leadership and greater responsibility."[20]

The Whiteheads also suggest that "steward" might more fully describe a next phase in lifelong faith development.[21] They propose a stage theory that describes the maturing faith of believers: "No relationship" characterizes the first stage, with "child" following. At the next stage, a believer becomes a "disciple" and in the final manifestation of spiritual maturity, the believer becomes a steward. They offer this summary thought: "The central characteristic of stewardship is the ability to trust the authority of one's own maturing convictions."[22]

Spiritual director and social activist Janet Hagberg and Robert Guelich, former professor of New Testament at Fuller Theological Seminary, apply Hagberg's work relating stages of power to matters of stewardship. At later stages, stewards realize the power of personal transformation, embrace reflection, and cherish their abilities to influence and mentor others toward good. In some cases, they become the conscience of an organization and risk becoming "irregulars"—leaders whose inner vision sometimes sets them apart from others.[23]

How could disciple/steward relationships remain useful? Because stewards are mature disciples, "stewardship" does not require you to ignore or repudiate the strengths of being a disciple. Stewards emerge from the ranks of disciples, just as leaders emerge from among groups of followers.[24]

Lively Stewardshifts

Let me suggest some possible changes in the ways you might proclaim or practice stewardship in your congregation. Some may fit your situation.

- *Keep at stewardship:* Throughout the year, your stewardship team can create and offer a variety of themes, programs, opportunities, or

challenges. You can also tie together yearlong stewardship-related
themes—e.g., "Transformed to Transform"—with learning and fellowship opportunities.

- *Keep at fund-raising:* When it's limited to only a short period of intense
  focus, mission-funding can get lost for the rest of the year. When
  extended into a continuing emphasis, fund-raising can inspire people's
  vision and sense of purpose, both of them necessary components of
  missional identity.

- *Communicate with relevance:* If stewardship language has become
  deeply habituated and ritualized, think how you might gently critique,
  shape, or edit your congregation's stewardship-related vocabulary so that
  the term can connect to a greater variety of life-related tasks and roles.

- *Repot your mission in stewardship soil:* If your congregation would
  benefit from a single, unifying identity, how might a more lively understanding of stewardship be helpful in transplanting evangelism, witness,
  or service efforts?

- *Talk about stewardship:* Most change begins with heartfelt conversations among people who respect and admire each other. Locate formal
  study of stewardship theology and practice within the informal setting
  of personal conversations. Lay leaders may be both teachers and learners.

- *Spend time in the Bible:* Reexamine time-honored stewardship Scriptures with more insistent, more contemporary interpretations. Pay close
  attention to the social and economic scene in which Jesus's life and
  witness were located.

- *Conduct an audit:* Assess every aspect of your congregation's stewardship teachings and practices, perhaps comparing them with members'
  actual beliefs or behaviors. If it is thorough and honest, the audit will
  suggest what to do next.

- *Start with historical strengths:* Look for and celebrate your shared
  stewardship assets. For example, your congregation may have always
  responded to victims of natural disasters; you may have the deserved
  reputation of welcoming people; or you may be known as the place
  where families learn to navigate financial difficulties.

It's (Not) about You

The broad biblical and historical images of *economos* and *stywaerden* may
be difficult to take into your life. Why could that be true? If you think of

yourself as an *economos*, you assume enormous responsibility. You function with authority in the middle of ambiguity, making decisions about things you don't own. If you're a *stywaerden*, you deal with the mess and muck of unpleasant circumstances, perhaps in relative obscurity. Both roles require humility, honesty, and resolute determination to be faithful. Both are leaders. Either role entails risk, and compels continuing courage and hope. In both cases, the rewards may seem small.

Thankfully, your stewardship does not start or end with you. What lies at the heart of this broad concept and role has remained true over its historical development: Stewardship starts and ends with God's will, God's ways, God's gifts.

In Summary

As a stewardship leader, you live out God's economy in the places and times where you operate most effectively. You can strengthen your congregation's unique position to equip stewards for daily lives of worship, service, and grace. You continue a history that began eons ago; you stand on many shoulders.

The fisherman disciple Peter put all these matters into perspective when he wrote:

> Like good stewards of the manifold grace of God, serve one another with whatever gift each of you has received . . . so that God may be glorified in all things through Jesus Christ. To him belong the glory and the power forever and ever. Amen. (1 Pet. 4:10–11)

Amen, indeed!

Notes

1. God's plan has been described in the term *heilsgeschichte*—salvation history—or what Reumann calls "God's arrangement to save us." See Ephesians 3:9ff. John Reumann, *Stewardship and the Economy of God* (Grand Rapids, MI: Eerdmans, 1992), 32, 44.
2. Leonard Sweet, "Freely You Have Received, Freely Give: Toward a Post-Tithing, Post-Stewardship, Postmodern Theology of Receiving," *http://www.leonardsweet.com*.
3. Reumann, *Stewardship*, 67ff.
4. Reumann, *Stewardship*, 16.

5. See especially the implications of God's stewardship of nature in Isaiah 55:6–11; 58:11; and 61:3b.

6. Amos 4 and 6 are good examples, as is Micah 2.

7. The practice of the tithe was likely adapted by Israel's priestly class from societies such as Babylonia, Persia, and Egypt. Leonard Sweet, "Freely You Have Received," 2–3.

8. The three tithes of Old Testament agrarian society may have disappeared by Jesus's time. But the religious elite in the Temple still maintained a healthy income through the Temple tax—based on the Atonement Offering of Exodus 30:11–16. Sweet, "Freely You Have Received," 3.

9. For a compelling exposition of this and other parables, see *Parables as Subversive Speech: Jesus as Pedagogue of the Oppressed* (Louisville, KY: Westminster/John Knox Press, 1994), by American Baptist New Testament scholar William R. Herzog II.

10. Luke 16 presents one such steward, a shrewd man who uses his wiles to please both his employer and his customers while still taking advantage of both. Luke 12:35–48 may seem to reflect on the wisdom of a faithful steward, but can also be interpreted as Jesus's critique and comparison of Jewish religious leadership. Herzog, *Parables*, 17.

11. One of Paul's converts, Erastus, sent greetings to Roman Christians from his position as treasurer (*economos*) of the city of Corinth (Rom. 16:23).

12. Reumann, *Stewardship*, 11–12.

13. To be historically accurate, the "households" of Old Testament times were not comparable with New Testament–era understandings of this socioeconomic term. Reumann, *Stewardship*, 12–13.

14. Reumann, *Stewardship*, 19, 30.

15. The larger idea of *economia* as God's "grand design" for human history also survived as the province of some theologians, philosophers, and other scholars. Reumann, *Stewardship*, 38ff.

16. See George Salstrand's *The Story of Stewardship in the United States of America* (Grand Rapids, MI: Baker Book House, 1956), for a detailed recounting of these matters.

17. Salstrand, as cited by Reumann, *Stewardship*, 53–54.

18. In whatever number, the "marks of discipleship" usually include some reference to generosity or participation in the funding of the Church. An example, "But (stewardship) is really a fundamental aspect of Christian discipleship. It is a way of discipleship embodying God's grace and love to people and a world in need." "Financial Stewardship," Ann L. Fritschel and Steve Oelschlager, *The Lutheran*, August 2014, 14.

19. Gerhard Lohfink, *Jesus of Nazareth: What He Wanted, Who He Was* (Collegeville, MN: Liturgical Press, 2012), 73.

20. Evelyn Eaton and James Whitehead, *Seasons of Strength: New Visions of Adult Christian Maturing* (Winona, MN: Saint Mary's Press, 1995), 56.

21. See Whiteheads, *Seasons of Strength*, especially chapter 4: "A Vocation Matures: The Emergence of Stewardship."

22. Whiteheads, *Seasons of Strength*, 63.

23. For a fuller application of her stage theory applied to stewardship, see chapter 12, "Stages of Power and Stewardship," in Janet O. Hagberg and Robert Guelich, *The Critical Journey: Stages in the Life of Faith*, 2nd ed. (Salem, WI: Sheffield, 2005).

24. "Disciples are still learning about the best of our heritage as believing people; stewards have matured to the point where they are able to—and need to—care for the worst of religious heritage. Stewards remain disciples, but carry with them the realization that they are responsible for what they do not own." Whiteheads, *Seasons of Strength*, 63.

chapter 2

Assured Foundations:
Scripture Shifts

In the preceding chapter I presented my understandings about the history of stewardship theology and practice. I also pointed out some gradual changes that might have taken this valuable practice and identity in directions that may not have proved helpful. In the following chapters I add to that probing, this time examining places where the scriptural witness about stewardship may also benefit from some shifting.

It might be difficult for you to approach the possibility that previous Scripture stewardship interpretations may not have served the church as well as you had imagined. As it has been practiced over many decades, steward-ship theology seems to have been well-integrated and thoroughly biblical. Proof-texts have seemed self-evident and biblical wisdom has appeared to be consistent. So any ruffling through stewardship texts with an eye bent on reinterpreting their meaning—that can feel like playing fast and loose with the Bible. You might even worry that, once it is dislodged from its scriptural moorings, the whole enterprise of church-oriented stewardship could be destroyed. These concerns are understandable.

Benefits of Scripture-Shifting

At the same time, I think that this work—considering traditional and new biblical material with newer scholarship in mind—is worth the effort. As you approach Scripture with fresh and insistent inquiries, you might:

- Appreciate more fully the life and times of early believers.
- Gain clearer perspective about the mission and teachings of Jesus and Paul.
- Answer difficult questions that earlier scholarship may have left untouched.

- Discover new insights—word meanings, cultural contexts, connections to broader messages—that might have lain dormant for decades.
- Reestablish the bases for your strongest convictions about the biblical witness.

These benefits will help you free your personal stewardship beliefs and practices from cultural history that might not have been as strongly biblical as you first thought. You will find courage to reexamine and change your stewardship practices.

Underlying Hermeneutical Assumptions

Biblical scholars continue to approach stewardship-related texts with high standards of intellectual honesty and strong adherence to hermeneutical principles, including the following:

THE FIRST MEANING IS THE BEST MEANING.

As much as possible, you can gain a truer meaning of scriptural sources when you consider how the first hearers or readers experienced the words, stories, or events portrayed in a passage.

CONSIDER THE FULL CONTEXT.

Over the past few decades, biblical scholars have increased their skill in using newer hermeneutical tools. As they have added to their knowledge of biblical circumstances and settings, exegetical scholars have discovered new layers of meaning in textual material. One Roman Catholic theologian states the matter thusly, "The text has no meaning outside of an historical context."[1]

New Testament scholar William R. Herzog II speaks about "compelling discrepancies" as a reason to apply this kind of interpretive care. His idea is simple: When the interpretation of a text requires contorted logic, suspension of disbelief, or even magical thinking, there may be a greater need to consider the context even more closely.

Herzog is direct about this matter: "The discrepancies between these social scenes and the spiritual messages assigned to them reveal a host of problems ranging from incongruities to hidden contradictions." And he adds this further warning: "Just as it is possible to interpret the parables without regard for their social scenes, it is also possible to conduct ministry without regard for its social context."[2]

The beauty of any compelling interpretation comes from the interpreter's respect for the smallest details. For example, consider the relevance of the fact that New Testament scribes and Pharisees were able to read and write, and to work with mathematical matters in a society in which the vast majority of people lacked literacy and numeracy.

Eisegesis Is Not Exegesis.

There is a vast difference between forcing meaning into a text (eisegesis), and letting a text speak for itself (exegesis). You could also think of *eisegesis* as "purposed retheming." But Scripture is not served well when original texts are backfilled with meanings from centuries later.

Beware Speaking to Silence.

Where Scripture is silent, you remain silent. Filling in the holes—of motivation, meaning, psychology, science, etc.—with contemporary knowledge can diminish the witness of Scripture. Still, as biblical scholarship increases in sophistication and accuracy, some earlier silences have disappeared. The intentions and observations of the original writers may have become clearer.

Proof-Texting Entails Risks.

In its rawest form, "proof-texting" consists of pulling bits and pieces of Scripture out of context and reassembling them into a newer perspective not intended by the original writers. The continuing risk: covering a more important meaning with a blanket of interpretive detritus.

The Old Testament Is Not the New Testament.

Part of what is sometimes called "progressive revelation," this interpretive principle can remind you that the movement of the Spirit through time sometimes resulted in strong differences within the witness of Old and New Testament writers.

Scripture Is Source and Norm for Faith and Life.

What you read in the Bible is more than a collection of good ideas. Its meaning for God's people is derived from a deep respect for God's work in inspiring teachers, prophets, and writers. What the Bible says about stewardship is truly inspired and true for God's people throughout times. The Spirit's hand is wonderfully evident.

SCRIPTURE INTERPRETS SCRIPTURE.

Within the bounds of contextual realities, scriptural truths about stewardship can gather greater meaning when they stand together with other parts of Scripture. Two examples: You can better understand Paul's views on sacrificial living if you examine the rich history of sacrifice as an element of Judaism from its earliest origins. Or you can identify with Jesus's disapproval of the Temple cult's fund-raising practices by reviewing the prophetic writings of the Old Testament.

Notes

1. Robert O'Toole, SJ, *Reading Ecclesiastes: Old Testament Exegesis and Hermeneutical Theory* (Rome, Italy: Editrice Pontificio Instituto Biblico, 1988), 217.

2. William R. Herzog, *Parables as Subversive Speech: Jesus as Pedagogue of the Oppressed* (Louisville, KY: Westminster/John Knox Press, 1994), 265.

chapter 3

Shifts in Familiar Passages, Stories, or Concepts

In this chapter, I present what contemporary biblical scholars seem to be saying about well-known passages, stories, or concepts. From these examples you might be able to approach other time-honored stewardship texts.

The Parable of the Talents

This is perhaps the most frequently cited scriptural encouragement for the wise use of money in the service of God's will. The moral seems fairly straight-forward: God requires a return on any investments or gifts we receive. A closer look reveals something completely the opposite. (Here I am indebted to the interpretative skills of New Testament scholar William R. Herzog II, who has reframed this story as "The Vulnerability of the Whistle-Blower.")[1]

Matthew's version of the story (25:14–31) is a parable about the plight of "retainers" in elite households.[2] In this story, one comes to realize his role in an unjust economic system and decides to tell truth to power. Rich enough to take a journey, "a man"[3] trusts three retainers with vast sums of money. His expectations are simple: "However it happens, double my money."[4]

The first two servants accomplish this feat, and the third retainer—motivated to act justly—puts the money only in a safe place. On returning, the master asks for an accounting from these trusted servants. He rewards the two retainers who have fattened his coffers, and condemns what he believes to be the lack of good business sense on the part of the third servant.

The parable gets even more interesting when the retainer talks back to the returned master, naming him as unjust and even cruel in his exploitation of others. With no apologies, the master agrees with the assessment of this whistle-blower, but still banishes him from the security of his former occupation. Even though he is the hero of Jesus's story, the third servant is punished severely.

In this retelling, the parable now fits closely with Jesus's overall message about righteous justice associated with the coming of the kingdom of heaven. The story also shows his abundant love for those who are downtrodden. His listeners understood clearly the kind of society in which widespread injustice destroyed the covenant with God. Because his listeners knew only too well the context and details of the story, they would have taken heart from this teaching. They would see that they were *not* dependent on the landed aristocracy whom they both envied and despised. They might even have been challenged to deal more courageously or caringly with retainers in their own locale.

Those original meanings can help today's Christians address similar contexts. The parable calls God's people to speak truth to power, even at great risk. Growing income inequality, subtle class warfare, dispossession of the poor, and unjust economic policies or practices—all require the church to remain vigilant, prophetic, and bold. God's people can also be "pedagogues of the oppressed" as well as advocates on their behalf.

The Jerusalem Offering

Early in its history, the Church faced an economic crisis: The Christians in Jerusalem were dealing with a famine. In an attempt to prove his loyalty to this primarily Jewish congregation, Paul rallied the Gentile congregations in Macedonia and Achaia to gather a collection—likely of money—to help the Jerusalem Christians. Thus the Church's first hunger appeal was planned and partially executed.[5]

Paul's administrative letters to the Corinthian congregation—particularly 2 Corinthians 8 and 9—address this situation, offering quotable maxims about giving and generosity. The applicability of these teachings changes slightly, though, when you step back and look at the larger picture that Paul was dealing with.[6]

Paul faced a troubling reality in this congregation: The Corinthians had agreed to collect the offering, even showing eagerness for the idea. But after about eighteen months they still had not completed the task. This wealthy and gifted congregation was troubled by immaturity, shallowness, disorganization—neediness of the highest order.[7] By comparison, the Macedonian congregations were living out the ancient ideals of simple living: sincerity, honesty, morality, and liberal generosity.[8]

Gift-giving was an integral part of accepted social norms in Paul's day. Because it was rooted in the rituals of religious sacrifice to the gods, gift-giving also pervaded social expectations regarding friendship and the conduct of business.[9]

Paul's writing about this one-time gift reflects Paul's rhetorical skill, his persuasive logic, and his knowledge of the accepted conventions of gift-giving in the larger society.[10] In chapters 8 and 9, Paul put all of these assets to work:

- He employed common rhetorical techniques such as comparison, praise, "testing," and example.[11]
- He filled his arguments with terms and concepts from law, sports, military matters, education, commerce, agriculture, administration, and even pagan religions.[12]
- He appealed to "friendship," in both its business and relational meanings.[13]
- He bolstered his arguments with quotations from familiar Old Testament proverbs and allusions to Jewish history and customs.[14]

Paul's appeal to the Corinthians applied familiar norms of generosity and gift-giving to even deeper matters. He reminded his readers that God is the true benefactor and thus deserved the ultimate honor (of a reciprocal gift).[15] Paul emphasized that God's gift-giving can result in self-sufficiency, which in turn enables the accumulation of reserves from which to do good deeds for others.[16] He credited God as a seed-multiplier, and then named the Corinthians' anticipated gifts as another kind of seed.[17] Perhaps most importantly, he grounded his logic in the reality of the Christ's self-sacrifice, an anchor point that was fresh and newly important for his readers.[18]

What can you take from this summary of Paul's instructions, pleas, and arguments about the Jerusalem collection? The scriptural shift here might be a movement that adds big-picture thinking to the weight of beloved adages. The larger mental landscape could include these elements:

- In matters of giving and generosity, it makes sense to consider well-known wisdom and practice in the worlds outside of the church.
- Asking people for contributions requires a full range of skills and experience. Mere techniques and tactics may not be sufficient.
- All giving comes back to God's goodness and our response. This "case statement" has remained true through eons.
- It's a good thing to speak frankly, openly, and at length about these subjects.

- Giving is primarily a matter of "the heart," but can also be complemented by logic and reason.
- The dynamics of giving to special circumstances may or may not apply to regular giving that support congregational ministries.

However you consider the scriptural witness surrounding the Jerusalem Offering, it remains a helpful example of how God's people can be encouraged in their giving of money to honor God's purposes.

The Widow's Mite

Traditionally considered as evidence of Jesus's admiration and encouragement of selfless generosity, this event may instead exemplify his continuing critique of a society—especially its religious systems—that had lost its spiritual moorings.[19]

In the Marcan version of the story (Mark 12:38–44), Jesus's observation of the widow's actions was preceded by his stinging condemnation of the behavior of religious leaders and followed by his words about the destruction of the Temple.[20]

Within that context, another possible picture emerges: A widow with no inheritance rights drops two small copper coins (*leptas*) into one of the Temple's trumpet-shaped metal alms-collection chests. Her physical appearance and the sound of her meager offering hitting that receptacle could have told Jesus that she had given her whole life savings. Exploited by scribes—who were also regarded as theologians—and by the Temple cult's expectations of almsgiving—the widow was perhaps generous to a fault.[21]

Her simple gift contrasted sharply with the pretentious offerings of rich donors. This could have been one reason for Jesus to criticize or lament the results of her piety. In one interpreter's mind, "The widow epitomizes Israel's ruin. The nation has been robbed (by Roman occupiers and their lackeys) and it now lives in a state of death, for the 'devourers' have taken the last two pence."[22]

Seen in this light, this story can serve as a reminder of the perils—or even injustices—that might accompany some aspects of mission-funding in congregations. How strongly should a congregation encourage "sacrificial giving"? Where else can generosity find expression? And perhaps most directly, in what ways could any religious leader, knowingly or unknowingly, take advantage of those who are poor?

The Lord's Prayer

With millions of Christians each day, you offer this prayer to God but may not have considered its stewardship implications. When you remember that stewardship is a way of describing your entire life of serving God's will, it may make sense to reexamine this signature prayer to see where stewardship considerations can be found.[23]

According to New Testament scholar Steven F. Plymale, the prayer is a "rehearsal (review) of the salvation history experience" and "a statement of one's dependence upon God for the things requested." Implicit in each of the petitions of the Lord's Prayer is the understanding that what we pray for is already occurring, and will continue into the future.[24]

Several parts of the prayer (Luke 11:1–4) seem worthy of attention. Briefly stated, they include the following:

- *Your kingdom come:* Then and now, Jesus's followers can be "instruments whereby God will accomplish and complete his salvation history." God's *economia* comes to pass when stewards of that plan remain at God's disposal, answerable to God's call and will.[25]

- *Give us each day our daily bread:* We need sustenance, safety, and support for our lifework as stewards. Considered literally and eschatologically, "bread" is always a continuing gift from God. Our bodies, minds, and spirits are filled by God's gracious provision for our lives.[26]

- *Forgive us our sins, for we ourselves forgive everyone indebted to us:* Forgiveness from God is always linked to forgiveness of others. ("The forgiven community is a forgiving community.") Without practiced forgiveness in place, the life of a steward would devolve into fear of failure, anxiety about punishment, or false reliance on God-pleasing actions (works righteousness). Within the household of faith, forgiveness is "an absolute pre-requisite for such a diverse community to exist."[27]

- *Do not bring us to the time of trial:* Jesus's words about trial—or the more familiar "temptation"—are not directed at matters of daily morality, but toward deeper questions that stewards face. Among the most important is the matter of apostasy—the temptation to deny, relinquish, or diminish our role in God's larger *economia*. Quiet, insidious voices can distract us from our resolve to fulfill God's purposes for the world.[28]

Understanding this prayer as a fundamental resource for sustaining your stewardship can add to its importance each time you voice its words and consider its meaning. The Lord's Prayer can remind you of God's wider intention and plan for your lifework as a steward.

Sacrificial Living/Giving

Let's shift now from examining specific texts and stories to considering broad scriptural themes that are stewardship-related. The first is "sacrificial giving," a concept that appears throughout the Bible.

For Old Testament believers, the archetypical sacrifice was that of Abraham, who obeyed God's call to sacrifice his beloved son. Both Abraham and his willing son Isaac epitomized "the sacrificial man."[29]

The Pentateuch spends about half of its words devoted to sacrificial theology and rituals. The themes of Old Testament sacrificial law include these:

- Death and life are in opposition to each other. Death is the great evil, the ultimate enemy.
- Israel has been specially chosen by God for God's purposes.
- Sacrifices are not only spiritual in nature, but involve the common things of daily life—food, drink, crops.
- The material sacrifice is a stand-in for the donor.
- When engaged in sacrificial worship, a worshiper identifies with the sacrificial animal or substances, and thus surrenders to God.
- Whatever the sacrifice—animal, cereal, wine, oil, wheat—the same basic truths are being proclaimed and lived out.[30]

How did sacrifices please God? The texts seem fairly clear: God was pleased by the aroma of the burning sacrifice.[31] But why would a pleasant smell satisfy God? We may never know exactly, but it seems that the sacrifice was acceptable because it indicated God's people were giving up or giving away something valuable. God understood and accepted the forfeiting of their well-being as an act of humility and surrender to God's primacy. By their sacrifices, worshippers implored God for forgiveness in a tangible way, trusting God's gracious mercy.[32]

By the time of the New Testament, sacrificial practices were less clear. Because of the apostasy of several generations of irreligious rulers and the destruction of both the First and Second Temple by invading armies, the rituals of sacrifice were intermingled with the practices of pagan religions.

By Jesus's time, those disruptive influences had corrupted sacrificial theology to the point that some of its underlying benefits and truths had been lost. Even though the sacrifices were still offered in Herod's Temple up until the destruction of Jerusalem, their meaning had been minimized and politicized to the point that many otherwise observant Jews could not or would not participate: The sacrifices of the elite and wealthy maintained higher importance; Temple taxes generated enough income to pay for the religious enterprises centered on the Temple; and because the Pharisees had preserved Judaism during the captivities, their interpretations of the rituals held sway.[33]

Trained as a Pharisee, Paul believed that sacrifice was a key element of worship and faith, and so centered much of his theology on these concepts. He was certainly aware of the dimensions of sacrifice in the pagan religions of his day,[34] but saw in Jesus's self-sacrifice strong reasons to reinvigorate and reintegrate sacrifice theology with the life, death, and resurrection of Jesus the Christ. One key feature of that theology: Because of Jesus, the sacrifices of the Old Testament were no longer necessary.

In Paul's thinking, Jesus's willingness to face a tortured death was not just a symbolic or metaphorical example for his followers, but corresponded to the torture and death those believers would face in the ensuing decades. For them, sacrificial living was a literal concept, one that helped them understand how they might follow Christ is his living and dying. (The letters of Peter echo those sentiments, written to believers perhaps already facing persecution.[35])

Sacrificial giving became an important concept for Paul when the need for a famine-relief collection for the Jerusalem church arose. He invoked the example of the Macedonian Christians who, though poor, were still able to contribute generously. He wrote eloquently about "giving yourselves as living sacrifices" (Rom. 12:1ff). He also instructed the Philippian Christians to have the same mind as Christ Jesus, one that included humility and self-sacrifice in all things (Phil. 2:3–8).

Given the long history and continued importance of "sacrifice" throughout biblical history, how can this ideal retain meaning in your life of stewardship? "Sacrifice" and "sacrificial living" go to the heart of your stewardship. These concepts can describe your identity and temperament—fundamental motivations for other attitudes and actions. If you aren't living sacrificially, less godly motivations might influence your deepest brain structures, decision-making processes, skill sets, or outlook on life.

What can sacrificial living mean in observable traits and actions? Let me take a stab at some ideas that have instructed my own stewardship:

- Your self-talk—thoughts that come to mind when you're not engaged in attention-demanding activities—can shift from self-absorption to other-mindedness, even God-mindedness. (Because self-talk may comprise about one-third of your daily thinking, this shift might make a sacrificial mindset into a habit.)

- A life of sacrificial stewardship can repurpose your sense of personal power. When you realize the amount (and limits) of your influence, you then choose how and where to apply it. In a self-sacrificing modality, your choices can show God's love to others.

- It takes imagination to live outside the gut instincts of self-preservation and egocentricity. As you begin to imagine yourself living sacrificially, your actions and attributes can follow more easily. Creativity and ingenuity can accompany those shifts in thinking.

- Sacrificial living involves some loss, some diminishment, some giving away, or giving up. You can't layer self-sacrifice over a lifestyle that's governed by "more." Paul's take on this: What you relinquish is not as valuable as what you gain.[36]

- As you remain a steward throughout your life, your sacrifice remains a thanksgiving for gifts received, not a self-denial from which you expect to gain something.[37]

Abundance

In their religious life, people faithful to Yahweh shared with other ancient religions the desire to be materially blessed by their god(s). "Abundance"—however it is understood—is a consistent theme in the Old Testament. The Hebrew *rabh* ("to increase") or its cognates occurs over 145 times in the Old Testament. All of those meanings flow from the idea of "overwhelming, overflowing plenty."

For Old Testament believers, the idea of abundance emanated from the marvel of the Creation stories, appearing over and over again in the examples of righteous men and women who were rewarded materially for their faithfulness. (Think here of Noah, Abram, or Job. Or see Deuteronomy 30:9, Psalm 132:15, or Amos 9:13 for more specific promises from God.) The worship-related book of Psalms and whole sections of Proverbs are unswerving in their proclamation that God's favor for Israel could be seen in material blessings. The prophets connected the prosperity of their nation(s) with the people's obedience to the Law, behavior that contrasted starkly with yielding to the alluring practices of pagan cults, which promised fertility as one form of abundance.

Particularly important to God's people during those centuries was the idea that their inheritance—the Promised Land as a source for assured well-being—was a dependable feature of God's covenant. This promise is scattered throughout the Old Testament, as an assurance of God's love. For examples, see Genesis 12:7ff (God's initial promise to Abram); Leviticus 20:24 ("A land flowing with milk and honey"); or Joshua 1:6 (God reiterates his promise and commission to Joshua).

God-given abundance was always connected to Israel's righteousness, however. When Israel disobeyed or ignored its original agreement with God, the nation could expect God's punishment: scarcity in several forms. The price for disobedience, injustice, or immorality could be seen in the decrease of prosperity. For examples, see Joshua 24:20 (God's direct warning); 1 Samuel 12:14–18 (Israel's disobedience punished immediately by a crop-destroying storm); or Jeremiah's ongoing warnings and laments (chapters 2–7 or 14 for starters).

Over time, the idea of rewarded righteousness became firmly entrenched in Jewish theology. (Proverbs 10:16 [CEV] summarizes this seeming wisdom: "The wage of the righteous leads to life, the gain of the wicked to sin.")

Well before the time of Jesus, the Pharisees had distilled the entire body of sacrificial laws into purity codes that were at the core of their spiritual practices. The intent: that God's people would remember and honor the full dimensions of God's covenant with Israel. "Clean/unclean" and "pure/impure" were carefully described in both literal and symbolic terms. Obedience was rewarded by material blessings, and disobedience was punished by poverty.

By the time of Jesus, written Scripture, tradition, and history seemed to prove that abundance was connected to consistent obedience to God's law. That made it easy for those who were wealthy to claim that their abundance was proof of their righteousness. Those living in poverty? They were obviously being punished for their ritual impurities—the Pharisees' way of describing disobedience to God's law. Given the specific practices of purity— e.g., washing of one's hands before eating or avoiding the handling of unclean materials—it follows that only those who were wealthy could afford the time and money it took to adhere to these religious practices. These rituals were economically impossible for the poor to undertake.[38]

Abundance remained an honored theme in the New Testament, although perhaps muted by the economic stranglehold and corruption that came from Roman oppression in Palestine. Occurring only about forty times in the New Testament, the Greek term for abundance (*perisseuo* and its various forms) was used mostly in a literal sense: referring to full and overflowing quantities of material goods.[39]

Jesus's teachings can be seen as a pivotal point in the evolution of abundance-based theologies. On one hand, Jesus enjoyed the pleasures of good company and good food, and he preached about truly righteous abundance. (You can read the entire Sermon on the Mount from that vantage point.) He spoke of abundant living—likely laced with eschatological assurances—as a reason for his coming among humankind (John 10:10).

On the other hand, Jesus criticized false ideas about abundance. (See the Parable of the Rich Fool [Luke 12:13–21] or Jesus's direct critiques of the corrupt materialism that governed Palestine's economy in the Parable of The Dishonest Manager in Luke 16:1–13). It may be accurate to characterize Jesus's views as warnings about dependence on material abundance.

In his lifestyle, preaching, and writing, Paul continued to scrape away the encrustations of self-serving abundance theology. Perhaps because he was aware of Greco-Roman understandings of this matter,[40] Paul employed the term in more deeply spiritual ways. His deft revisions of abundance thinking—especially related to God's grace in Jesus—made this idea a fundamental part of his proclamation.[41]

Over the centuries, this stubbornly persistent principle—righteousness is rewarded with abundance—has continued to circle back to its most crassly selfish meanings. Taken to its logical extremes today, abundance thinking continues to shape-shift into subpar theologies known as "the prosperity gospel" or "works righteousness." Thoroughly enmeshed in the so-called Protestant work ethic, these thought patterns can sometimes masquerade as legitimate stewardship principles.[42]

Let me suggest some possible Scripture shifts about abundance that you might apply in the larger landscapes where you live and work.

Perhaps most obviously, it seems necessary that you continue to name and root out any supposedly scriptural notions of causality, reward, or deservedness when it comes to abundance. You entered life as a naked beggar, and will exit in a similar condition. In between those moments, any imagined deservedness—your righteous behaviors or exemplary stewardship included—is a form of self-idolatry. That's why, in any disguise, a prosperity gospel is never good news.

Instead of relying on overly literal readings of abundance-related Scriptures, look for those meanings of abundance that do not foster selfishness, materialism, greed, and their ilk. Start by mining the Wisdom literature of the Old Testament for memorable aphorisms, or consider how Jesus's commentaries on wealth-seeking might apply to your life. The stark warnings of the prophets might help you apply these ideas to the cultural tides you want to resist. Spend some time in biblical material that refers to contentment, a possible antidote to the poison of false abundance thinking.

You may see gathering evidence that materialism—abundance run amok—and growth-oriented philosophies of economic well-being will soon choke the planet. In that case, hold dear those Scriptures that can help you persevere and prosper even when severe shortages—of food, water, arable land, clean air, safety, or peace—become a prevalent reality throughout the world economy.[43]

Contentment

Although "abundance" seems to be part of most world religions, a balancing concept—contentment—has also firmly embedded itself into the precepts of those religions. The Buddha is widely credited with the statement, "Contentment is the highest wealth." For its adherents throughout the world, Islam offers assurances (and warnings) that contentment is preferable to acquisitive materialism. Among Hindus, the Second Niyama (observance or practice) is contentment (*santosha*). In each of these belief systems, contentment is related to happiness or joy.

Next to their proclamations about God's abundance, Old Testament writers inserted signals about the foolishness of full-bore acquisitiveness or greed. Contentment themes began early in Israel's history, most notably the practical and spiritual warnings about gathering too much manna (Exod. 16:15–26). The writers of Wisdom literature seasoned their observations with similar thoughts.[44]

Among those Wisdom writers, the author of Ecclesiastes—"The Preacher"—makes the Old Testament's strongest case for contentment. Dominated by irony, his writings use understatement to note the incongruity between acquisitive expectations and a life of contentment. The Preacher, most likely speaking from personal experience, directed his comments to a community of faithful followers of Yahweh.[45]

In the New Testament, only a few passages address contentment directly. Jesus charged (Roman) soldiers to be satisfied with their pay and named food and clothing as sufficient for one's life. Paul assured the Philippians (4:11–12) that he was content in whatever state (of physical well-being) he found himself. "Godliness with contentment" comes from Paul's First Letter to Timothy (6:6), as does the pragmatic idea that we can be happy with just food and clothing (6:8). Hebrews 13:5 echoes that thought.

Contentment is easily understood: You can find satisfaction, pleasure, and joy in your present state of mind or body. So it may not seem that this element of stewardship needs much shifting. You receive gratefully whatever you are given, count it as a blessing, and don't complain to God, the Original and Ultimate Giver. Contentment is like a passive verb: Stuff happens and you take it in stride.

The ideals of contentment get a bit more shift-inviting when you look at the attitudes and behaviors that are connected to contentment. Let's examine some of these matters now.

For Paul, "self-sufficiency" was a useful character trait. In his roving ministry, Paul took care of his necessities, rarely asking for aid or support. Thus he could establish credibility with his congregations. Because it implied contentment as well as an independent and plucky temperament, self-sufficiency made "being content" more like an active verb: A state of mind could also become a way of behaving.[46]

Complaining and murmuring are the opposite of contentment. Some examples: The wanderings of the Children of Israel gave them occasion for these behaviors, which God condemned and even punished (see Exod. 14:11ff and 16:2, as well as Num. 11:1–11ff.) Jesus scolded the bread-seeking multitudes for their murmuring (John 6:43). Paul invited the beloved Philippians to "do all things" without murmuring—and connected that idea to "not arguing" (Phil. 2:14). Jude characterized false teachers by their grumbling and complaining (Jude 16).

Knowing and practicing "enough" seems another good way to characterize contentment. The Hebrew and Greek terms for "enough" appear over ninety times in the Bible (including the deuterocanonical writings). Most uses are fairly practical or ordinary—enough flocks, enough time in a place, or enough horses for chariots.[47]

But "enough" can also indicate satisfaction or dissatisfaction; sufficiency or insufficiency; abundance; satiation; and the finality of a good or bad situation. When inserted into a conversation or prayer, the word "enough" sometimes indicates a person's desire to end something unpleasant, sad, or dangerous. (My favorite word-picture of "enough" in the Scriptures: Isaiah calls people who can't ever get enough "a pack of hungry and greedy dogs" [56:11, CEV]).

Another strong collection of scriptural wisdom about contentment encourages God's people not to worry. The psalmist talks about "eating the bread of anxious toil" (Ps. 127:2). The writer of Ecclesiastes exposes the folly that comes from overthinking things—a possible precursor to worry. (See

5:10–12, 7:10 or 8:16–17 as examples.) In both Matthew and Luke, the discourses known as the Sermon on the Mount include a lengthy treatment of anxiety (Matt. 6:25–34 and Luke 12:22–31). Jesus also scolded Martha for her seeming fretfulness. Paul summarized the matter neatly in his letter to the Philippians: "Do not worry about anything, but in everything by prayer and supplication with thanksgiving let your requests be made known to God" (4:6).

The entire letter of Paul to the Philippians might function as a foundational Scripture if you want to understand contentment.[48] Within its easily read prose are contentment-related themes such as these:

- The example of Christ as a faithful, humble steward who was not self-serving (2:6–11, the "Christ Hymn").
- True gain and loss (3:7–11).
- Seeking "maturity" in pressing toward life's spiritual goals (3:12–16).
- Being steadfast (3:16).
- Rejoicing continually (1:18, 4:4, and 4:10).
- Thanking as a way of displacing worry (4:6).
- Truly valuable thoughts (4:8–9).
- Contentment regardless of circumstance (4:11–13).
- Assurance of God's ability to satisfy all needs (4:19).

However you understand contentment, and however you shift in your use of contentment-related Scriptures, it makes good sense to include this concept and practice in your personal and congregational stewardship.

Giving

We come next to what may have originally compelled you to read this book: the relationship between stewardship and giving, especially giving money for the support of congregations.

It's understandable that this matter would merit your attention. Your congregation depends on financial resources to engage in ministry. It's also understandable that you might approach "stewardship equals giving" with some discomfort. Effective approaches to financial support of congregations may seem mysterious, difficult, or at least elusive. And you may still harbor some theological or practical misgivings about the conflation of "stewardship" with the necessities of your congregation's financial well-being. In any case, the following pages may prove helpful.

First, a review: In their strictest biblical roots, neither stewardship nor financial support for congregations had much to do with the other. As you have gathered from the previous chapter, the secular New Testament–era *economos* was probably not a church member. He was not likely commissioned to give away assets that didn't belong to him. (This would have been the prerogative of the owner or ruler.) The actions of the steward were based on the owner's *economia*—a larger plan or vision. To include "giving" as a part of that plan—especially giving to support a religious gathering—would depend on the largesse of the owner, NOT the steward.[49]

The complicated nature of financial support for religious enterprises in the Old and New Testaments makes the time-honored equation "stewardship is about giving" even more difficult to defend scripturally. Several kinds of giving characterized Jewish piety. One kind of giving—various sacrifices— supported Tabernacle and Temple worship. Those sacrifices were supplemented by one of the biblical tithes. Later in Jewish history, the sometimes heavy burdens of religious taxation were added.

Synagogues were a different matter. Begun during the Babylonian Captivity, these local gatherings of devout Jews offered religious instruction, prayer, and fellowship. Led by rabbis instead of priests, these "houses of assembly" (*beit k'nesset*) were supported financially by regular contributions—in today's culture, "membership dues"—from their constituencies. Alms may also have been collected. Tithes and sacrifices were not brought to synagogue gatherings; those additional offerings were instead reserved for the Temple.[50]

Perhaps more deeply engrained in Jewish theology, almsgiving was aimed at those who were poor or otherwise needy. Beginning with the *Peah* in Leviticus 19:9 —literally, the corner of one's land that was left as a place where the poor could glean food—Jewish theology was insistent that the poor would not be forgotten.

Scriptural evidence seems consistent in this regard.[51] In the Old Testament:

- The Torah states that almsgiving to the poor was equivalent to sacrificing to God. (Prov. 19:17 summarizes this matter thusly: "Whoever is kind to the poor lends to the Lord, and will be repaid in full.")
- The ideal of a "Sabbath Year" included invitations to liberal, ungrudging almsgiving to alleviate poverty, and also the command to "open your hand to the poor and needy neighbor in your land" (Deut. 15:10–11).
- The Year of Jubilee was aimed squarely at justice for those who were poor. (Lev. 25 spells out this larger form of almsgiving.)

- Wisdom literature directed God's people to care for the poor. (See Ps. 82:4, Prov. 22:9, or Prov. 21:13 as examples.)

In the New Testament, almsgiving is similar to contemporary ideals regarding charitable giving:

- Jesus's admonition to the rich young man (Mark 10:17–22) illustrates the ultimate evidence of devotion to God: giving to the poor.
- Prominently placed in the Jerusalem Temple were the trumpet-shaped alms-collection receptacles where the widow contributed the last of her sustenance (Mark 12:41ff).
- One of the first organizational tasks of the early church was managing the distribution of alms to the Greek widows (Acts 4:34–35 and 6:1–6).
- Luke singled out Tabitha (Dorcas), an early believer in Joppa, for her "good works" as well as her "acts of charity" or almsgiving (Acts 9:36–43).
- Paul's collection was targeted for the relief of the famine-ravaged Christians in Jerusalem.

Perhaps the most striking theological principle related to almsgiving is the Torah's assertion that giving to the poor is equal to obeying all the commandments of God! The Mishnah—the final compilation of the Torah in the late second or early third century—names five "commandments" that included no specified limits: the *Peah*; first fruits giving to the Temple; festival offerings to the Temple; almsgiving; and study of the Torah. The Mishnah's supplement, the Tosephta, offers this startling declaration, "The giving of alms and works of charity are equal in value to all of the commandments of the Torah."[52]

A logical fallacy that makes it difficult to equate "stewardship" with "giving": The two ideas were separated by centuries and cultures. "Giving" predated the establishment of the role and behaviors of the steward in Greco-Roman economic life. Thus the writers of the Old Testament did not consider "stewardship"—a later economic concept—in their perceptions of sacrifice, tithing, Temple taxes, or almsgiving. They could not proclaim or practice a doctrine that had not yet developed.

The New Testament scriptural witness includes a large number of Greek terms for giving or the one who gives. But the majority of these expressions do not refer to money. When money is involved or inferred, the Greek words describe down-to-earth matters such as the wise men's gifts, the widow's mite, or honoring your parents.[53]

Paul's writings established the historical antecedents for "giving of money" in four major passages: 1 Corinthians 9:1–23 (a discussion of his financial rights as an apostle); 1 Corinthians 16:1–4 (a brief reference to the Jerusalem Collection); 2 Corinthians 8–9 (longer observations about this collection); and Philippians 4:15–17 (grateful remarks about financial support from this church). But his wider appreciation of gifts and giving reveal another set of propositions: God is the giver (of all material and spiritual blessings); Jesus sacrificed/gave himself for our sake; and God deserves our giving of self. We depend on Paul for these wider applications of "giving" to a life of serving God's will.

One other giving-related matter deserves our attention: How can followers of Christ be givers if they are not first receivers? Theological polymath, author, and speaker Leonard Sweet addresses this question, suggesting a "theology of receiving": He insists that, absent a well-formed sense of your dependence on God for blessings of every kind, the basic principles of giving won't take hold. Sweet grounds his ideas on 1 Corinthians 4:7, "What do you have that you did not receive? And if you received it, why do you boast as if it were not a gift?" Riffing on this passage—and connecting it to a host of related Scriptures—Sweet explores other fundamental matters such as God's ownership and extravagant generosity; tithing; the spread of "gifts" throughout all of our lives; the arrogance and dangers of a theology of stewardship based on giving; Jesus's receipt of gifts and wisdom in receiving God's gifts. His points are well-taken and necessary for any sense of mature stewardship.[54]

How might you shift your understanding about "giving" in the Scriptures? In my estimation, the changes could include the following:

1. Fewer previously acceptable passages about "scriptural stewardship principles" may now be available to you. (Some of these principles may function less like theological foundations and more like culturally bound strategies, tactics, or methodologies.)

2. When it comes to changing mission-funding practices, you may need to turn to the wisdom available in secular fields of knowledge and practice such as philanthropy.

3. Scriptural themes that undergird giving will remain true and useful. For example, invitations and descriptions regarding generosity, self-sacrifice, other-mindedness or altruism, gratitude, and pragmatic appreciation of what God grants you. Also instructive are passages that expose self-idolatry, greed, or materialism; scriptural threads that strengthen your resolve to carry God's will forward and winsome adages that undergird joyful living.

However you interpret Scriptures about giving—and however you shift in your understanding and application of this biblical theme—you can be assured that the Spirit will continue to fill God's people with generosity (Gal. 5:22–23).

Tithing

In many approaches to financial support for congregations, the tithe—an offering of one-tenth of one's income—is presented as a biblical imperative or at least a strong expectation. Tithing seems to be well-supported by Scriptures that are literal, direct, and easily understood. Tithing practices (and accompanying attitudes) offer tangible benefits to tithers. Scriptural bases for the church's presumed understandings of tithing may not be as strong or as deep as they first appear, however. The following pages outline this matter.

Prior to Mosaic Law, tithing was not a systematic process, but mirrored the ancient cultural practice of bringing an exceptional gift to an honored person or a deity. Abram gave a tithe (of the spoils from his battle against the five kings) to Melchizedek (Gen. 14:20 and Heb. 7:4). Jacob promised a tithe (Gen. 28:22) as part of his negotiations for God's blessing. In Abram's cases, this tithe was not repeated; in Jacob's case, there is no record that it took place.[55]

As you weigh the scriptural bases for tithing, you might first focus on which of the biblical tithes you are contemplating. There were three tithes in the Old Testament: the Levitical Tithe, the Festival Tithe, and the Welfare Tithe.[56] Each had importance for the Israelites, and each was expected or commanded as part of Israel's faithfulness to Yahweh.

- The Levitical Tithe (Num. 18:21–26) was first given in support of the work of the Levites, who offered daily sacrifices to God. The Levites turned over to the priests one-tenth of the amount they had received, thus extending the benefits of this tithe to all those who carried out the functions of the Tabernacle (and later, the Temple). The tithe could be satisfied by the offering of animals, land, grain, oil, or fruit—and by money later in Israel's history.
- The Festival Tithe (Deut. 14:22–27) had an exceptional outcome: The celebration of a large feast that included both the Levites and those bringing the offering. The Festival Tithe could be brought as money, enabling tithers to purchase "whatever you wish," including meat and strong drink! (v. 26). The Levites were not directly supported through

this tithe, but tithers were encouraged to share with them. In later centuries the celebration made possible by this tithe—also called the Deuteronomy Tithe—was held in Jerusalem.

- The Welfare Tithe (Deut. 14:28–29) is the third offering commanded by Mosaic Law. This tithe was gathered every third year and given to orphans, resident aliens, and widows. Because they shared some of the same economic disadvantages as those who were poor, the Levites were also beneficiaries of this tithe. This offering may have been the precursor or archetype for almsgiving in Judaism. It is unclear how universally this tithe was observed and which other tithes, if any, it displaced during that third year.

When calculated as annualized percentages, these three tithes amounted to about 23.33 percent of the income of the Israelites. The tithes were not voluntary offerings—those were a separate category of giving—but were required of every observant Jew in addition to sacrifices. During the dynasties of the Judean kings, the tithes were exacted from the population in addition to taxes. Tithe collectors were employed to collect these offerings.

The tithe was not strictly a tax. In its early years, Israel was a theocracy, administered by religious authorities—the priests and Levites—whose work was supported by the tithe. When the monarchy developed, the tithes still supported one pillar of society—the Tabernacle/Temple—and taxes supported the monarchy. Still, tithing resembled a tax because it was not voluntary.[57]

The Destruction of the Temple and the Babylonian Captivity likely caused tithing—along with other religious practices—to disintegrate temporarily. On their return from captivity, the exiles funded the initial phases of the rebuilding of the Temple with a generous free-will offering (Ezra 2:68–69). The latter phases of this building project were underwritten by the royal treasury of Darius (Artaxerxes), and by other personal offerings from the king and his counselors. The people, including "heads of ancestral households," made additional offerings to the building fund. (See Ezra 6:3–4 and 7:15, as well as Neh. 7:70–72.) Nehemiah instituted the annual Temple Tax—one-third of a shekel (Neh. 10:32–39). It is unclear if any of these contributions could be considered as forms of tithing.[58]

The New Testament says little about tithing—as a religious observance or as a form of funding. At the time of Jesus, the Temple tax fulfilled that function instead. Tithes may still have been collected among parts of the population, especially among some economic cohorts.

The Gospel writers record only two observations about tithing by Jesus—neither prohibiting nor encouraging the practice, instead condemning the shallow motives and minimal spirituality that were associated with the tithe. (See Matt. 23:23, its parallel in Luke 11:42 and Luke 18:9–14.) Jesus narrowed his criticism to the behaviors of the scribes and Pharisees, whose piety was considered exemplary. His major critique: While tithing, these devout Jewish leaders had missed other important qualities of devotion to God or had forgotten their need for repentance.[59]

Jesus did not tithe because he owned no land, raised no crops or animals, nor had any income. His contribution to the Temple? The required shekel his disciple Peter would find in a fish (Matt. 17:27). Jesus's lack of wherewithal from which he could tithe does not mean that he was unwilling to tithe. The Gospel writers are mute about this matter.[60]

Paul was completely silent on the matter of bringing tithes. "Proportional giving"—giving as you are able—is the closest he came to the idea of tithing. This concept, well-known to Gentile readers because of their familiarity with similar ideals in Greek philosophy, included an emphasis on voluntary giving. It seems clear that Paul "would have regarded tithing requirements as similar to other laws . . . from which Christ has set people free (Gal. 3:23–26)."[61]

Paul's silence is understandable. He related primarily to a Gentile constituency as well as Jews of the Diaspora, so tithing—to support the work of the Jewish temple in faraway Jerusalem—may have seemed distant from the weightier matters Paul considered and proclaimed. (See the earlier treatment of "gifts" and "sacrifices" in this chapter.[62])

How can we view what the Bible says about tithing? The scriptural witness about tithing as a requirement for God's people is strong only when the passages are taken literally or grouped together without attention to context. Finding scriptural support for tithing sometimes involves other exegetical contortions or outright omissions. These may be examples of the purposed retheming I've noted earlier.[63]

In the case of tithing, these approaches to Scripture do not adequately answer important questions such as these:

1. If tithing was part of the Mosaic Laws that Jesus transcended (Gal. 3:23–26 or Eph. 2:15), how is it any different from Old Testament civil or religious laws regarding clean/unclean foods, sacrifices, ordination rites, health practices, the Year of Jubilee, penalties for violating the Sabbath, women's vows to the Lord, or cities of refuge?

2. What other Old and New Testament contexts have *not* carried forward into today's society (e.g., an economy based on agriculture, a priesthood not able to own property or work for wages, or a single, central location for religious observances)?

3. If tithing includes only the Levitical Tithe, what are we to make of the command to observe the other two tithes, whose purposes remain equally important?

4. What does it mean that Jesus was relatively silent about this method of supporting Jewish religious enterprises?

5. What other approaches to funding God's mission have endured throughout scriptural history or are supported in Paul's theology?[64]

What might be some summary shifts in your understanding of the scriptural bases for tithing? These ideas come to mind:

1. As a requirement for faithful living, tithing does not meet high standards of biblical interpretation.

2. At the same time, tithing can be a helpful benchmark for your commitment to support your congregation's part of God's mission.[65]

3. Tithing does not encapsulate all of your gratitude to God. Your generosity, offerings, or sacrifices for God's purposes also show themselves in other faith practices.

4. Whether you tithe or not, you remain a steward.

Some practical considerations can accompany these scriptural shifts. Among them are these actions:

1. Frame your references to tithing in invitational language rather than as expectations or requirements.

2. Steer away from theological nostrums or teachings that ignore tithing's contexts or place in Jewish theological life.

3. Stress proportionate giving—perhaps even the concept of "fair share giving"—a practice perhaps closer to the spirit and letter of the Scriptures.[66]

4. Continue to explore additional methods of funding God's mission in your congregation (e.g., mission endowment funds, bequests, sponsorships, sale or rental of assets, investments, designated giving, or extracongregational program grants.)

5. Spend time in Bible conversations about the history of mission funding. Talk about the actual contexts of earlier times. Look at the emotional

and spiritual expectations of biblical leaders, and how gratitude or generosity were manifested in their lives. Examine carefully what happened as the original concept of "willing contributions" morphed into "institutional expectations."

Finally, don't despair about the seeming loss of tithing as an assured piety for supporting your congregation. Your hopes can supplant those worries: New generational cohorts of devout believers will continue to develop as mature disciples. They will find God-pleasing ways to financially support local congregations and the larger alliances that congregations form.

Notes

1. For a detailed and persuasive explanation of this entire parable—and its meaning for Jesus's hearers—see chapter 9 in Herzog's *Parables as Subversive Speech: Jesus as Pedagogue of the Oppressed* (Louisville, KY: Westminster/John Knox Press, 1994).

2. Herzog uses this term to refer to the highly placed servants who worked for privileged elites, managing their household economies, especially in matters of income generation. Although not named as *economos*, the retainers essentially functioned as stewards. Herzog, *Parables*, 157ff.

3. Although this pivotal character in the parable is traditionally considered to be God, Jesus nowhere refers to him as such. His actions and self-description later in the parable suggest the opposite of godly traits. Newer interpretations of this parable pivot on this clear shift, characterizing the master as less-than-admirable. Herzog, *Parables*, 154–55.

4. This seemingly amazing investment return was considered normal among the super wealthy in Jesus's times. Rich landowners would loan money to smaller landowners or tenant farmers, perhaps to purchase seed stock or to serve as bridge loans. At the time of harvest, the retainers would collect the loaned amount, plus a hefty fee for the use of the money, ranging upward from 100 percent. Should the borrowers be unable to repay their overloaded loans, the rich landowner would foreclose on their property, adding it to his holdings—for the purpose of planting crops with higher returns (e.g., vineyards and orchards). The hapless borrower would become landless and slip into servitude or abject poverty. The elite would gain wealth quickly and assuredly. Herzog, *Parables*, 159–62.

5. This was a special offering that was gathered over time. Its purpose was *not* for the maintenance of Paul's ministry or any of the congregations he established.

6. These familiar and helpful aphorisms from 2 Corinthians come to mind: "Now as you excel in everything . . . so we want you to excel also in this generous undertaking" (8:7); "For your sakes he [Jesus] became poor so that by his poverty you

might become rich" (8:9); "The one who sows sparingly will also reap sparingly, and the one who sows bountifully will also reap bountifully" (9:6); "God loves a cheerful giver" (9:7); or "Thanks be to God for his indescribable gift!" (9:15).

7. Their cultural context perhaps allowed or engendered some of that neediness, which hid a larger, more important truth: These believers possessed an abundance of material and physical gifts. Hans Dieter Betz, *2 Corinthians 8 and 9: A Commentary on Two Administrative Letters of the Apostle Paul* (Philadelphia: Fortress Press, 1985), 48.

8. Greek culture extolled the popular ideal that simple folks could live generously, in response to a divine grace. In the case of the Macedonian Christians, that grace was seen in their salvation through Christ. Betz, *2 Corinthians 8 and 9*, 44–45.

9. The gift-giving process Paul describes also fit the standards of other religions familiar to his readers: You receive a (divine) gift or grace. You reciprocate by dedicating yourself to that god. Animals could be the substitute for your self-sacrifice. Betz, *2 Corinthians 8 and 9*, 47.

10. Among the customs and beliefs Betz notes are these: Both stinginess and profligacy were considered the opposite of generosity (p.108); reciprocity in gift-giving was expected (p. 109); a lack of response (to a received gift) was a sign of greed (p. 97); gift-giving was considered an emotional act (p. 108); wealth was a blessing that enabled generous response (p. 97); and a gift was considered acceptable not because of the size of the gift but because of its relationship to the giver's ability to give (p. 66).

11. Paul's arguments and techniques were constructed to accomplish the desired result: The Corinthian church's willing and generous completion of its collection. Even his avoidance of the direct mention of money was employed as a part of his overall strategy of persuasion. Craig S. Keener, *1–2 Corinthians* (New York: Cambridge University Press, 2005), 202–5.

12. According to Betz, *2 Corinthians 8 and 9*, among the ideas already familiar to Paul's readers are these: provoke (p. 93), bountifully (p. 103), zeal (p. 56), willingness (p. 66), equality (pp. 67–68), redundant (p. 90), partnership (p. 46), scattering seed (p. 114), multiplying the harvest (p. 114), and reciprocity (p. 109). Keener (*1–2 Corinthians*) adds eagerness, privilege, sharing, fruit, abundance, and friendship to the list (pp. 203–5, 213).

13. The Greek term for "friendship" can be understood either as a business or personal relationship. Both Betz and Keener contend that in these chapters Paul alluded to the business sense of the term but focused on its more important relational elements. Keener asserts that Paul considered equality and sharing things in common to be part of true friendship (*1–2 Corinthians*, 203, 206).

14. Paul quoted or paraphrased Psalm 112:9; Proverbs 22:8; Exodus 16:18; and Isaiah 55:10. He alluded to the story of manna in the desert and the furnishing of the Tabernacle. Betz, *2 Corinthians 8 and 9*, 69, 106; Keener, *1–2 Corinthians*, 203, 213.

15. In Paul's theology, God alone deserved the honor. Thus the collected gifts of the Corinthians would result in thanksgiving, praise, and honor (from the Jerusalem congregation) being directed to God. Keener, *1–2 Corinthians*, 213.

16. Paul expanded this notion from Greek philosophy and referred to himself as a primary example, perhaps to refute possible accusations that he would use the collected gifts for his own well-being. Betz, *2 Corinthians 8 and 9*, 110.

17. Here Paul recalled the mythology regarding Dionysius, a kind of "corn god." Dionysius made sure that the harvest multiplied seed so that there was enough for both consumption and for planting the following spring's crop. Betz, *2 Corinthians 8 and 9*, 114.

18. Implicit in 2 Corinthians 8:5 and 8:9, the redemptive sacrifice of Christ calls for the response of self-sacrifice from the Corinthians. Betz, *2 Corinthians 8 and 9*, 47.

19. "While Christians have usually read this story as a tribute to the woman's piety . . . it is more likely in the context of Mark's world that Jesus singled her out to signify the horrific consequences of the economics of the Temple." Mitzi Minor, *The Spirituality of Mark: Responding to God* (Louisville: Westminster John Knox Press, 1996), 87.

20. Note especially Jesus's biting criticism of evil scribes who "devour the households (*oikos*) of widows." They accomplished this by seeking attention for their ostentatious piety, which justified their appointment as trustees of widows' estates. Thus they could exploit defenseless widows for their own gain. John R. Donahue, SJ, and Daniel J. Harrington, SJ, *The Gospel of Mark* (Collegeville, MN: Liturgical Press, 2002), 362–63.

21. In order to fulfill their religious obligations, peasants could be forced to sell their lands (and even family members) in order to pay the debt of their tithes and religious taxes. Minor, *Spirituality of Mark*, 87.

22. Peter G. Bolt, *Jesus' Defeat of Death: Persuading Mark's Early Readers* (Cambridge: Cambridge University Press, 2003), 252. Bolt also reminds his readers that the Temple aristocracy—including the scribes Jesus condemns—depended on the crushing presence of the Roman occupiers, and joined those oppressors in plundering the people under the guise of religious duty.

23. Robert Jewett (New Testament Interpretation Professor Emeritus at Garrett-Evangelical Theological Seminary) summarizes the matter thusly: "Luke-Acts uses its eleven explicit prayer texts to present the distinctively Lucan understanding of God's plan of salvation, the divine method for activating that plan and the proper human response to it." Flyleaf blurb from Steven F. Plymale, *The Prayer Texts of Luke-Acts* (New York: Peter Lang, 1991).

24. Plymale, *Prayer Texts*, 55–56.

25. Plymale, *Prayer Texts*, 54.

26. Luther is practical in his understanding of the wide range of God's continuing gifts. He included in his godly gift list the following: "Food, drink, clothing, shoes, house, home, fields, livestock, money, faithful rulers, good government, good weather, peace, health, decency, honor, good friends, faithful neighbors and the like." Quoted in Timothy J. Wengert, *The Contemporary Translation of Luther's Small Catechism* (Minneapolis: Augsburg Fortress, 1994), 36.

27. Plymale, *Prayer Texts*, 54.

28. Plymale, *Prayer Texts*, 55.

29. Some contemporary Jewish scholarship calls this supposedly exemplary behavior into question. An interesting Midrash accompanies Genesis 22:7 (Isaac's apparent consent to be sacrificed). In this reverential addition, Isaac adds, "But I grieve for my mother." Perhaps Isaac has some second thoughts? Tova Hartman and Charlie Buckholtz, *Are You Not a Man of God? Devotion, Betrayal and Social Criticism in Jewish Tradition* (New York: Oxford University Press, 2014), 37–39.

30. The sacrificial rituals—and their foundational themes—are not as much evidence of individual piety as they are expressions of the values of the entire worshipping community. Gordon J. Wenham, "The Theology of Old Testament Sacrifice," in *Sacrifice in the Bible*, ed. Roger J. Beckwith and Martin J. Selman (Grand Rapids: Baker Book House, 1995), 76–79.

31. More accurate translations of the Hebrew *nih.ōah.* might include "soothing," "pacifying," or "quieting." Thus God's uneasiness—with idolatries and other sins—could be alleviated by sacrifice. Wenham, "Theology of Old Testament Sacrifice," 80.

32. "Sacrifice" also calls attention to a host of related matters—e.g., theologies of atonement, the symbolism of blood, human sacrifice, similarities/differences with pagan cults, and the role of priests in these rituals. Wenham admits that although the sacrificial rites are clearly described in the Old Testament, their derivation or deeper significance is not as clearly outlined or generally agreed upon. Thus the matter of sacrifice remains a difficult concept to bring forward into the context and behaviors of contemporary Christianity. Wenham, "Theology of Old Testament Sacrifice," 76–78, 80–82.

33. Their faithfulness included preservation of the Law, the establishment of synagogues, and their zeal for purity in the face of corrupting foreign influences. Roger T. Beckwith, "Sacrifice in the World of the New Testament," in Beckwith and Selman, *Sacrifice in the Bible*, 107.

34. These could be termed "sacrifices of greed": Worshippers offered sacrifices out of thanksgiving to the more predictable deities, but also sought to appease the capricious avarice of the less-than-admirable gods and goddesses. Beckwith, "Sacrifice," 105.

35. These dynamics continue to play out in the lives of Christians around the world in these times. Their suffering, torture, and death continue, both as horrific tragedy and also as a witness to the enduring power of Jesus's example.

36. For Paul's witness in this matter, see Philippians 3:8–9, "More than that, I regard everything as loss because of the surpassing value of knowing Christ Jesus as my Lord. For his sake I have suffered the loss of all things, and I regard them as rubbish, in order that I may gain Christ and be found in him." (Luther's scatological translation of "rubbish" frames this personal confession even more bluntly.)

37. By sacrificing, you are not buying anything from God or causing God to act on your behalf. In sacrificial living, there is no earning nor paying back. Martin J. Selman, "Sacrifice for Christians Today," in Beckwith and Selman, *Sacrifice in the Bible*, 159.

38. For a detailed exposition of these matters, see Herzog's interpretation of the story of the Rich Man and Lazarus (Luke 16:19–31), chapter 7, "The Unbridgeable Chasm," in *Parables*.

39. Abundance-related words describe the leftovers from the Feeding of the 5000 (John 6:12); the Prodigal Son's memories of his father's servants' lifestyle (Luke 15:17); Jesus's comments about the poor widow's offering (Luke 21:4); and even the increasing number of Christians after Pentecost (Acts 16:5).

40. It would be easy to characterize Greco-Roman religious life only as the worship of a rogues' gallery of gods and goddesses who deserved adoration primarily because they could (literally) deliver the goods. (Copia, Euthenia, Abundantia, Diana of Ephesus, Cybele, Dionysius, Demeter, Eros, Gaia, and Fortuna are examples.) As a balance to unrequited abundance-seeking, the Greek philosophers also held to the principle that wealth was granted by the gods as a commission to share with others. Paul echoed and deepened that viewpoint. Betz, *2 Corinthians 8 and 9*, 110.

41. For Paul, ideas related to "abundance" and "abound" could apply to God's truthfulness (Rom. 3:7); the grace of God (Rom. 5:15); the value of the sufferings of Christ (2 Cor. 1:5); the Philippians' love for Paul's ministry (Phil. 1:9, 4:18); and thanksgiving to God (Col. 2:7). Even though he lived a Spartan existence, Paul wrote reassuringly about God's abundant blessings (2 Cor. 9:8; Phil. 4:19).

42. The sacrilege of the Prayer of Jabez—and its attendant semitheologies—remains a painful memory in Protestant Christianity. Another sobering evidence of this pernicious way of thinking: the enduringly high percentage of Bible-loving believers who are certain that "God helps those who help themselves" is an actual Bible passage!

43. For a sobering treatment of this matter, read carefully and prayerfully the continuing work of Bill McKibben, especially *Eaarth: Making a Life on a Tough New Planet*. (New York: Henry Holt and Company, 2010). Similar themes fill entire psalms and the laments of several prophets. See Psalms 113 or 117, and Joel 2:12–17 or Habakkuk 3:17–19 as examples.

44. See Proverbs 5 for direct counsel about being satisfied with one's spouse; Proverbs 11:24 for a warning about the results of greed; Proverbs 12:9 for a reminder about

an overexalted self-image; Proverbs 30:15–16 for an example of dissatisfaction from the natural world; or the summary encouragement of Proverbs 14:30 (CEV), "It's healthy to be content, but envy can eat you up."

45. The author's target audience may have been believers who were tempted to reconcile Greek notions (of the good life) with biblical truth. The entire book may have been a kind of textbook, particularly directed at young males. O'Toole, *Reading Ecclesiastes*, 261.

46. The moral philosophy of the Stoics held that only basic necessities—food and clothing—were sufficient for one's well-being. That virtue was related to another personal trait that Greeks sought: self-sufficiency. *Autarkes* meant a competence for both self-sufficiency and being satisfied with one's state of life. W. Hulitt Gloer, *Smyth & Helwys Bible Commentary: 1&2 Timothy-Titus* (Macon, GA: Smyth & Helwys, 2010), 197.

47. Even though its dictionary meanings number only a few, "enough" functions linguistically like the utility infielder on a baseball team, who can play any number of positions in order for the team to win. Utilitarian at its roots—a quantifying adjective—the word can also carry subtleties of description and relationship. Its synonyms—adequate, sufficient, full, quite, satisfactory, tolerable, rather—do the same, spreading into adverbial forms and uses as well.

48. Some background information may illustrate the importance of this letter as you seek contentment: (1) The standard of Jesus in the Christ Hymn takes advantage of an accepted piece of pagan moral philosophy. Seneca addresses the importance of example, "The way is long if one follows precepts, but short and helpful if one follows examples." From Seneca's *Moral Epistle 6.6*, translated by Frederick Weidmann in *Philippians, First and Second Thessalonians and Philemon* (Louisville: Westminster John Knox Press, 2013), 71–72. (2) In this letter, "holding fast" does not denote static, passive determination to remain in a fixed place or position. Instead, it is a military term implying forceful movement, as in a battle formation. This wording would have set well with Paul's readers, who lived in a Roman colony settled by military veterans. Weidmann, *Philippians*, 71. (3) The verbs in 3:12–16 are voiced as present tense participles. Paul encourages actions—e.g., pressing on, straining forward—that continue as an ongoing process, an enduring "now." Weidmann, *Philippians*, 70. (4) Gain and loss are framed by their relevance to the "knowledge of Christ." Contentment is rooted in acknowledging that Christ is Lord. Weidmann, *Philippians*, 67. (5) Paul was glad to say that he could be content regardless of circumstance. The term for "content" is closer to "self-sufficient," with its connotations of thrift and self-control. Paul's thoughts here transcend the similar principle in Stoic moral philosophy because he gave credit for this personal character trait to "the one who strengthens me." Weidmann, *Philippians*, 83–84.

49. In a metaphorical or metaphysical meaning of stewardship, God is the "owner." Part of God's plan—perhaps all of it?—is devoted to giving (to the world and its

people) blessings of every kind. God *gives* his only Son; God *sends* rain on the just and unjust; God *grants* salvation to undeserving humankind; and God *offers* the gifts of the Holy Spirit. As stewards of God's mysteries—God's giving?—we participate in that part of God's overall will for the world.

50. It is important to remember that the priests and Levites could not own property or engage in agricultural enterprises. Thus the sacrifices, tithes, and later Temple taxes were necessary. Mark Allan Powell, *Giving to God: The Bible's Good News about Living a Generous Life* (Grand Rapids, MI: Eerdmans, 2006), 156–57.

51. See chapter 11, "Sacrificial Giving," in Gary A. Anderson, *Charity: The Place of the Poor in the Biblical Tradition* (New Haven, CT: Yale University Press, 2013).

52. Anderson, *Charity*, 155–56. Further proof of this statement is the fact that "the Hebrew and Aramaic term for commandment, *mitsva*, can often mean simply alms-giving." Twentieth-century Talmudic scholar Saul Lieberman, as quoted by Anderson, *Charity*, 156.

53. Some New Testament examples can illustrate this point. *Carivzomai*—freely give, deliver, or forgive—usually refers to God, but never to money. *Dovs* and *Dovths* denote monetary gifts, but *dwrevomai, dwreavn, dwvrhma, dwreav*, and *davrisma* do not ever refer to money. Appearing over 150 times in the New Testament, *cavris* refers to money only once. Andreas J. Köstenberger and David A. Croteau, *Reconstructing a Biblical Model for Giving: A Discussion of Relevant Systematic Issues and New Testament Principles* (Wake Forest, NC: Southeastern Baptist Theological Seminary, web-published paper, 2006), 9–10.

54. Leonard Sweet, "Freely You Have Received, Freely Give: Toward a Post-Tithing, Post-Stewardship, Postmodern Theology of Receiving," 5–10.

55. Andreas J. Köstenberger and David A. Croteau, *"Will a Man Rob God?" (Malachi 3:8): A Study of Tithing in the Old and New Testaments* (Wake Forest, NC: Southeastern Baptist Theological Seminary, web-published paper, 2006), 2–8.

56. Köstenberger and Croteau, *"Will a Man Rob God?"* 9–11.

57. Sweet, "Freely," 2–3.

58. In addition to the imposition of taxes to support the Temple and its workers, Nehemiah also required the collection of firewood for the Temple and reinstituted the concept of "first-fruits giving." He also appointed tithe collectors to go from town to town to collect unspecified tithes. Köstenberger and Croteau, *"Will a Man Rob God?"* 14–16.

59. Köstenberger and Croteau, *"Will a Man Rob God?"* 19.

60. Sweet, "Freely," 3.

61. Powell, *Giving to God*, 155.

62. The author of Hebrews—possibly Paul?—compared Melchizedek to Christ and included a mention of a tithe given to Melchizedek by Abram (Heb. 7:1–3). This

offering came from Abram's battle spoils and was given as a one-time gift. Using this single passage as a proof for the institution of tithing among God's people stretches the Genesis event past its context and far beyond the purposes of the larger Christology of Hebrews. Köstenberger and Croteau, *"Will a Man Rob God?"* 24.

63. For example, turning Abraham (in his tithing encounter with Melchizedek) into an allegorical prefiguring of contemporary Christians, or naming Abel's superior sacrifice as the beginning of tithing. Köstenberger and Croteau, *"Will a Man Rob God?"* 2–3. 24. Among scriptural truths somehow exempted from critical scrutiny: the tithe's devolution into a virtual tax or the enormous economic burden tithing placed on poor people. Sweet, "Freely," 2, 4.

64. Perhaps the strongest examples are the principles of proportional giving and a willing heart. Powell, *Giving to God*, 155, 162ff.

65. In the Scriptures, tithing has a matter-of-fact purpose: Religious enterprises required financial support. No matter what piety is attached to tithing, this pragmatic reality remains. As you consider your responsibility to maintain your congregation's active participation in God's purposes, you can benefit from this 10 percent standard, thinking of it as a goal or habit. Powell, *Giving to God*, 162.

66. Lutheran theologian Mark Allan Powell outlines details of this practice, essentially a way to determine how much to contribute to a congregation's part of God's mission. Based on Paul's notions of fairness—giving according to one's means (2 Cor. 8:3; 11–13)—you can develop a system of financial pledging that expects larger contributions from those with higher incomes and lower contributions from those with lesser earnings. Neither tithing nor sacrifice is excluded by this approach. Powell, *Giving to God*, 162–66.

Chapter 4

Promising Stewardship Scriptures

In this chapter I invite you into some places in the scriptural witness where stewardship-related wisdom might not be as easily seen. What might you discover? Fascinating, motivating, and inspiring testimony that has been waiting for your stewardship spirit all these years! Whether these Scripture passages, stories, or concepts are familiar or not, they might become:

- Missing pieces that complete stewardship puzzles.
- New answers to old questions.
- New questions that challenge old answers.
- Wormholes to new universes of stewardship thinking.
- Backdoor approaches to stewardship.
- Sources for new metaphors, analogies, or word pictures.

Each of the following concepts or Scripture verses comes with this encouragement: Do some more digging and thinking! While avoiding the traps of proof-texting—"Everything in the Bible is about stewardship!"—you can still find encouragement for your congregation's stewardship ministries.

The Role of Churches in God's Economy

Perhaps the most basic proposition to explore is the idea that your congregation— a "body with many members" (1 Cor. 12:12–31)—fulfills God's *economia* together. Neither "steward" nor "stewardship" calls solely for acts of individual piety or responsibility.

Much of your congregation's stewardship is carried out through its programs, ministries, and proclamation. An even more effective stewardship occurs as members fan out into their circles of influence and responsibility. In their daily life ministries, the members of your congregation get God's work done in places where no pastor or church program could ever reach.

Your congregation could be a steward of stewards. Your congregation can be the place that equips stewards to carry out their individual ministries in the world. Members carry the stewardship of the congregation into every nook and cranny that they inhabit, in every relationship that they hold dear, and every situation that needs God's love (see Eph. 4:11–13). It's possible that this "equipping of the saints" for their stewardship could become your congregation's primary mission.[1]

The Ephesians text also suggests that "unity and maturity" might be an outcome of this viewpoint. Because every member has a stake in carrying God's work into their daily lives—using their unique gifts—this central focus of the church might enable unity and maturity more easily than other cherished or historical purposes of the church. However they are measured, the unity and maturity of a congregation might transcend the sometimes chaotic promises of the church-growth movement. Both unity and maturity find their strength in diversities of gifts, not in an invisible or *de facto* homogeneity among members.[2]

Jesus as Steward

Jesus is the prime example of faithful, righteous living, so it makes sense to consider how Jesus behaved as a steward. Even though the stewards of his day were nonexemplary functionaries in a corrupt economic system— meaning that Jesus did NOT identify himself as a steward—it's still possible that Jesus behaved as a steward in several ways. (See Phil. 2:6–11 for Paul's take on Christ's faithfulness as a steward.)

You might approach these questions in your study of Christ's role as a steward:

- How strongly did Jesus understand his role in God's *economia*?
- What do Jesus's teachings suggest about his understanding of the positive uses of possessions, wealth, or power?
- How did Jesus stay content, joyful, purposed, and humble?
- In what ways was Jesus a sacrificial giver?
- What evidence do you find about Jesus's sense of ownership, trusteeship, or management of resources?
- What stewardship-related excesses or problems did Jesus criticize?
- What can you learn from Jesus's stewardship that could work in your context? What might be difficult?

- Which of Jesus's commands, observations, parables, or experiences fit well with Paul's theology of stewardship? Which of them fit well with your self-concept as a steward?

Wealth

The Bible is full of observations about wealth. It's not that difficult to find passages that condemn or warn about wealth, especially fortunes amassed by injustice of any kind. (Jer. 17:11 minces no words.) Other sections of Scripture caution those who are wealthy about the dangers or follies of being rich. (Eccles. 5:13–17 is an example of this viewpoint.)

It would be easy to name Jesus as a critic of wealthy people and their riches. In several of his parables, the villains are rich people—Luke 16 features both the Dishonest Manager and the Rich Man who ignores the beggar Lazarus. His warnings about riches are specific and direct (Matt. 6:19–20).

At the same time, Jesus spent time in the homes of rich people. One of his disciples (Matthew) was a former toll tax collector. Jesus's ministry was likely funded by the generosity of patrons such as Mary the Magdalene. The wealthy tax collector Zacchaeus was a beneficiary of Jesus's call to repentance. Among his quiet followers in Jerusalem was the influential religious leader Nicodemus, most likely also rich.

Paul's message of Christ to the Gentiles attracted those who were downtrodden or oppressed, but it also appealed to those who were well-off. Those who accepted Christian beliefs and lifestyles included rich merchants (Lydia [Acts 16:14–15]), government officials (Erastus, the treasurer of Corinth, [Rom. 16:23] and the proconsul Sergius Paulus [Acts 13:4–12]), the lawyer Zenas (Titus 3:13), and synagogue officials (Crispus [Acts 18:8]).[3]

Paul's view about riches and those who were wealthy is perhaps best exemplified in his first letter to the young pastor Timothy (see 1 Tim. 6:6–11a and 6:17–19.) Although he reminded Timothy about the perils of acquisitive expectations—and named "the love of money" as the source of all evil—Paul also observed that opportunities for service are made possible by wealth.[4]

In our times, the growing income disparity between the very wealthy and the rest of the population has become a source of conflict and condemnation. At the same time, some of our country's wealthiest individuals have taken The Giving Pledge—a promise to contribute the majority of their wealth to philanthropy. Formalized in 2010 by Warren Buffett and Bill and Melinda Gates, this growing cohort of the world's richest people—currently numbering over

125 individuals or families—continues to offer a compelling testimony about the power of wealth to change the world for good purposes.

Scriptures about wealth might suggest that your congregation could consider "ministry to or among the wealthy" as part of your mission. You might also include those who are wealthy in deliberations about how best to serve God. (If your congregation regards those who are wealthy only as assured contributors, you will soon learn that this approach dishonors the fact that they can also follow Christ and serve God's will *outside* of your congregation's ministries.)

Possessions

In a country as wealthy as the United States, the materialism that the Scriptures warn against is not just the province of the wealthy, but afflicts all of us. Scriptural invitations to live simply—"If we have food and clothing, we will be content with these" (1 Tim. 6:8)—include strong suggestions that possessions can pose problems for godly living.

Perhaps the strongest example is Jesus's epigrammatic proverb, "Where your treasure is, there your heart will be also" (Luke 12:34). The causality in this passage is correct. Your core attitudes and identity—implied in "heart"—are framed by your material contexts, especially "treasures." You are not only what you eat, but also what you see, touch, chase after, surround yourself with, or immerse yourself in. Possessions can be instrumental to God's purposes, certainly, but Jesus's warnings about materialism are consistent. The story of the Rich Young Man—who could not follow Jesus and "grieved, for he had many possessions"—may be an accurate description of a universal phenomenon today (Matt. 19:22).

Even as materialism—seeking a way of life centered on possessions—drives the world economy, this embedded human characteristic also leads increasingly to the destruction of the world's environment. Injustice, hunger, disease, and war are the long-term results of unrequited acquisitiveness. As these economic realities bump up against each other, your congregation cannot ignore the fact that members' hearts could more likely be found in their treasures and toys. Stewardship ministries can address this matter directly.

Individualism and Self-Idolatry

What can most easily confound or block our identities as stewards is simple: Self-idolatry lies at the heart of all apostasy. We believe ourselves to be minor gods come to Earth. Smart enough to disguise our obvious idols, we can easily succumb to philosophies that proclaim the primacy of individuals in systems of belief and practice.

Stewardship rests on exactly the opposite propositions: We are not God(s), our lives are not our own, and so we live to serve God's purposes. In communities of gathered stewardship—churches—we accomplish together what we cannot accomplish alone.

Paul's writing supports this social philosophy. In Romans 12, his nearly poetic words invoke a steward-like way of living and being. He talks about giving away our lives as communal sacrifices for the will of God. (This is something we can discern better when we're transformed beyond individualism.) He prefaces a long metaphor—the church as a body—with "a call to change the way in which we assess ourselves and others." This ideal undercuts competition for honor and undermines any status system based on the presumption of individual excellence.

Paul was writing to a house church in Rome—likely a diverse collection of people from among various social and economic cohorts—who were newly joined together in this new faith. Most were Gentiles, familiar with their cultural context but still learning about The Way that centered on Christ. His readers would have known well the value of cooperative trade associations and communal meals. They were already banding together in anticipation of coming persecution. They would not have understood individualism as central to their faith life. The church-as-body-of-Christ comparison seals the matter in this text.[5]

Let me say this again for emphasis: The scriptural stewardship witness does not support—or even suggest—individualistic approaches to faith. Paul is even more blunt in this matter, "We do not live to ourselves, and we do not die to ourselves. If we live, we live to the Lord, and if we die, we die to the Lord; so then, whether we live or whether we die, we are the Lord's" (Rom. 14:7–8).

Self-idolatry—an ultimate disobedience of the First Commandment—is the root of all other sins. So it makes sense that stewardship also suffers when that overinflated self-concept remains unchallenged. Individualism calls for continuing repentance and forgiveness. However it manifests itself, this attitude does not bode well for the health of your congregation. (For example, in matters of congregational funding, "It's my money, and I'll decide what to do with it" is evidence of this inadequate understanding of stewardship.)

A good place to find scriptural support for combating individualism: any passage that reminds you of God's power, primacy, or protection. (The last chapters of Job—starting at chapter 36—are bluntly, irrefutably honest.)

Economic Behaviors and Systems

Stewardship begins and ends with economics, especially when that term is understood as broadly as "stewardship." Economic behaviors of individuals—their decisions and resulting actions—collect together to form intricately balanced systems that ripple toward us throughout geography and history.

What was economically troublesome or evil in Scripture continues into our lives today. The warnings of Proverbs and Ecclesiastes continue to show themselves in contemporary selfishness, greed, and economic folly. Amos's sharp rebukes of prevailing economic corruption and injustice in Israel and Judah apply equally well in our times, in our locales, in our ears (see Amos 5 and 6). In other prophetic utterances, widespread economic inequities still bristle at our touch. Many of Jesus's most relevant teachings concentrate on the economic sins of his (and our) times. The writer of the New Testament book of James sounds warnings about unjust wage payments, stories that could have generated news headlines this morning (James 5:1–6).

To retain its integrity, your congregation might also focus on larger economic questions that can impede the fulfillment of God's *economia* for the world. These matters might include disproportionate income distribution; unfair taxation; disregard of workers; misshapen notions of "freedom"; hidden fraud; or the undue influence of oligarchs.

Coming Scarcities

One of the more difficult elements of stewardship in the coming decades: The reality that the Earth's resources are being consumed at a rate that does not allow for them to be sufficiently replenished. So scarcity could likely become a factor in your congregation's stewardship.

I don't use the term "scarcity" lightly, nor am I defining it in merely metaphorical or metaphysical ways. When I write about scarceness, I refer to diminishing supplies of natural resources—water, arable land, forest, animal and plant species, minerals, clean air—as well as the common ingredients of life that are derived from them—food, manufactured products, sanitation. And with those scarcities can come larger societal disintegration—civil unrest, anarchy, failed states, or wars. General truths that are hard to avoid:

- In major crop-growing regions, the world's supply of groundwater is being depleted faster than surface water can replenish it.
- Air pollution threatens the economic and political stability of China.

- As birth rates decline in Russia, China, and India, their consumer base is less able to drive worldwide economic growth.
- Rates of increases of worldwide food production are not keeping pace with rates of population growth.
- The number of failed states—nations with minimal or nonexistent governments—has continued to increase.
- Significant global warming is already affecting the entire planet.[6]

A careful look at scriptural coverage of this subject yields this equation: "Blessing" is not the same as plentitude, which is not the same as abundance. "Our God is an Abundance God" pronouncements—sometimes blithely proclaimed as though they were nostrums or narcotics—cannot hide what most people are already aware of: Food prices are higher; the effects of bad weather seem to grow; fear and hyperprotectiveness continue to increase; and the rates of worldwide unemployment are edging stubbornly higher. Half-full glasses don't discount the probability that pessimism, mistrust, and doubt also seem to be prospering.

The stewardship witness of Scripture can be a vital source for wisdom in coming times of scarcity:

- God's people have been at the ends of their ropes before, in circumstances not unlike what you're facing now. When deeply probed, their experiences can be a source of hope—as in "people like us have faced this before and still lived faithfully."
- Miracles of rescue and deliverance dot the landscape of the Bible, as do hard-nosed condemnations about the states-of-mind that made God's rescue necessary. (A sobering sample: Jeremiah's über-frank account of his lifelong prophetic mission.)
- Jesus counsels against worry and invites us to "ask so that you will receive" (Matt. 6:25–34 and 7:7–11). He teaches his followers about contentment and warns against the perils of acquisitiveness.
- Paul reminds his readers of God's ability to grant abundance (Eph. 3:20–21) as well as God's working toward an eventual purpose (Rom. 8:28).
- In one little-known gem of Scripture, Peter writes to martyrdom-bound believers, "We have everything we need to live a life that pleases God. It was all given to us by God's power, when we learned that he had invited us to share in his wonderful goodness" (2 Pet. 1:3, CEV).

These Scriptures address the reality of scarcity with assurances about God's nature, God's promises, and God's history. The passages provide solid grounding for a kind of "abundance thinking" that can help you make sense out of the factual data that pours into your brain each day:

- There may be less water for crops—but congregation members can eat less and still be healthy.
- Carbon-based pollution may start to drag disease into your lungs, but God's people can adjust their thermostats and limit their automobile use.
- Selfish disregard might characterize too much of politics and business, but your congregation can help parents raise children with simple living precepts burned into their brains.
- Your lifestyle may be threatened, but that may turn out to be a good thing for the entire planet.

In all these cases, abundance is the godly attitude even when scarcity approaches the factual reality. Both are true, and both are reasons for action.

Hope and Courage

Stewardship flourishes where hope and courage are embedded in self-identities. Think again about the original first-century role from which stewardship theology is derived: To fulfill their responsibilities, stewards had to exhibit shrewdness, practicality, bold action regardless of circumstances, and trust in the future—all ingredients or correlatives of hope.

Hope is as hope does. With courage in hand, hopeful people act on their fervent wishes for the future. In that sense, both stewardship and hope/courage result in—and cause—actions that can be measured and felt. That's why hopeful, courageous stewardship can be seen in the lives of admirable and active people. (See Job 4:6 for a poetic comment.) Always hopeful people, stewards can't get stuck in competitive cynicism or "learned helplessness."[7] (See Gal. 6:9 for Paul's take on not giving up.)

The source of hope is perhaps best summed up in Paul's blessing to the small band of Christians in Rome: "May the God of hope fill you with all joy and peace in believing, so that you may abound in hope by the power of the Holy Spirit" (Rom, 15:13). Joy and peace—gifts of God—are the causes for abundant hope. They may also be its outcomes.

Hopeful, courageous mindsets undergird and motivate stewardship actions of every kind, in every arena of life. When you identity, affirm, and strengthen hope and courage, your congregation can strengthen communal and individual stewardship. Your decision-making, your priorities, your programs, your proclamations—all can be tinged with language and actions that promote hope and courage. In doing so, you remain faithful stewards.

Love

Undeserved love—a gift of the Spirit and an essential quality of all spiritual matters—is connected to stewardship ministry. How does love inspire contentment? How does love motivate when "dutiful obedience" tails off? When does love trump selfishness? Where did Jesus's sacrificial love show itself in his stewardship?

Jesus's life and teaching are filled with examples and exhortations to love. Paul uses chapter 13 of his First Letter to the Corinthians to extol the virtues and necessity of love in the Christian life. Perhaps the most concentrated description of love's value comes in the letters of John. First John 4:7–21 assumes an almost creedal character as the writer connects God's love to salvation in Christ and to relationships essential for the community of faith. Part instruction, part poetry, and part praise hymn, this text could also serve as a basic training manual for apprentice stewards.

Love takes on down-to-earth importance when you consider how love connects to giving. A secular aphorism for fund-raising suggests this truth: "Fund-raising is friend-raising." The resulting logic seems apparent: Where love is easily found in a congregation, gratitude and generosity will also be in ample supply.

Love welds together people in common purpose, especially when difficulties threaten to overwhelm their mission or devotion to God. It may be true that Paul was proclaiming a first-century sociological truth when he wrote: "And now faith, hope and love abide, these three; and the greatest of these is love" (1 Cor. 13:13). Because love lasts, loving stewards can remain committed to their work.

Quick-Takes on Individual Passages

Stewardship shines out of smaller pieces of Scripture—not as proof texts, but as evidence how stewardship can soak into the witness of the Bible. Some examples follow here.

PSALM 34

Written at the time David was pretending to be mad—in order to escape his enemy Abimelech—this psalm expands abundance into other approaches to life. The psalm writer wants deliverance and protection; he speaks of God "tasting good" and he voices assurances about "lacking no good thing." Wickedness will be punished, and the fear of the Lord will result in contentment. This could be a good psalm to pick up when you're wondering where along your life path you lost track of the meaning of true abundance.

PSALM 90

This psalm presents long-view wisdom based on Moses's life experience, and offers a sobering-yet-hopeful testimony about the eternal nature of God's stewardship of human existence. The psalm deserves more than its customary use at funerals or New Year's Eve services. Perhaps some of the language in this psalm could be reworked to form your congregation's next stewardship theme.

ECCLESIASTES 2:1–11

Incessant pleasure-seeking may be a disease with no cure—the human brain easily habituates or becomes addicted to reward neurotransmitters. This section of Scripture details the futility of self-indulgence, and can serve as a starting point for whole-scale changes you might be seeking. The writer speaks candidly about his own desires—uncannily mirroring our own times—and relegates them to the trash heap of human existence. Good content for rites of passage, these verses could also be helpful in twelve-step programs aimed at acquisitive disorders or addictions.

ECCLESIASTES 3:1–8

Disturbed or disoriented daily schedules characterize much of the poor stewardship in our society. Time—in its smallest and largest manifestations—is a gift of God, so mindless use of this precious resource probably requires correction. This passage provides solutions, but not time-saving tips. Instead, the writer reminds readers about a *kairos*-oriented sense of time. In this passage, the eternal question, "What time is it?" gets a different answer, one that can slow you down and get you thinking. A good place to start stewardship disciplines for the time-trodden.

1 CORINTHIANS 9:3–18

When confronted with questions about his legitimate rights as a spiritual leader, Paul drew on Deuteronomic laws—the unmuzzled oxen—and secular models of soldiers, shepherds, and those who plant. His logic was as clear as its desired outcome: Like them, he had a right to be compensated for his labor. For the Jews among his readers, Paul also included in his argument the ways in which the Levites and priests had been compensated for centuries. The passage can address the fiduciary responsibility of congregations to their pastors.[8]

ROMANS 12:9–21

Stewardship themes fill this section of Romans, sometimes subtitled, "Marks of the True Christian." A possible manifesto for a stewardship of relationships, this text also contains subthemes concerning humility, alms-giving, hope, love, patience, and overcoming evil. When combined, these directives paint the picture of gifted stewards going about their work with wisdom.

THE BOOK OF JAMES

Regardless of Luther's "strawy epistle" opinion, this letter could be a helpful source for understanding stewardship ministry in practical terms. A quick reading of the NRSV subheads illustrates this possibility:

- Faith and wisdom (benefits of endurance)
- Poverty and riches (transience of riches)
- Trial and temptation (ultimate source of generosity)
- Hearing and doing the word (actions that flow from faith)
- Warning against partiality (perils of disregarding the poor)
- Faith without works is dead (stewardship as an action verb)
- Taming the tongue (stewardship of speaking)
- Two kinds of wisdom (personality traits for stewards)
- Boasting about tomorrow (the future determined by God's will)
- Warning to rich oppressors (moth-eaten and rusted possessions)

The writer of this letter did not have first-century stewardship in mind. But broad stewardship elements fill his plain-talking epistle. He offers pragmatic directives to Jews dispersed throughout the Roman Empire, gathering already known wisdom from their ancient traditions and laws into a body of practice that could be useful in their new faith context. God's grace may hide behind God's requirements in this book, but grace is never far removed from this basic supposition about stewardship: You serve a God unlike no other, a deity who is always working on your behalf. (See 1:5–7; 1:17–18; 4:6; and 5:13–16 as examples.)

1 Peter 4:10–11

You could post this passage on your refrigerator or cubicle wall as a summary statement about your congregational or individual stewardship: "Like good stewards of the manifold grace of God, serve one another with whatever gift each of you has received . . . so that God may be glorified in all things through Jesus Christ. To him belong the glory and the power forever and ever. Amen."

Notes

1. The lists of (four or five) gifts in this passage can be added to the twenty-plus gifts noted in other New Testament writings. Here the gifts connect to God's *economia* directly: "The building of the body is inextricably linked with (Christ's) intention of filling the universe with his rule, since the church is his instrument of carrying out his purposes for the cosmos." Peter T. O'Brien, *The Letter to the Ephesians* (Grand Rapids, MI: Eerdmans, 1999), 297–98.

2. Allen Verhey and Joseph S. Harvard, *Ephesians* (Louisville: Westminster John Knox Press, 2011), 168, 169.

3. Although there is ample evidence that early Christians were deeply concerned about people who were poor, the term *ptōchos* (the poor) is not found anywhere in Acts. "If the poor do not have a prominent place in the Acts narrative, the rich do." John Gillman, *Possessions and the Life of Faith: A Reading of Luke-Acts* (Collegeville, MN: Liturgical Press, 1991), 94.

4. Paul's stark word choices reveal his insistence about the dangers of wealth. Some examples from 1 Timothy 6:9: "Fall into temptation" might also be translated "to be defeated by, succumb to, or be overcome by temptation." The "plunge into ruin" can also mean a sinking or drowning. "Ruin" and "destruction" include connotations of an extensive, severe destruction filled with violence. The root words for "do not be haughty" (v. 17) carry a warning about self-exaltation. Paul's direct language also shows his deep understanding that wealth can accomplish godly possibilities. The wordplay on "rich" (vv. 17–18) changes material wealth into spiritually mature actions. "Ready to share" connects with *koinōnia* (fellowship), a mark of the early church and Greco-Roman sensibilities. W. Hulitt Gloer, *Smyth & Helwys Bible Commentary: 1 & 2 Timothy-Titus* (Macon, GA: Smyth & Helwys, 2010), 197–98, 209–10.

5. Peter Oakes, *Reading Romans in Pompeii: Paul's Letter at Ground Level* (Minneapolis: Fortress Press, 2009), 73–74, 99–102.

6. For specific examples, statistics, and detailed analysis, see Lester R. Brown's monumental work, *Plan B 2.0: Rescuing a Planet Under Stress and a Civilization in Trouble* (New York: W.W. Norton & Company, 2006). Perhaps most troubling about his account: Conditions have only worsened since the book was first published. *World on the Edge: How to Prevent Environmental and Economic Collapse* (New York: W.W. Norton & Company, 2011) continues his warnings and hopes.

7. Brain researchers have discovered that, when subjected to random shocks, mice give up trying to determine the causes of their extreme discomfort. They retreat to the corners of their cages and quiver continuously. Their neurobiology deteriorates and—if mice can be hopeful—that part of rodent self-identity probably disappears as well. The experience and personality trait can occur among humans. Bob Sitze, "Mice That Don't Run Away," in *It's NOT Too Late: A Field Guide to Hope* (Herndon, VA: Alban Institute, 2010), 66–67.

8. George T. Montague, SM, *First Corinthians* (Grand Rapids, MI: Baker Academic, 2011) 151–54.

Chapter 5

What Can Happen Next

In this final Scripture-focused chapter, let's see how all these matters could work together to strengthen your use of the Bible in stewardship ministries. The ideas are presented as invitations to action.

Don't Despair about Losing Cherished Stewardship Passages.

Yes, some familiar texts may not carry all the meanings that you've been taught or have used for years. But the changes you've seen here still honor the applicability of those passages, although in different ways. If you accept the proposition that "stewardship" is a concept and practice much broader than you may have considered in the past, you'll begin to see that the Bible is packed full of meaning for your life as a steward. Scores of practical texts can help you answer fundamental questions—about your relation to God, your purpose in life, your identity, your gifts, or your sins. What's left after you "lose" beloved Scriptures? Perhaps more than you imagined!

What You Might Do:

1. Remain open to the possibility that you have not learned enough about treasured stewardship Scriptures, or that you may have missed their deeper meanings.
2. Trust that newer passages you're now examining will show you their applicability for your service to God's will.
3. If you choose to shift more securely into your long-cherished views of these Scriptures, take comfort in having studied other meanings or uses with an objective and appreciative mind.

Insist on Accurate Interpretations of the Bible.

Theologians look at the Bible with a variety of interpretive rules and tools in hand. When you hold those generally agreed-upon rules in high regard, you won't be easily tempted to force into the Scriptures what was probably *not* in the minds of the writers or the first hearers/readers. And when you use a full range of exegetical devices—historical or literary criticism, for example—you can move beyond the limits of only literal or devotional interpretations.[1]

WHAT YOU MIGHT DO:

1. Consult commentaries, Bible dictionaries, concordances, and other reference materials that reflect current knowledge and practice. Some useful approaches to biblical interpretation have come into full bloom only recently.

2. When possible, read and study Scripture in translations rather than paraphrases. Translations are more insistent that the meanings of the original languages remain intact.

3. Continue to ask questions about any stewardship text. Two that characterize my personal study of Scripture: "What's really going on here?" and "What's the writer really trying to say?"

4. If your questions elicit only metaphorical, allegorical, or eschatological answers, you might reexamine the passage's context or the original meanings of its words.

5. Learn more about new approaches to scriptural interpretation. Look for news about new archaeological discoveries. Buy and use a newer Greek or Hebrew lexicon. Regularly read theological journals or websites devoted to Scripture interpretations. Look for continuing education possibilities—some online—offered by seminaries or denominational offices.[2]

Separate Out Church-Focused Stewardship.

One of the major difficulties in approaching the stewardship witness of Scriptures is the default assumption that stewardship is primarily concerned with the state of the institutional church. When that interpretation can be refined out of a passage, hold to it dearly. But when that interpretation might reflect a contamination of the passage's meaning, rethink its utility in your life.

WHAT YOU MIGHT DO:

1. Verify that the context of a passage applies to current ecclesiastical matters. (For example, methods for funding the First Temple in Jerusalem have to be understood in that context, and cannot automatically be flung forward into the settings of contemporary congregations.)

2. Assume that an institutional church bias may still be coloring a large share of the interpretation of stewardship Scriptures. You may need to look for subtle shifts in logic. (For example, even though the text nowhere states this fact, "the man" in the Parable of the Ten Talents is automatically presumed to be a figure for God.)

3. Let Scripture be silent in the places where it does not speak. The writers of the Bible could not have known about automatic bank deposits, charitable deductions on income taxes, clergy housing allowances, or Supreme Court decisions about the place of churches in our democracy. When Scripture speaks in broad terms, listen carefully but don't wait to hear culturally specific details.

Embrace Scriptures That Critique Ecclesiastical and Secular Matters.

Many Old Testament passages were written within the context of the continuing struggles of the prophets with the Temple Cult. Those disagreements focused on whether Temple-oriented laws and observances were central to the worship of Yahweh. It's fair to say that Jesus and Paul joined the critique of the Temple cult. With the prophets before them, they saw practices and beliefs that pulled God's people away from more basic understandings of the Law. (For example, Jesus disputed the relevance of the Purity Codes in the Torah, aiming his message instead toward the Torah's insistence on justice.)

The prophets—joined by the writers of Wisdom literature—also turned their gaze on evils in the world around them. Jesus and Paul carried those warnings into their teaching and writing. What did they condemn? Idolatry of any kind, but also greed, economic malfeasance, sexual immorality, arrogance, selfishness, and indulgent living. At any time in history, these ways of living obstruct the fulfillment of God's will. As you encounter the prophetic warnings of Scripture, you may also be gathering wisdom and courage to confront these evils in your own setting.

WHAT YOU MIGHT DO:

1. If you're already inclined to give your attention to justice-related Scriptures, see how you can connect the meanings of those passages with other stewardship Scriptures. See how you can marry your fervent hopes for righteous integrity with your strong self-identity as a steward.

2. If justice-and-peace passages haven't yet attracted your attention or prayers, consider seriously reframing your approach to these texts so that you're more appreciative of their stewardship implications. The will of God for the world—God's *economia*—also includes God's battle against or elimination of evil.

3. Look carefully at places where a modern-day "temple cult" mentality might be present. (Clericalism—the clergy comprise the core of the church—is one persistent example.) See how the warnings of the prophets—Jesus and Paul included—might apply to your own assumptions or behaviors as a congregational leader.

4. Where evil or sinfulness exist elsewhere in the church, be ready to call out of Scripture the wisdom you need to combat these stewardship-defying practices.

5. As you read stewardship Scriptures of any kind, try not to get caught up in anger or condemnation. Yes, anger can be righteous, but the role of steward is not the same as that of a prophet. You can be prophetic, certainly, but your calling goes further than truth-telling or warning. Remember that you're dedicated to accomplishing the will of the Owner. When anger or condemnation take over your brain, it might be hard to be shrewd, wise, creative, cooperative, or powerful.

Trust the Spirit's Working in You.

Even if cherished or familiar stewardship texts don't carry as much weight or inspiration as they have in the past, remember that the Holy Spirit works in all parts of the Bible. Paul summarizes the matter nicely: "All scripture is inspired by God and is useful for teaching, for reproof, for correction, and for training in righteousness so that everyone who belongs to God may be proficient, equipped for every good work" (2 Tim. 3:16–17). This means that you can be as heartened by the stewardship implications of the story of Samuel's mother Hannah as you are motivated by invitations to care for the poor. Jesus's Sermon on the Mount could become as instructive as all the passages on sacrificial giving combined.

WHAT YOU MIGHT DO:

1. Start any Bible reading or study with a prayer for openness to the Spirit. This helps you approach a text expecting to be surprised or delighted.

2. Expand the number and quality of questions you bring to a text. This will help open the meaning of a passage after the most obvious ideas come to mind.

3. As a further discipline, write down both the questions and possible responses that develop as you read and study a text. Look at what you've written to see what patterns or new discoveries are now evident.

4. If you intend to spend more time and effort in a larger search—e.g., looking for new approaches to giving—consider mapping your work. Concepts, questions, and connections are more easily seen in a map than in a list. "Ahas!" are now available to you in a different way.[3]

Read for Your Life.

When you put it to work, stewardship theology can be as big as your life. As you approach Scripture, you're also asking the text to answer this enduring question, "How can I live my life?" You can think of any encounter with the Bible—stewardship-related or not—as an opportunity to learn about God's *economia* and your place in it. Stewardship is tilted toward pragmatic matters, so it's good and godly for you to ask "How does this (passage) make sense for my life?" and to expect answers!

WHAT YOU MIGHT DO:

1. Read or study Bible passages in physical settings that are closely associated with your daily living. Before morning routines, at lunch, during breaks, during your commute, after a meal, before or after chores, at the end of the day—any of these times offers you the benefit of recent experience, which can help color the questions and answers you bring to a text.

2. If Bible reading or study are new or languishing faith practices, start your stewardship searching in the books of Ecclesiastes, Proverbs, or Job. Each is rooted in the daily life experiences of wise people of God.

3. Devotional materials might provide another beginning for your Scripture pursuits. These books, journals, or blogs can offer you the life-related insights of other stewards.

Put Stewardship Scriptures to Use in Your Congregation.

It's possible that you have underestimated the ways in which you could employ the witness of Scripture in your congregation's ministries. To help you strengthen your stewardship ministries, think about some possibilities that might work in your setting:

1. *A working group:* Members meet weekly—Sunday mornings or mid-week before work for breakfast—to consider the meaning of a particular text or book of the Bible for their workplace ministries. Case studies, testimonies, word study, skill development—all are brought into focus by a section of Scripture.

2. *Pauses in worship:* Sunday worshipers take advantage of a five-minute gap between the reading of the day's text(s) and the sermon. During the silence, they meditate on the question, "What part of this text helps me carry out God's plan in my setting(s)?"

3. *Stewardship committee work:* As you plan annual stewardship campaigns, programs, or emphases, see what happens when you rethink which Scriptures you'll use as part of this work. If this book is expanding your understanding of "stewardship ministry," you may have much more scriptural material to work with.

4. *Stewardship "skunk works":* Some forward-thinking companies form informal teams of free-wheeling staff members who dream, wonder, conjure, or explore possible products or services. It might be valuable for you to bring together some bright-eyed folks to rethink your congregation's whole approach to stewardship. The best place to start might be some of the texts you've encountered here.

5. *Stewardship writing:* If you have a congregational newsletter, consider the possibility of putting some stewardship Scriptures onto paper or screens. New thoughts, hard questions, down-to-earth explorations, personal reflections, poetry, or cartoons—forms of communication that go beyond a simple, earnest description of scriptural texts. Start with the basics—passages about gratitude, stewardship as lifework, God's ownership, purpose, and meaning. Think of this as a gentle series of teaching moments—cozied into your newsletter. You might ask selected congregation leaders to develop some of this material—*after* they've done some studying and thinking about the texts.

6. *Personal correspondence:* As you write notes to people, use themes or memes that come from stewardship-related Scriptures as the content for thanks, blessings, or reflections. For example, who might exemplify a faithful steward or whose day would be brightened if you commended them for "sowing contentment"? Cite or paraphrase the relevant Scripture verse so that your correspondents can find and read the text.

7. *Renewing your congregation:* If you're interested in rethinking your congregation' mission or reason for existing, consider stewardship as *the* central organizing principle for the revitalization you hope will happen. Any number of the texts in the previous chapters could suggest core values for your congregation's ministry, and might also give you fresh language to use in this necessary task.

Summary

You've come to the conclusion of the first major section of this book. Before you and I move on, let's go back over the major ideas I've proposed in the previous chapters.

1. Because Scripture functions as source and norm for faith and life, you must interpret texts carefully, using established exegetical methods and rules.

2. Where the church may have misinterpreted or misapplied some portions of Scripture to serve justifiable goals—e.g., funding congregational mission—you may have to reexamine those texts and some of the cherished principles or practices you have derived from them.

3. Alongside "giving" emphases, Scripture encourages and advises several other attributes or actions for your lifework as a steward.

4. Given the broad expanse of stewardship themes, it also makes sense for you to explore previously overlooked stories, concepts, and texts that can provide support for the entire expanse of stewardship theology and practice.

5. Your rethinking of familiar Scripture texts does not diminish their usefulness. The emphases may shift, but they still retain their powerful witness.

These strong invitations bring this section to its close. These challenges come from my fervent hopes for the well-being of your congregation.

Notes

1. Literal and devotional uses of Scripture are important to a life of faith. The meaning of Scripture can be richer—and more applicable to your life—when you reach beneath the literal meanings of individual words or phrases.

2. You might want to exercise caution that these opportunities reflect newer and more insistent views of stewardship Scripture and theology.

3. A web search—*mind map* or *visual mapping*—will yield any number of software applications or downloadable templates. My favorite resource: *Mapping Inner Space, 2nd ed.*, by Nancy Margulies (with Nusa Maal) (Tucson, AZ: Zephyr Press, 2002).

PART II

Secular Stewardshifts

Chapter 6

Continuing Revelation: Secular Wisdom

Introduction

You've already considered possible shifts in the way you view stewardship-related Scripture texts and themes. Now I invite you to turn down a different path: Seeking secular stewardship wisdom and applying it to the stewardship ministries of your congregation. This task will fill the rest of the book.

In these next few pages I want to set the context for this "secular wisdom" way of thinking, so that your reading of the coming chapters will be helpful. These observations:

1. It might be important for you to rethink your views about sacred and secular.
2. God's wisdom can be found both in and outside the Scriptures.
3. A good portion of secular wisdom is already known and practiced by members of your congregation.
4. Your congregation will benefit from acknowledging the usefulness of extrascriptural wisdom.

An Underlying Yearning

Most people—you, too?—dearly want to be wise. Down deep, you know that anecdotes do not equal data, and that data do not equal facts; that facts are not the same as knowledge, and that knowledge does not ensure wisdom. Most of the time you don't want more information—it's the sorting and soothing capacity of wisdom that you really hope to find.

In a world overfilled with data, stories, facts, and knowledge, it seems even more difficult to hold onto wisdom. When it comes to living out your daily routines as a steward of God's *economia*, you depend on wisdom to sort out truth from fiction, fact from fantasy, achievable goals from wishful thinking, what's godly from what's selfish-and-stupid. That wisdom comes from the sacred Scriptures *and* secular sources where you can find God.

Time-Out for Terms

Take a few moments with me to think about the ideas embodied in the terms "sacred" and "secular." Each holds obvious meanings while also harboring other useful truths in its quiet alcoves.

With the rest of its linguistic family, "sacred" is derived from the Latin *sacrare*, a verb that means "to make holy, consecrate or set apart; dedicate; hold sacred; or immortalize"—all presumably in relation, worship, or service to a deity. The actions within the rites, rituals, and practices are deemed sacred. Sacredness is important because the god in question is preeminent or transcendent. What is sacred deserves veneration, reverence, or respect because of the ineffable nature of the divinity. "Sacred" fills in the empty spaces that remain when descriptions end.[1]

The word "secular"—sometimes a synonym for "world" or "worldly"— also has a Latinate root. Its original meaning came from *saeculum*, a term referring to a generation, age, or period of time. Implicit in the original meaning was the idea that an event, person, emphasis, or train of thought occurred only once during a generation or age. Therefore, anything "secular" had special character because it was a rare event. Over time, the term may have come to imply inferiority in relation to "sacred": Anything *not* sacred was impermanent, transitory, fleeting—and thus not completely trustworthy. A god is presumed to be everlasting; what is "secular" lasts only for a finite period of time.

It wasn't until the 1850s that "secular" came to entail the absence of a belief in God that was rooted in humanism. "Secular humanism" is still a paired expression that evokes disdain in some parts of the Christian family.

When secular and sacred are used in opposition to each other, anything *not* ecclesiastical—sacred, and therefore connected with the Church—must be considered profane. (Other synonyms or connotations of profaneness— blasphemy, disrespect, obscenity, contamination, abuse, impiety, or perversion—add to the negative cast of "secular.") This spread of meanings can create mistaken gulfs between people who live in sacred or secular contexts.

Worse yet, the imagined disconnect between those two ideas can create inner conflict for people who live in both sacred and secular worlds—basically every member of your congregation!

Sacred Better Than Secular?

The pseudoconflict between sacred and secular may force you to choose which side of this imaginary divide you most identify with. As a loyal congregational leader, you may think and behave as though sacred is always better than secular. That opinion seems logical: Religion is about the things of God, which are always preeminent. What's holy works better than what isn't. What's sacred is set apart—by God's own ordaining—for God's special purposes. (The *economia* of God is vast, covering everything it touches.) You are loved by—and serve—a God who stands out from among all other (imagined) gods of antiquity, as well as those still worshiped at the present moment. You don't want to be separated from that God.

It makes sense that you would want to stay inside the protective bubble of sacred because much of Scripture's apparent view of the world is not favorable. Many of the Bible's teachings presume that "the world"—e.g., anyone not following Yahweh or Christ—is evil, and therefore deficient or dangerous.

The history of Israel can be described as the story of a people wrestling with their set-apartness in the middle of pagan cultures. This theme appears in the Old Testament: in commands to avoid the temptations of pagan religions (Deut. 12:29–32); warnings from the example of Solomon's later life (2 Kings 11:1–4); reflections regarding the folly of wisdom (Eccles. 1:12–18), and the warnings about foolishness peppered throughout the book of Proverbs. (See 13:20, 14:9, and 21:20 as examples.)

Jesus speaks about "the hatred of the world" regarding his teachings (John 15:25). In his High Priestly Prayer, Jesus seems to differentiate himself from that evil world—and its presumed menace—when he prays, "The world has hated [his disciples] because they do not belong to the world, just as I do not belong to the world. I am not asking you to take them out of the world, but I ask you to protect them from the evil one" (John 17:14b–15).

Paul brought this matter into sharp focus in several places in his writings. He characterized "the wisdom of the world" as foolishness with God (1 Cor. 3:19). He implored believers not to conform to the world (Rom. 12:2) and urged Christians to "come out from them [the world] and be separate from them" (2 Cor. 6:17). In some ways still a Pharisee, Paul reflected a sentiment that had remained strong within Judaism since the Return from Captivity, when Ezra and Nehemiah commanded the dissolution of mixed marriages with foreigners. (See Ezra 9–10 for the complete story.)

The writer of the First Letter of John voices this train of thought most directly: "Do not love the world or the things in the world. The love of the Father is not in those who love the world; for all that is in the world—the desire of the flesh, the desire of the eyes, the pride in riches—comes not from the Father but from the world" (1 John 2:15–16).

At face value, then, the preponderance of Scriptures seem to say that "the world"—a loose set of terms characterizing the pagan cultures with whom God's people interacted—was evil because its ungodly religions compelled or allowed widespread immorality, idolatry, and other selfish behaviors. "Worldliness" constituted the core of folly, not wisdom. Taken into our times, this logic still holds true: Following Yahweh (and Christ) probably embodies a better wisdom.

"Sacred" Not the Only Kind of Wisdom

Under these biblical understandings about true wisdom may also be quiet indications that secular wisdom was valued and practiced during Bible times. Some examples follow.

Solomon was known for the thousands of proverbs and songs he composed. People came from "all the nations" to hear his wisdom. When you look closely, though, something different than purely religious/sacred sagacity emerges. Solomon "would speak of animals, and birds, and reptiles, and fish" (1 Kings 4:29–34). Solomon's wisdom seems to have been centered on the natural world.

The beginning chapters of Proverbs place wisdom inside the general rubric of "the fear of the Lord" (Prov. 1:7). God is named as the source of wisdom (Prov. 2:6) and the applications of wisdom to daily living are intertwined with devotion, honor, and worship of God (e.g., Prov. 3:9–10). With that background in place, though, the writers of Proverbs sprinkle the rest of the book with the kinds of wisdom that could also be sourced in the secular worlds of commerce, parenting, relationships, the natural world, governance, and healthy lifestyles.

The value of much of Ecclesiastes seems to rest on the fact that wisdom is proven or disproven by its practicality. (Lacking pragmatic outcomes, wisdom is "vanity" or "a chasing after wind" [Eccles. 2:11].) Here again, God is the source of wisdom, but its dimensions are not colored in purely sacred hues.

Some examples from Jesus's teachings: The "Sermon on the Mount" (Matt. 5–7) is one place where Jesus's wisdom teachings are distilled. Here you read a mixture of sacred wisdom—the discourse on the Law and Prophets (5:17–20)—and commonsense maxims that draw on daily life—Jesus's words concerning anger (5:21–26). In a textual gloss added to his story about the Dishonest Manager (Luke 16:1–13, CEV), Jesus offers this observation, "The people of this world look out for themselves better than the people who belong to the light." If wisdom is manifested in shrewdness, this passage might suggest a more appreciative view of a character trait not often associated with "sacred" (Luke 16:8b). Jesus sends his disciples out into a temporary ministry with advice to "be wise as serpents and innocent as doves," probably not alluding to anything sacred (Matt. 10:16).

Although his view of "the world" was not generally positive, Paul regularly adapted Greco-Roman secular philosophy into his teachings. (Recall from the previous chapter how Paul built much of his case for mission funding from existing practices in pagan temple worship.) And in his writing, Paul appropriated into Christianity a wide variety of secular images, language, and constructs. Paul seemed able to distill from his secular context what was truly wise, useful, and even godly.

Three Questionably Sacred Ideas

Three not-so-sacred actions or attributes may wall you off from seeking or finding wisdom in the secular realm. Expressed as adjectives, the three ideas are: sacralized, sacrilegious, and sacrosanct.

When you sacralize something—perhaps in a ritual or a rite—you give it a sacred character. That event, person, object, or subject presumably becomes more holy than it was before your designation. This is not necessarily a bad thing: Sacralizing sets apart for admiration and respect what you have named as holy. (So a "sacred moment" might burn itself more firmly into your cherished memories. Or a rite of commissioning people for a mission trip might add to the spiritual weight of that project.) But when sacralizing actions occur too readily or too frequently, the idea of "holy" or "sacred" might lose its focus.

"Sacrilege" originates from the Latin *sacrilegium*—literally temple robbery, the stealing of sacred things. This etymology might explain some of the understandable indignation that can accompany a sense of sacrilege: Real or imagined disrespect, irreverence, searching questions, or minimal piety might look like blasphemy or apostasy. The indignant persons might not see others as part of the community of Christ, even imagining themselves "holier than thou" (Isa. 65:5, KJV).

When sacralizing operates full-bore, and sacrilegious filters are turned to their highest settings, it's a short conceptual/behavioral step to hold everything holy as sacrosanct—inviolable and immune from criticism, untouchable by questions or doubts, and protected by its set-apartness.

All three of these attitudes or behaviors about sacred matters may embody circular arguments: An event, object, person, or idea is holy (not holy) only because someone thinks so. Taken together, those ways of thinking might also form one of the cornerstones of fundamentalist thinking. Wisdom may get lost in a quasi-sacred shuffle.[2]

Secular Wisdom Can Be Part of God's Revelation

God's revelation also includes wisdom found outside the Scriptures. God inspires and God reveals. Wisdom is available to humankind in both instances. The doctrines of inspiration and revelation are connected to and support each other in these ways:

1. God's inspiration (of the Scriptures) is the preeminent means by which God reveals God's self to humanity.
2. The truths of Scripture are normative and actionable, the primary source for your faith and life.
3. At the center of the scriptural revelation is the redeeming work of Jesus Christ, "the Word made flesh" (John 1:14).
4. The general shape of God's nature, intent, or providence is also revealed in other places where God exerts power, agency, and grace.
5. What you can learn in these other places can also be useful in serving God's will.

Truth Enshrined in Time

In Scripture—God's inspired word—God opens the window on timeless wisdom. In one sense that wisdom is confined to specific contexts—of time, geography, or personality. At the same time, the Bible can float free of contexts—offering knowledge that applies across a broad range of circumstances. Where the biblical conditions match contemporary affairs, the wisdom of Scripture is useful in specific settings. Where biblical states of affairs only minimally connect to today's context, the Scriptures still carry the weight of universal wisdom that you can plug into almost any situation.

As you search for God's wisdom, you can find basic precepts by which you can strengthen your identity as a steward. As you come upon God's truths in Scripture, your work is to interpret its meaning—in general and for all time—as well as its applicability to your life.

Specific Truths Still Unfolding

God's revelation continues through other means—certainly the natural world but also in human enterprises. The God revealed in Jesus Christ is also present as human knowledge develops and intertwines with the Scriptures. Some of that knowledge is obviously godly—it readily harmonizes with Scripture. In other places, it is hard to discern whether what humans name as wisdom actually lives up to that claim.

In some doctrinal formulations—those of Martin Luther, for example—God's dominion extends into both sacred and secular realms: A kingdom of glory (roughly akin to sacred matters) and a kingdom of power (roughly corresponding to the secular world) are both places where God continues to work God's will.

As knowledge accumulates, it meshes together to form acceptable truth. As this knowledge stands the test of time—and as it passes through the checkpoints of scriptural truth—it becomes part of the gathered revelation of God. Some theologians call this "progressive revelation": We gather more information, knowledge, and wisdom—means by which God continues to reveal God's self.

In his classic treatment of this concept, *The Meaning of Revelation*, theologian and ethicist H. Richard Niebuhr was also quick to voice a key caution: "Revelation is not progressive in the sense that we can substitute for the revelatory moment of Jesus Christ some other moment in our history, and interpret the latter through the former. . . . Jesus cannot be rightly regarded as the son of the god of modern culture."[3]

Examples of Progressive Revelation

You can see the continuing development of God's revelation in the increasing sophistication of biblical scholarship—e.g., linguistic analysis, archaeology—and in the lives of the saints. In the first case, scholars today know more about biblical languages and cultures than previous generations. In the second case, the lasting example of these faithful believers provides additional understanding about how you might live a godly life under difficult circumstances.

Three other examples might help you see how the usefulness of Scripture has expanded over time because of the Spirit's work in the secular world.

CARE FOR THE POOR

In the previous chapter, you read about the extensive biblical mandate to almsgiving that extended basic kindness to widows, orphans, resident aliens, and those mired in poverty. Throughout Bible times, that command was fulfilled in various ways. In our day, that form of care—direct charity—is now just one means to fulfill the biblical command. Today we can analyze the causes of poverty with some precision. We know how to apply specific remedies—e.g., appropriate technology, community development, education and health programs, food-for-work—that have been proven effective in eliminating poverty. Thus the scriptural requirement of care for the poor is being satisfied by means of programs and systems unknown to the biblical writers.[4]

LIVING ETHICALLY

The wisdom and prophetic literature in the Old Testament show God's specific intentions for righteous living. The teachings of Jesus and Paul bring those precepts into even sharper focus. Today, most of those elements of scriptural virtue still apply—e.g., showing kindness and patience, refraining from idolatry, sexual immorality, avarice, and violence. In our times, psychology, sociology, and neurobiology have shed new light on upright living. Behavioral sciences have constructed clearer pictures of habit formation, change, addiction, and altruism. In these cases, the scriptural elements of a godly life have been supplemented by scientific discoveries and therapeutic practices.

CONTENTMENT

As you saw in the previous chapter, this element of stewardship is proclaimed throughout the Bible. In recent decades—mostly in response to the self-destructive ways by which our materialistic culture is fouling the Earth—an entire body of knowledge has arisen to provide specific practices and techniques that support "simple living." Neurobiology and positive psychology have described contentment more fully.

Some Secular Wisdom Requires Discernment

Astute observers of the secular world can find useful stewardship wisdom in places that have their sources outside of Scripture. In these cases, it requires careful judgment to find the revelation of God. Consider the following three examples: mindfulness, the movies, and the "secular life."

MINDFULNESS

Traced to the meditation and wellness practices of Buddhism, mindfulness techniques are valuable for reducing stress, improving concentration, and increasing personal effectiveness. Whether practiced as a spiritual act—prayer/meditation—or as a spiritually neutral practice, mindfulness benefits the brains and bodies of people mired in reactivity or multitasking.

The Scriptures contain only a few passages about anything resembling mindfulness, and the techniques of mindfulness could easily morph into subtle self-idolatry. Still, it seems obvious that this way of living provides distinct benefits to anyone who wants fewer distractions, less stress, and more purposed activity. Mindfulness seems to be a good thing for humankind, even though its roots lie outside Scripture.

GOD AT THE MOVIES

Sometimes the "scripture" of God's revelation can occur outside of the written words of the Bible. Dr. Robert K. Johnson, professor of theology and culture at Fuller Theological Seminary, considers movies as one of those sources in contemporary culture. He terms them "divine encounters" and "experiences with the Numinous," part of God's wider presence.[5]

Johnson summarizes his students' testimonials regarding the spiritual experiences that resulted from their viewing of films. Three categories of responses emerged from his interviews:

- Students deepened their understanding of a particular spiritual reality. Films with religious or quasi-religious themes helped students make connections with spiritual truths they already had encountered.
- Students reported life-changing moments. Movies put students "in touch with something greater or other than their everyday lives," offering experiences that were "extraordinary and illumining, but not necessarily divine."
- For some students, movies provided them personal encounters with God's presence. Students felt that "God had revealed his presence to them through the truth, beauty and goodness (or lack of it) portrayed on the screen."[6]

In Johnson's opinion, these experiences deserve strong consideration as more than echoes of Scripture. He writes, "While not having to do with one's salvation in any direct way, and occurring outside the church and without direct reference to Scripture or to Jesus Christ, such encounters are foundational to life." He suggests that, in a culture "seeking beauty and goodness before truth," God's wider witness in movies could be an important feature of the Church's respectful outreach, and as a possible reason for rethinking our theology of revelation.[7]

My Bias about the "Secular World"

In my comments at the beginning of this book, I admitted a bias—born of consistent life experiences—that some of God's wisdom is available outside of the Scriptures. Let me add a few comments here, so that you understand my approach to the remainder of this book.

Although I accept fully the notion of Scripture as "source and norm" for faith and life, I also understand how a narrowed approach to God's wisdom can result in missed opportunities for spiritual conversation and witness with those who still search for God. If others see me as arrogant or dismissive about other sources of wisdom, they might understandably reciprocate by disregarding my personal testimony to God's beauty, goodness, wisdom, and truth. Hardly the stuff of "good news" sharing!

Because I do not share in the opinion that Christians should retreat from the secular world in abhorrence of its utterly ungodly character, I hope never to wall myself off from encounters with any part of God's created world. And I always want to honor the vast majority of devout Christians whose entire ministries take place deep inside of worldly contexts.[8]

My example? The life of Jesus. He could have chosen to secede from his culture—joining the Essenes or completely adopting the teachings and lifestyle of the Pharisees. Instead, he wandered purposefully into the nooks and crannies of his worlds, bringing good news to everyone he encountered, no matter how secular or profane they were!

A quiet caution has stuck with me throughout my own search for God's revelation in Scripture and in the secular world: The God who gave prophetic voice to Balaam's donkey can certainly speak truth in many other ways. (See the entire story in Num. 22–24.) This saying has helped me remain curious, respectful, and humble about God's voice, and has kept me ready to be surprised and expectant about God's continuing revelation.

The Chapters Yet to Come

The remainder of this book will present individual areas of human enterprise or expertise where you might find stewardship wisdom. Each of the chapters is based on the premise that this knowledge can be useful to your congregation.

In each chapter you'll find a description of some elements of stewardship wisdom that seem especially cogent for congregational life. In some cases, what you read will be familiar material; in other cases, you may be surprised by new ideas. Each chapter will also feature specific suggestions—sometimes formed as questions—that will help you act on what you have read.

The Shifts to Come

In the previous chapters, "shifting" could be several kinds of movement—from one viewpoint to another, from knowledge to action, and from discomfort to comfort. In the following chapters, shifting will be much simpler: learning perhaps new ideas and putting them to use. In order to take advantage of what you will soon read, I offer these two preparatory thoughts:

1. Secular wisdom is always vulnerable—to new discoveries, trends, or analysis. Any of these chapters could become quickly dated—by the next scientific discovery, theory, scandal, or political shift!
2. You may not be able to apply everything you discover to your specific situation. Your congregation may lack the assets to turn an idea into actions.

You the Steward

Whether sacred or secular, stewardship wisdom is not a set of mystical incantations that work their magic because you wave them at some vexing situation in life. Instead, the wisdom to which I direct you—in Scripture and the worlds of human enterprise—is valuable only as you put it into use wherever God has called you.

You're the steward. It's a continually active verb. You have work to do!

Notes

1. Other parts of this linguistic family include words assocsiated with *sacrament* or *sacrifice*, such as *sacramental, sacerdotal, sacrificial,* or *sacristy.*
2. It's possible that the content or intent of this book feels to you like disrespect for time-honored stewardship principles and practices. What I write could be sacrilege because sacralized elements of stewardship have become sacrosanct.
3. H. Richard Niebuhr, *The Meaning of Revelation* (New York: Macmillan, 1941), 99.

4. Nongovernmental agencies around the world that are chipping away at hunger and poverty cite this maxim: "Give a man a fish and he eats for a day; teach him how to fish and he eats for a lifetime." In some places another sentence is added: "And give that fisherman the pond so that he will become a landowner."

5. Robert K. Johnson, "Meeting God at the Movies," *Christian Century* 131, no. 17 (August 20, 2014); 24. Excerpted from Johnson's *God's Wider Presence: Reconsidering General Revelation* (Grand Rapids, MI: Baker Academic, 2014).

6. Johnson, "Meeting God," 24–26.

7. Johnson, "Meeting God," 26.

8. I find support for my viewpoint from Brookings Institute Senior Fellow Jonathan Rauch's description of the failed premises of contemporary Christians who seek legal recourse in removing themselves from laws that require involvement with what they feel is an evil society. Jonathan Rauch, "The Great Recession," *The Atlantic Monthly* 314, no. 1 (July/August 2014): 19–20.

Chapter 7

More Than Household Rules: Wisdom

Introduction

Wisdom is a critical part of a steward's personal traits. Wisdom becomes useful where "household rules" come up short. Absent the owner, the steward must discern the particulars of an *economia* that offers only general descriptions of the owner's intent.

Whether you consider yourself wise or not, you probably yearn for greater wisdom. The process of seeking wisdom can help you make the world better—fulfilling God's will. Wisdom helps you compare your actions to your best intentions. It can serve as a motivating force that compels you to live beyond mere selfishness. Your shortcomings, your history of decision-making, your capabilities, your life-purpose—all can come into clearer focus when you think or read about wisdom.[1]

Sacred Wisdom

God's people can consider wisdom as something we already understand well. In the original story of Creation, Eve's "looking at" the forbidden fruit could also be translated as "making one wise" (*lehaskil*). Her discernment might also explain how the Hebrew term for wisdom (*chokhmah*) was feminized.[2]

The Scriptures are full of useful descriptions and examples of both wisdom and folly. One entire section of the Hebrew Bible is designated "Wisdom." The book of Proverbs is filled with short maxims that function as wisdom appetizers. Longer treatises on the subject help readers consider wisdom in its wider context. (See Prov. 1–3; 31:10–31.)

In Proverbs 4, Wisdom has an "anatomy"—ears, eyes, heart/mind, mouth, and feet. The writer uses language that likens wisdom-seeking to movements—walking, running, stumbling, entering, avoiding, turning away, passing by—that suggest how wisdom is a lifelong journey down a particular path.[3]

At its heart, the story of Jesus's temptations in the wilderness is a story about wisdom. Similar to the "vision quests" of some Native American cultures, Jesus's time in the desert brought him face-to-face with larger questions—power, immediate gratification, spiritual depth, identity, and purpose—that correlate directly with qualities of wisdom. In all cases, Jesus's responses to the embodied temptations were wise (Matt. 4:1–11).

King Solomon is often presented as a prime example of godly wisdom. His prayers for wisdom were answered, and a lifetime output of proverbs and other wise utterances seems to prove his exemplary sagacity. The entire story of Solomon's life, however, presents more of a cautionary tale about how transitory wisdom might be. As he grew older, Solomon seemed to violate every part of Deuteronomic law. By the end of his life, his excesses and other arrogant behaviors—most noticeably, his taking too many wives and concubines—disallowed any claim that wisdom remained his identifying attribute.[4]

Beginnings of Secular Wisdom

As a body of written knowledge and practice, wisdom probably first appeared in the Upanishads—writings that later formed the core of Indian philosophies and religions—about a century earlier than the earliest Greek philosophers. (Heraclitus, one of the "fathers of philosophy," formulated his teaching and writing in the sixth century BCE.) About the same time, the Chinese philosopher Confucius began to understand that wisdom could help reduce human misery and conflict; societies could change because of wisdom.[5]

Sacred and Secular Redux

One way to characterize the development of Western wisdom: the ongoing tension between theological and nontheological forces. Greek philosophy may have emerged as a reaction to the notion that the magical mystery and capriciousness of the gods were sufficient sources for understanding life's deeper meanings. The struggle can be framed as a simple question: "Does all wisdom emanate from the divine, from beyond human capacity for thought?"[6]

That question spills over into contemporary arguments about the primacy and inerrancy of Scriptures, the trustworthiness of science, or the nature of human consciousness. To oversimplify the tension: Sacred wisdom comes from on high, and requires only to be well interpreted. Secular wisdom emerges from human thought, and so deserves questioning and exploration. Sacred wisdom is relatively inflexible; secular wisdom is malleable. Sacred wisdom provides its own proof—the nature of God—while secular wisdom searches for validation.

The Nature of Wisdom

How might you describe wisdom? These summary statements might help you grasp this desirable-but-elusive part of stewardship:

1. Wisdom is always about the process and results of decision-making. Wisdom begins when your knowledge is incomplete, or when it contradicts itself. In order to make wise decisions, you also have to be wise about the process.[7]
2. Wisdom begins with awareness. You take in the wider world, reflect on what you learn, and explore the relationships between your outer and inner worlds.[8]
3. Wisdom is associated with both knowledge and emotion. "Knowledge" includes the full range of your life experiences and your ability to analyze those experiences within the boundaries of verifiable truth. Your brain's default decision-making process depends on your emotional well-being. Both intellectual and emotional capabilities balance each other's influence on the direction and strength of your decisions.[9]
4. Wisdom is contextual. Because change is continuous, chaotic, and complex, wisdom requires you to continually assess the contexts of decisions—including possible outcomes.[10]
5. Wisdom is frequently self-contradictory. Uncertainty in the face of unpredictable change is always present in human endeavors. So minimarkers of wisdom—e.g., proverbs, maxims—can promote opposing sides of the same dilemma. A bedrock principle in one context may turn into foolishness in a different setting.[11]
6. Wisdom is not predicted by the levels of your cognitive intelligence. High intellectual levels may tilt your decision-making toward reactivity about purely factual matters.[12] In his continuing research on intelligence, Robert J. Sternberg, professor of human development at Cornell University, proposes a "balance theory of wisdom" that integrates

ethical, social, and empathic elements of wisdom into what has traditionally been measured as only intellect or aptitude.[13]

7. Wisdom is ordinary. Although it may seem that wisdom is granted to only a handful of acknowledged sages, it is also present in the day-to-day counsel and observations of friends, family, and colleagues.[14]

8. Wisdom is grounded in what's practical. If wisdom were a pipeline, what would emerge from its end point would be decisions that are useful. In that sense, wisdom is approachable, tangible, and realistic.[15]

9. Wisdom invites action as well as inaction. Wisdom helps you find a path from dilemma to action, at times coloring a possible action with caution, or even prohibiting it.[16]

10. Wisdom comes with age. Because it depends on reflected experiences, wisdom grows as those experiences accumulate over a lifetime, helping you discern what is truly important. Capabilities that increase with age include inclusivity, acceptance, forgiveness, self-knowledge, prioritizing skills, a sense of time's passing, contentment, and self-control. Until the point of senility, your brain continues to regenerate neuronal connections, enabling new thought patterns.[17]

11. Just as individuals can be wise (or foolish), so can groups of people. A caution: Wisdom does not consist of the rule of the majority or suggestions of overwhelming data. When it comes to wisdom, there is no crowd-sourcing.

12. Wisdom is not always accepted or honored. History relates the stories of wise people who were also regarded as traitors, misfits, or at least dangerous to the accepted order of society. (Pythagoras, who first coined the word "philosophy" so alienated the population of Croton, his adopted hometown, that his house was burned down and Pythagoras was forced to flee.[18])

An Explanatory Side Note

Permit me this brief explanation of the reasons why I have chosen to use "stewardship wisdom" throughout this book instead of the more prevalent "stewardship principles." A principle-based identity might mean that you can live your life as a steward with assurance. ("Adhere to the principles, and you will be successful.") But the image of the steward's role is based less on principles than on wisdom. When the owner is absent, the exact details of his *economia* are not available. Knowing the broad outlines of that plan, however, provides enough of a context for the steward to be observant, nimble, flexible, courageous, shrewd, intuitive, and discerning. Individually and collectively, these personal traits describe wisdom! Thus "stewardship wisdom" is one of my desired outcomes for your reading of this book.

Eight Neural Pillars

In the second section of *Wisdom: From Philosophy to Neuroscience*, science writer Stephen Hall describes wisdom by what he terms "neural pillars." These are generic components of sagacity that have some basis in neurobiological sciences. His premise is clear: Neuroscience must certainly extend into wisdom. The pillars are: emotional regulation, knowing what's important, moral reasoning, compassion, humility, altruism, patience, and dealing with uncertainly. He suggests that accumulating empirical evidence shows how particular cognates of wisdom might be also described as elements of the brain's continuing functions. Each of the pillars deserves consideration.

EMOTIONAL REGULATION

Because emotional elements of wisdom are tied to its core decision-making functions, it seems logical to examine your emotional capabilities for being wise. Your ability to remain focused, calm, and rational under duress is a mark of strong leadership. You can also think of your ability to regulate your emotions as composure, even-mindedness, emotional resilience, or coolness in the face of challenging circumstances. Given the hard-wired strength of emotions such as fear, anger, or pleasure-seeking, emotional regulation is a remarkable capability of your brain.[19]

This kind of wisdom is probably a function of your age or stage of life. Facing mortality more realistically, older adults are more apt to value emotional depth and social connections as important elements of their well-being. When you are older, false urgencies or knee-jerk anxieties don't crowd out your sense of time. "In the shortened time perspective that comes with aging, people are motivated to focus on what is most important."[20]

KNOWING WHAT'S IMPORTANT

Another component of wisdom consists of your ability to weigh the benefits of differing courses of action—part of the lightning-quick decision-making process. As yet not completely understood, this brain function attaches proven or anticipated value to a choice well before the decision-making is finished. This process is subjective, fraught with idiosyncratic complexities. Description, memory, emotion, prediction, evaluation, reward—all play into an evaluation process that may or may not involve consciousness or free will.

You can't make important decisions in a vacuum, so some amount of knowledge—about a subject, an encounter, or experience—is necessary for decision-making. Confronted with what's novel or unexpected, your brain sorts out vast amounts of sensory and remembered information so only what is relevant will be considered. The attention system of the brain—which includes strong capabilities for inattention—comes into play as well.[21]

MORAL REASONING

Perhaps least well described by neurobiology are the ways in which you exhibit the wisdom of "moral" choices. In the realm of religious truth, "right and wrong" are lived out in obedience to time-honored precepts or commandments. (Wise people obey the laws of God.) But no clear consensus has yet emerged from the study of the biological markers of moral judgment. (Discovery of a "conscience" has not yet been announced with certainty.)

Neuroscientists know that moral reasoning occurs in several brain structures, and that it involves both emotion and reason. The conflict and coordination between these two large-scale systems requires both significant experiences and significant decision-making time. Moral reasoning may be connected to the brain's wider capabilities for disgust or repugnance. The social consequences of moral decisions may also impact when and how sometimes-difficult choices are made. Moral reasoning may consist simply of your ability to know when to trust emotion and when to trust rationality.[22]

COMPASSION

Wisdom benefits more people than just the wise person, so any attitude or skill that enhances your personal relationships—compassion among several others—must necessarily be wise. Writes Hall, "Compassion rounds and softens the hard-edged lessons of experience; compassion warms human thought when intelligence becomes too impersonal and chilly; compassion motivates action in the direction of social good."[23]

Your compassion is comprised of recognizing the perspective of others, feeling some emotion regarding that perspective, and acting on that experience. Roughly akin to empathy, perspective-taking seems hard-wired in the brain because of the widespread presence of "mirror neurons." (These nerve cells enable you to sense other's intentions, even their physical experiences.) Sometimes encapsulated as "theory of mind," this capability of your brain enables you to mimic and resonate with others. Compassion enables helpful social relationships, strengthening the social intelligence that is fundamental to wisdom.

Humility

Subject to a great deal of definitional fervor, humility has been universally regarded as a core component of wisdom. Its roots extend deep into Eastern and Western philosophy. Hall speaks of the etymology of humility—*humus*—as an illustration of its "rich, organic, nose-to-the-ground pragmatism."[24]

Sacred and secular understandings of humility differ in one major way: In its biblical sense, humility is connected to obedience and submission to God. Adoration, loyalty, self-denial, and piety come when you realize that you are small, weak, and foolish in relation to God. Considered from a secular point of view, humility acts "like a social lubricant, greasing the wheels of group interaction, minimizing interpersonal friction and enhancing the odds for cooperation." Its markers include humor, helpful self-deprecation, resistance to avarice, and a broad worldview.[25]

Humility becomes a useful component of wisdom—especially wise leadership—when it allows you to balance your esteem for others with your personal power, your self-awareness with other-centeredness, and your self-confidence with the acknowledgment of your lack of knowledge.

Humility has attracted little neurobiological research. Instead, social scientists have examined its opposite, narcissism, at length. Narcissists exhibit hyperinflated self-regard, false superiorities, and a lasting appetite for attention and regard. Even though they may easily emerge as leaders in social situations, narcissists are not considered wise.

Even with a lack of neurobiological connections, humility seems well understood by psychologists and social scientists. According to June Price Tangley, professor of psychology at George Mason University, humility includes these features:

- An ability to acknowledge your limitations and mistakes.
- Openness to new ideas and knowledge (that may be contradictory).
- Skill in avoiding self-aggrandizement.
- Perspective about your achievements.
- Awareness of your strengths and weaknesses.[26]

One cautionary note: Humility is not characterized by low self-worth, self-deprecation, a sense of incompetence, or worthlessness. These attitudes subtract from the usefulness of wisdom—its ability to attract and inspire those you lead.

ALTRUISM

Related to both empathy and compassion, altruism can be thought of as your nearly automatic tendency to sacrifice yourself for the good of others, especially larger groups of people.

The nature of supposed selflessness has been the center of socio-psychological debate for decades. Some psychologists have considered supposed altruistic behaviors as a façade for "reciprocal" or "kinship" altruism: You behave selflessly because of anticipated rewards that will eventually come from your social group or family.[27]

Other voices differ slightly. UCLA professor of psychology Shelley E. Taylor thinks of altruism in terms of "heroisms" of several kinds—including the quiet valor of sturdy caregivers. In her judgment, altruism is impulsive and wired into your brain's circuits. "Altruism may be . . . so fundamental, so essential to the survival of human beings that it has taken root in neurocircuitries designed for other purposes, finding its expression in numerous unexpected, but largely successful ways." Taylor proposes that bonding mechanisms are primary among brain systems, underlying much of human flourishing.[28]

PATIENCE

Expressed in neurobiological terms, patience consists of your brain's ability to weigh immediate and delayed rewards. Veterans Administration research psychiatrist George Ainslie calls patience "a debate between our present and future selves" in a process that he calls "intertemporal bargaining."

Patience helps you temper restless reactivity to stimuli and situations. What makes patience a component of wisdom is the presence of willpower—the skill of knowing and acting wisely in the face of temptation.

In his experimental work, Ainslie has come to see that self-control—another way to name willpower—is really "the art of making the future bigger." Giving in to the promised pleasure of a temptation is actually a devaluation of the future in favor of an immediate outcome. Your brain may be trapped in the false perception that, as you approach a smaller (immediate) reward, it seems greater than it really is. Imagination becomes a useful skill in that discerning process, a way of organizing for the future.

To be patient means to learn to delay gratification, trusting the promise of a greater future reward. "Wisdom isn't just an insight," Ainslie says. "It is a budgetary skill." Prudence—considering the future outcomes more deliberately—takes the place of impulsivity.[29]

DEALING WITH UNCERTAINTY

Hall completes his gallery of neuronal cognates for wisdom by describing how your brain treats uncertainty. He credits Jonathan Cohen, director of Princeton University's Center for Brain, Mind, and Behavior, with the idea of "meta-wisdom," an overarching capability of the human brain to remain flexible and nimble in the face of change.

When encountering change, your brain employs two systems. In the first, you search for memories of similar experiences—Cohen's "models"—for the likelihood that a new situation corresponds closely enough to a familiar event that it can be trusted for assured, automatic reactivity. In the second approach, when there are few dependable models, the brain shifts into a more measured and time-consuming process. Perception, knowledge, memory, and emotion all become necessary ingredients in Cohen's "meta-wisdom," a kind of ultimate proof of wisdom. Decisions become like an inner conversation between intuition and reason. Premises are formed and analyzed for their present and future verity. Fundamental perspectives—for neuroscientists, "framing"—serve as scaffolds for a process that also takes into account the contexts of the situation and the likely results of a decision.[30]

The term "meta-wisdom" assumes that the flexible capabilities of the rational brain (neo-cortex) are able to modulate the rapid operation of the inflexible emotional brain. Brain structures loosely gathered under the designation "the social brain" add valued relationships to the decision-making process.

This balancing among brain systems may be an ultimate description of wisdom: the ability to take the time necessary in order to assess a situation before making a decision and acting on it.[31]

Shifting toward Wisdom

If you choose to concentrate your congregation's stewardship ministry on wisdom (or wisdom-seeking), you might consider some of the following approaches.

REVISE VISION, MISSION, PURPOSE, OR CASE STATEMENTS.

If your congregation's public or written declarations seem to be inadequate—their language doesn't inspire, they misrepresent reality, or they are difficult to carry out—include wisdom-related matters in necessary revisions or rewritings. Start with your case statement—a direct explanation of the reasons why your congregation deserves financial support.

RETHINK THE ASSETS OF BEING AN ELDERLY CONGREGATION.

The research seems clear: Older people are likely to be wise. Think what might happen if you unleashed the considerable wisdom already resident in the elderly members of your congregation. A simple start: Putting younger and older people together in situations where wisdom could be taught and caught. Think how you could insert life-wisdom testimonials into your worship times, your newsletters, or your programming. Depending on the distribution of generations in your congregation's population, you might have a wealth of elder wisdom that you could share with other congregations and organizations.

REARRANGE YOUTH MINISTRY.

One of the emerging trends in youth ministry is apologetics: study of creeds, confessions, and other doctrinal documents. It seems that the default purposes of youth ministry—fellowship, identity-forming, service learning—are now complemented by in-depth examination of the beliefs that form the core of faith life.

You might revise your goals for youth ministry around this simple proposition: Your congregation wants to help teens be wise. Although immature teen brains may not be completely ready to grasp or embody wisdom, those same young brains yearn for it. And they are more likely capable of learning how to be wise than may be evident.

TRANSPLANT WISDOM INTO MORAL TEACHINGS.

You might try to translate your teachings about morality into the language of wisdom-seeking. Start with an assessment of your congregation's communications and teachings—including prayers and sermons. To what extent do only Law-oriented pronouncements fill your congregation's message? How flexible are your ideas about what is ethical or moral? Wisdom's presence might fill the places where right vs. wrong are difficult to discern. "Seek wisdom" might nudge out "seek perfection" as a benediction.

Incorporate Diverse Wisdom.

See what might happen if your wisdom-seeking followed paths other than those defined solely by your denomination or faith family. With Scripture as guide, see where the wisdom of your Muslim neighbors might help you understand hospitality, where the witness of Jewish faith could instruct your practices of generosity, where Buddhist mantras might supplement your understanding of prayer's benefits, or where Roman Catholic worship practices could deepen your congregation's ability to find God in quiet reflection.

Dislodge "Assured-Results Thinking."

Implicit in wisdom-seeking is the likelihood that decision-making is fraught with complexity, change, and incomplete knowledge. No matter how scientific or logical any planning process might seem to be, one soggy fact muddies up the process and results: By the time that data is gathered and analyzed into patterns or recommendations, the facts have changed!

With wisdom as the guiding light, incorporate matters such as compassion, patience, altruism, emotional regulation, humility, or knowing what's important into a planning process that admits uncertainty as its basic assumption.

Shift from Charismatic to Wise Leaders.

"We need a charismatic leader" is one of the siren songs that can tempt congregational leaders. The logic seems clear enough: Charismatic gifts of any kind attract attention, which will presumably result in congregational growth and health.

Instead, you might identify potential leaders with wisdom as the guiding principle. Use some of Hall's eight neural pillars as clues. Consider both older and younger members—some teens are already wiser than some adults. When you invite possible leaders to serve, be honest about your reasons: "We value wisdom as part of being a leader. The people who know you tell us that you're a wise person."

As you choose a potential pastor or other professional leaders, use interview questions that include elements of wisdom. Adapt denominational processes so that wisdom-related traits are front-and-center. Remember that wisdom always retains a certain amount of mystery and ineffability, so precise measurement of this cherished attribute will always be elusive.

REARRANGE PARENTING SUPPORT.

If you offer programs, events, or other support for parents, they might also benefit from a slightly different focus: helping them raise wise children. Alongside their children, parents are regularly beset with "foolishness training," so your congregation might offer a welcome alternative to what they encounter each day. Involve them in the planning and execution of this effort.

AUDIT WISDOM IN YOUR MIDST.

What would happen if you named "wise" as one of the criteria for evaluating any part of your congregation's life? What might "wise evangelism" look like? How does wisdom color the ways in which you ask for financial support? How might you evaluate your congregation's annual statistics wisely? What have been the truly wise moments in the congregation's history? What wisdom do you seek as you plan for the future? Put your findings into writing, and talk together about what you discover.

TRANSPOSE WISDOM-SEEKING INTO WISDOM-WRITING.

If you have the assets to do so, offer a series of "wise writing" events. Participants might learn to write poetry or proverbs, both of which are compact literary forms that have wisdom as outcomes.

COLLECT WISDOM LEGACY STORIES.

Some of your older members may have a desire or need to pass on the legacy of their wisdom in story form. Collect oral history—written or recorded—from selected older members. Provide conversational or writing prompts so that these elders can focus on wisdom-related matters rather than purely historical narrative. Think how the results on this ongoing effort will be shared with others.

The End of This Subject?

It's possible that wisdom-seeking is a resting place—a plateau or oasis—in your lifelong search for effective stewardship. In that case, you've come to "the end of this subject"—at least for a while—and you can stop here. On the other hand, if you're still curious where else secular knowledge and practice might inform and invigorate your sense of being a steward, keep reading.

There's more to learn.

Notes

1. Stephen S. Hall, *Wisdom: From Philosophy to Neuroscience* (New York: Vintage Books, 2010), 9, 10 and 18. Throughout this chapter, I am deeply indebted to the monumental work of Hall. He has gathered together insights about this elusive subject in a way that is approachable and inspiring.

2. Hall, *Wisdom*, 44–45.

3. Christine Roy Yoder, *Proverbs* (Nashville: Abingdon Press, 2009), 52, 55.

4. Ironically, the kingdom that Solomon built up fell apart because of the lack of political wisdom in his son Rehoboam (1 Kings 12). Hall, *Wisdom*, 167–68.

5. Hall, *Wisdom*, 29–31.

6. Hall, *Wisdom*, 26, 34.

7. Hall, *Wisdom*, 7. Where there is abundant factual knowledge, decision-making becomes only a matter of applying known algorithms to a situation. In these Big Data situations, wisdom may seem to be less important than skill in building and applying predictive formulas.

8. Hall, *Wisdom*, 9.

9. Hall, *Wisdom*, 17.

10. Hall, *Wisdom*, 12, 27. Heraclitus first proposed the fluidity of change in his famous dictum, "You could not step twice into the same river; for other waters are ever flowing on to you."

11. Hall, *Wisdom*, 11, 50–51.

12. Hall, *Wisdom*, 43, 52. The original and continuing writings of Daniel Goleman (*Emotional Intelligence, Working with Emotional Intelligence, Social Intelligence*) provide ample evidence of the necessary functions of several other forms of intelligence. Any of them might also be considered a component of wisdom.

13. From "Conversations on Wisdom: Robert J. Sternberg," Wisdom Research Web Site, University of Chicago, *www.wisdomreserach.org/forums*, January 14, 2015.

14. Hall, *Wisdom*, 14–15.

15. Hall, *Wisdom*, 21–22.

16. Hall, *Wisdom*, 8.

17. Hall, *Wisdom*, 43, 52.

18. "True wisdom at some level is often an act of hostility against society." Hall, *Wisdom*, 12, 24.

19. Hall, *Wisdom*, 62–63.

20. Stanford University psychologist Laura J. Carstensen calls this capability a "time horizon." She is careful not to insist that only older adults can discern the times in a wise way. Hall, *Wisdom*, 63–64.

21. Researchers are especially interested in the function of dopamine—one of the brain's "feel-good" neurotransmitters—in the process of attaching value or desirability to a particular choice. Hall, *Wisdom*, 80–87.

22. Much of the difficulty in connecting neurobiology to morality lies in both the limitations of experimental evidence and the extreme complexity of the concept of "morality." Hall, *Wisdom*, 107–14.

23. Hall, *Wisdom*, 118.

24. Thus grounded, "humility shows its origins, its sense of scale and its point of view." Hall, *Wisdom*, 136.

25. Hall, *Wisdom*, 138–39.

26. Dr. June Price Tangney, in *Handbook of Positive Psychology*, as cited by Hall, *Wisdom*, 142.

27. Hall, *Wisdom*, 151–52.

28. Taylor is especially interested in the implications of the neurotransmitter oxytocin in bonding processes. Shelley E. Taylor, *The Tending Instinct: How Nurturing Is Essential to Who We Are and How We Live* (New York: Times Books, 2002), 147–58.

29. Ainslie, as referenced in Hall, *Wisdom*, 171–79, 188.

30. Cohen, as referenced in Hall, *Wisdom*, 190–203.

31. Cohen conceives of this balancing process as a choice between "exploitation"—using automatic habits—and "explorative"—tentative adjustment to change. Hall, *Wisdom*, 203.

Chapter 8

Neurobiological Nudges: Brain Science

In the previous chapter I suggested that secular wisdom could be the sum-and-substance of stewardship ministries, and that "wisdom-seeking" could be another way to describe the role of steward. In this chapter, I ask you to consider six stewardship-related subjects that can also be understood from the viewpoint of neurobiology. I'll add in a few summaries about other brain science that may turn out to be information streams of their own.

Why Neuroscience?

Let me start my answer with this invitation: "Wake up and smell the brain science!" (If coffee gets neurons firing, then brain science can get stewardship leaders revved up for their ministries!) My invitation has a little insistence to it because neurobiology continues to grow as a trend line in science. (Genetics and complexity physics are among the others.) It doesn't take a rocket scientist's mind to realize that neuroscience is coming out of the bright corners of research labs into the even-brighter atmospheres of boardrooms, planning venues, and classrooms.

Shortly after the Vietnam War, brain science grew from a trickle of earnest theories to a torrent of incredible facts. With the advent of imaging technologies, the data revealed patterns that invited further theories and research. In the past decade or two, those patterns have gelled into practices that benefit education, marketing, political campaigns, mind/body therapies, and technology—all practical applications of neurobiology that offer value to human enterprise.

You can't live without a brain, and you probably can't live wisely or purposefully without knowing how your brain works. Everything you attend to,

111

everything you hope to accomplish, everything you believe, and everything that frames your steward identity—all of it takes place inside the approximately three pounds of tofu-consistency gray/white matter that rests securely inside of the protective cave of your skull.

What's true of you is also true of your congregation—a collection of brains. Your congregation's identity, purpose, and well-being are dependent on how all those brains function. The ministries of your congregation all rely on brains attuned to spiritual matters. The functions of your congregation have their basis in how well the congregation's brain(s) work(s). You know God in your brain(s).

The Big Question

In each of the sections of this book, I try to answer "so what?" questions. In this chapter, I add a larger question, one that only you can answer: "What are you going to do with all these brains?" As a leader, you have the privilege of incorporating into your congregation's stewardship ministry the willing and capable brainpower of members. This is no small matter—marketers have to pay big money to learn how to persuade people to join in their efforts or purchase their product. The brains at your disposal are an amazing resource! You can't take them lightly or for granted—that would be a mistake. And, in these times, it's no longer possible for you to manipulate people's brains.

Attention and Inattention

Attention is your brain's way of concentrating on its inner and outer environments, in order to enhance your body's well-being. Attention is the first and most important commodity in human existence. No other brain activities can take place until the brain's attention sequence is engaged.

Attention occurs as a sequence of coordinated actions engaged by various brain structures for a purpose. The sequence begins when the body's senses—not confined to the sensory organs—take in stimuli and process them in a four-stage cycle described by the verbs *arouse, orient, detect,* and *execute.*[1]

The brain is always fully engaged with its surroundings. Whether in a background (automatic) mode or fully mindful, your brain is scanning its inner and outer contexts at all times. Full-frame attention is directed at what's new, surprising, or unique. Real or imagined danger warrants attention, as does any stimulus that engages the emotional or social brain systems. Most movement, physical or imagined, requires and focuses attention.

Your brain is also easily distracted. But because of the biology and chemistry of neuronal firing patterns, your brain can attend to and process fully only one stimulus at a time. Time is finite, so multitasking is a myth derived from the misapplication of technological metaphors onto human biology.

Your brain is also fully equipped for necessary inattention. Inattention is not the opposite of attention, but a complementary brain activity that helps regulate the amount and nature of information that can be processed. Your brain constantly filters which stimuli can be minimally processed and which require the full attention sequence. In a world in which too much sensory information tries to crowd into your brain, an inattention system purposefully avoids or deflects attention.[2]

It's essential that you understand how attention and inattention occur in congregational life. These quick observations:

1. Attention is rare, precious, and wonderful. You should treat willing attention as a gift.
2. Because of the strength of the brain's inattention system, it's probably correct to assume that most people are not paying attention to most things most of the time.
3. A corollary: Just because "you build it" doesn't mean that people will pay attention.
4. You are competing for members' attention. These competitors are working smart, using proven techniques to trick or wrest attention from consumers or constituents.
5. Although you can attract attention with similar methods, it's probably better to deserve attention than to manipulate people into giving it away.
6. If anyone pays attention to you willingly, you're a leader. Your success as a leader is directly related to the amount of attention you are given.
7. The core messages or stimuli that characterize your congregation are attention-worthy. They come from and appeal to some of the core matters of human existence. When it comes to godly things, people pay attention!

Three Attention-Related Matters

Let me introduce you to three attention-related matters that are currently being applied to other parts of human enterprise. They are self-talk, the spread of ideas, and boredom. Each may be important to your congregation.

SELF-TALK

Also called "metacognition" by some neuroscientists, your capacity for self-reflection is a critical survival skill. Incorporating emotion, memory, and relationships, self-talk helps you identify your limitations and compensate for them. Occurring during quiet or alone times, self-talk frequently focuses on your actions, emotions, or relationships. Self-talk helps you steer attention, tamp down galloping emotions, and remember social mores. Self-talk can motivate you to action or depress you. It assists you in learning from the past and preparing for the future. When systematized in the brain, self-talk is one element of "theory of mind"—your ability to construct a mental model of others' thoughts and intentions. The summary benefit of self-talk: an affirmation of who you are and what you are experiencing.[3]

THE SPREAD OF IDEAS

In our times, "going viral" is used to describe an idea or experience that races into the lifeblood of contemporary culture. Highly desired, this contagion depends on immediate attention and quick adoption of a cultural meme by a large number of people. According to University of Pennsylvania marketing professor Jonah Berger, ideas become infectious mostly because of word-of-mouth and its implied social influence. He credits the strength of "social epidemics" to six factors:

- Social currency (The remarkability, value, or uniqueness of a concept or experience, including qualities that make people look good among their peers).
- Triggers (Stimuli or prompts that remind or connect).
- Emotion (Any emotional set or proclivity, however reliable).
- Public quality (The visibility or availability of the idea or experience).
- Practicability (A value that is readily understood and accepted).
- Story-like (A broader narrative undergirds or surrounds the experience or idea).[4]

In Berger's analysis, matters as profound as awe, amusement, disgust, game mechanics, and herd mentality all play into the process by which a concept or encounter can move into the consciousness of a large number of people.

BOREDOM

First coined by Charles Dickens (in his serialized 1852–1853 novel *Bleak House*), boredom is a common attention-related phenomenon whose neurobiology is not completely understood. University of Waterloo neuroscientist James Danckert has been examining this subject carefully for several years. With his colleagues, he thinks of boredom as the inability to control attention. Boredom might thus be understood as a disconnect between inner expectations and one's external context.

Danckert categorizes two types of boredom: apathetic (couch potato) and agitated (distress-prone). In the first case, bored individuals can't seem to gain much satisfaction from internal stimulation and lack the motivation to seek external gratification. The second type signals other problems. People who experience this more severe form of boredom may show symptoms of ADHD, and perhaps experience inner turmoil that can lead to depression. Chronic boredom is linked to lower work and school performance, lower job satisfaction, increased rates of alcohol and drug abuse, and more frequent lapses in attention.

Some preliminary research in Britain has established a connection between levels of boredom and unhealthy outcomes such as cardiac issues, higher levels of cortisol, and higher heart rates. Boredom might be a sign (or cause) of poor health conditions.

Perhaps the most troubling research about boredom is its statistical connection to traumatic brain injuries (TBIs). TBIs are already implicated in unhelpful novelty-seeking (as experienced in drug and alcohol use and the practice of unsafe sex). TBIs may also cause a heightened sense of boredom among those who have experienced severe brain injuries such as concussions and front-end automobile crashes.[5]

What You Might Do about Attention-Related Neuroscience

Your congregation is one place where attention is routinely sought. (Think of worship as an opportunity to focus attention on godly matters, meetings as attention-contests, or sermons as appeals for deep attention.) To put attention-related neuroscience to work in your setting, you might address these invitations and questions:

1. Review all the ways in which your congregation attempts to garner its members' attention. How might your methods be manipulative—and therefore eventually doomed to failure or exposure? In what ways does your congregation deserve attention? How do you ask for it graciously— or inadvertently spurn or deflect it?

2. Construct an informal sociogram of present leaders that shows lines of leaders' likely influence. A simple question can help form the chart: Who's paying attention to a particular leader? How can you tell?

3. How could you help members' self-talk include your congregation's mission or identity?

4. Name or list all the distractions that pull members' attention away from core spiritual or religious matters. For example, how might feel-good worship direct worshipers away from confession? How might congregational conflict capture members' emotions? What will you do about those distractions?

5. At a more prosaic level, how attractive or visually accessible are your congregation's communication methods?

Fear/Stress

Next we turn to a universal descriptor of the human condition: our default responses to danger. Whether you name this process as "fear" or "stress" probably doesn't matter—your brain and body react similarly in both cases.

Fear and (dis)stress are woven together biologically, with similar patterns of reactivity. (The classic threesome—"fight, flight, freeze"—may be more male-oriented. "Tend and befriend" may describe female responses to fear or stress more accurately.) Any part of the fear/stress sequence—e.g., anger—is evidence of an entire state of mind. Two fear systems—the first one immediate and automatic and the second more analytical—operate within thousandths of a second of each other.

The biology of fear and stress can be understood as the behaviors of a brain seeking to protect itself and the body in which it is housed. In a situation perceived as dangerous, the amygdala sounds a general alarm, marks the threat, and stores it in memory. The pituitary gland signals the release of adrenaline; the thyroid gland raises the body's metabolic rate; normal-but-necessary body systems shut down; blood is redirected to muscles; the liver breaks down glycogen for increased energy; eye pupils and lung bronchioles dilate; and breathing quickens. The spleen contracts, heart and blood pressure rates increase, and the bladder and colon prepare to empty themselves. Throughout this process, the neurotransmitter cortisol is secreted into the brain. An "emotional hijacking" has occurred; fear has taken control of the brain for a while.

Mere moments after the danger has passed—fighting, fleeing, freezing, or tending and befriending have done their work—the brain is flooded with endorphins, and the pleasure of escape replaces the terror of possible danger. The fear/stress sequence is complete.

The biological reactions to fear/stress diminish soon after the sequence has completed itself. Fear is *not* quickly reduced by rational considerations, because at its height fear momentarily short-circuits the rational or sequential functions of the brain. (Hence a quiet aphorism of neuroscience, "Fear/stress makes you stupid.") Cortisol—a primary neurotransmitter in the fear sequence—dissipates in conversation, laughter, and touch. (Yes, "perfect love" casts out fear!)

Because it is valuable for the continued well-being of brains and bodies, fear is contagious and thus easily perceived or accepted. Fear is a quick and effective motivator, a fact well known to fear-mongers and fear-marketers. When accompanied by anger—a part of the "fight" reaction—fear can provide individuals and groups with a potent identity.[6]

Contemporary culture and continuing events are steeped in fear, so it makes sense for you to be cognizant of fear-related matters. These observations:

1. Congregations (or leaders) whose identity is oriented primarily toward danger will continue to draw in on themselves. They will find it difficult to appeal to a broad swath of believers.

2. Congregational ministries that are fear-filled will have a short shelf life, or will require the continual reintroduction of fearful stimuli in order to gather continuing attention.

3. When it comes to your decision-making, it can be helpful for you to name and analyze the causes for your fear, anxiety, or worry.

4. Angry, stressed, or fearful leaders—lay or clergy—will eventually destroy themselves and/or those around them.

5. When you see diminished trust, lack of empathy or civility, increased pettiness, minimal wisdom, decreased generosity, or broken communication links, you're likely seeing the results of fear or stress.

6. Because the wider culture is infected with fear and stress, most members approach congregational life with fear/stress already present in their minds.

7. One way to characterize Jesus is as a fearless Messiah.

8. A strong benefit that your congregation might offer: a place of refuge from fearful or fear-mongering influences.

Three Fear/Stress-Based Matters

Follow me into a brief exploration of the prevalence of fear in society, destructive fear and stress, and strategies for reducing fear/stress.

THE PREVALENCE OF FEAR IN SOCIETY

As a function of the human brain, fear has resided inside individual and collected brains since the dawn of civilization. (For example, words for *fear* appear over 750 times in the Bible. In Hebrew, there are 25 linguistic forms dealing with fear, and in Greek 10 different forms.) Times of wholesale panic have occurred throughout history and throughout civilizations. Fear is a universal, enduring phenomenon.

With the advent of digital technologies and twenty-four-hour news cycles, fear- and stress-related reactivity seem stronger, more contagious, and more prevalent. Misinformation and fear-mongering add to the strength and spread of fear. Because of its essential irrationality, fear (and stress) pushes decision-making processes toward pure reactivity—far from wisdom or reason. In our times, anything or anyone could be potentially dangerous—from immigrants to pandemics to those who dare to criticize the government. Political campaigns have continued to trumpet fear—and use it effectively to influence the electorate.

In the long run, no one wins by promoting fear, but the short-term gains are reason enough for some attention-starved people and enterprises—e.g., "news" networks, bloviators, politicians, business and religious leaders—to use fear as an effective method to capture the minds of others. And if these fear-spreaders want to extend the shelf life of fear, all they need to do is reinsert a supposedly fearsome stimulus to reignite the automaticity of the fear sequence.

DESTRUCTIVE FEAR AND STRESS

Fear and stress can become habitual—or even addictive—as the brain becomes more efficient at recognizing and responding to danger. Continued fear responses are harmful to the body over time. Physiological changes can cause the body's basic systems to deteriorate or weaken. Repeated doses of cortisol may cause the hippocampus—the brain's memory center—to atrophy. Habituated or addictive behaviors may rewire the brain to accept fear or stress as "normal"; both fear and stress can morph into continuing anxiety.

Medical literature has established the connections between stress and a variety of life-threatening conditions or diseases. Excessive or continuing stress is implicated as a factor in heart disease, stroke, diabetes, high blood pressure, asthma, addiction, autoimmune disorders, and a variety of cancers and psychotic conditions.

Fear and stress can also destroy relationships—and with that destruction comes the unraveling of institutions or enterprises. Fighting, fleeing, and freezing—the automatic responses of the brain (and body)—can ripple into friendships, work associations, family bonds, and any affiliation that depends on invisible connections based on trust, shared purpose, or affinity. Fear searches for causes, and with causation come blaming and shaming. Supposed victims look for supposed villains. Entire nations can be so gripped by fear that they lose their capabilities to conduct civil discourse or the necessary functions of a society. In these cases, we think of them as "failed states" and add them to our lists of dangerous places in the world.[7]

FEAR/STRESS REDUCTION

Because fear and stress have some usefulness in life—danger does exist, and some stress can motivate us toward our best efforts—it would be foolish for you to try to eliminate all causes or evidences of fear. Instead, you can diminish the amount of fear and stress in your life, and moderate your reactions to fearful or stressful situations. You might accomplish this feat in any of the following ways:

- Don't try to rationalize immediately all fear or stress reactions. (The rational functions of your brain take just a little longer to engage.)
- Stay attached to the company of supportive others. ("Perfect love casts out fear" because cortisol dissipates in the presence of loving words and touch.)
- Engage in conversations. (Your cerebral cortex—the rational part of your brain—finds words to assist in controlling the raw emotions of fear and stress. This activity can displace the brain space taken up in fear reactivity.)
- Keep your sense of humor active and fully functional. (Laughter is a whole-brain activity, engaging the parasympathetic system in positive emotions.)
- Where possible, avoid contact with fearful/stressful people or situations.
- Practice your own version of "fear conditioning"—experiencing and debriefing small doses of a fearful stimulus.[8]

Because death can inspire fear, it makes sense to deal directly with your feelings and experiences regarding your own mortality. For Christians, fear of death can be eclipsed by the certainty of you resurrection. One way to diminish anxiety about dying is to write your own obituary.[9]

What You Might Do about Fear and Stress in Your Congregation

Like it or not, fear- and stress-related matters lurk or linger in the corners of your congregational life. Because it's a universal human condition—not usually helpful or positive—fear's presence requires your action. Consider some of these possibilities:

1. Admit that fear exists in your congregation. Assay its presence and strength. Look for its tell-tale signs—most of them show up in your individual and collective health. Talk together about what you find.

2. Confess your individual and collective fears. Because some fear and stress reactions can approach the level of sinfulness, confession and forgiveness will be a welcome presence.

3. When you sense the presence of fear or stress—in a meeting, planning session, event—stop and address the effect that fear/stress is having on you at that moment. You might start with the question, "What are you/we afraid of here?"

4. Substitute fear-laden planning processes—that start with descriptions of enormous and fearsome neediness—with those that begin with capacities or assets.

5. Replace fearful leaders. (If you believe that they can be dissuaded from self-poisoning attitudes and behaviors, try that first.)

6. If fear is especially dominant in your congregation, plan a leaders' retreat so that you can deal with the fearful behaviors in your life together.

Social Cognition

As a subset of social biology, the field of social cognition (or social neurobiology) examines the ways in which human brains are primarily dependent on sociality for well-being and identity. The field is based on the generally accepted notion that the brain is a social organ. One simple way to describe social cognition: the innate skills of positive human relationships.

The "social brain" is actually an array of functions that take place in various places throughout your brain. The cerebellum—"the little brain" at the back of your skull—is now considered to be a mediator of attention, movement, emotion, and some language functions. The amygdala—a key structure that regulates emotion—adds capabilities for face recognition and mimicry. The storage and retrieval of memories is a function of the hippocampus. The anterior cingulate gyrus (ACG) plays a role in social behavior and motor function. As part of the limbic system, the ACG is strongly connected to the thalamus, the brain's sensory filter. Neurotransmitters such as dopamine and serotonin flood the brain's pleasure centers—notably the nucleus accumbens—to reward socially pleasing behaviors.[10]

Behaviors and traits associated with social cognition include:

- Altruism, the capability for self-sacrificing behaviors that benefit others.
- Empathy, the capacity to determine the emotional states of other people in relationship to your own identity or feelings.
- Face recognition, the ability to discern the meaning of hundreds of minute changes in the faces of others. Acquired within moments after birth, this skill is seen in mimicry, another form of social cognition.
- Bonding, the capacity to synchronize your behaviors with the identified emotions and behaviors of others. Beginning with the mother-child relationship, social bonding spreads past kinship into friendship and love.
- Free will, the (highly debated) ability to regulate your impulses or emotions purposefully.
- Language, the multifaceted capability to receive and understand meaning accurately.

Among the useful tenets of social cognition for your congregation's ministries are these:

- The human brain may be more strongly hardwired for altruism and empathy than selfishness.
- Humans are intricately equipped to mimic others, and to respond favorably to suggestion.
- Social rewards (approval, bonding, attachment) and punishments (shame, blame) are dependable motivators for action or inaction in groups.
- Social acceptance and bonding limit the risk of depression and anxiety.
- Except for a small percentage of the population, most people are "experts" in most social cognition skills, including self-recognition.

- When your brain's social cognition systems are in full play, other brain systems may not operate as well.
- Sociality begins within hours of your birth and continues throughout your life.
- Reciprocity is one of the strongest norms that you experience.
- Mirror neurons—now thought to be present throughout the brain, and not always associated with motor skills—are an important basis for social cognition.
- Autism may be better understood within the parameters of social cognition. (The functionality of the amygdala seems to be a hopeful focus for research about the autism spectrum.)[11]

Social cognition theory and research have strong implications for congregational life. In their message and activities, congregations can be primary sources for developing and strengthening social intelligence. Congregations provide a safe place for members to connect the wisdom of scriptural stewardship with the wisdom of the secular world. Some observations:

1. The vast majority of scriptural wisdom about relationships corresponds favorably with the findings of social neuroscience. The battles of religion versus science need not be fought on this territory.
2. Congregational leaders might be selected, trained, and evaluated on the basis of their socializing skills. For example, how adept are they at gratitude, admiration, leadership development, listening, or generosity?
3. Because members will mimic them, what kind of examples do congregational leaders exhibit?
4. Denominational leaders and other spiritual pundits might want to reexamine their subtle condemnation of congregations that are "inwardly turned." (Social cognition could be stronger in these places!)
5. Those elements of "the Good News" that correspond to social intelligence—e.g., forgiveness, empathy—should also be proclaimed and celebrated.

Three Big Ideas in Social Cognition

This growing field can offer insights into many important features of human relationships. Among the more intriguing of those ideas are social/physical pain, shaming/blaming, and self-deception.

SOCIAL AND PHYSICAL PAIN

Neurobiological research strongly suggests that the brain deals with both physical and social pain in similar ways and within similar brain structures. We are so sensitive to rejection and separation that our brains consider both those phenomena as painful. Our bodies also treat these two forms of pain in similar ways. The language of social pain shares the language of physical pain: *Hurt, broken, punched in the gut, knifed in the back, hungry for love, kicked to the side of the road.* Social pain—threats to our connection to others—motivates us to seek, cherish, and strengthen those connections. The biochemistry of social rewards—praise, forgiveness, undeserved favor—is similar to that of sensory or physical rewards. Social pain is not a metaphor: Sticks and stones will break our bones, *and* names will always hurt us.[12]

SHAMING AND BLAMING

Active deep within the human brain, the social mechanisms of shaming and blaming are pervasive in relationships. Blame is a spoken belief about a wrong deed, and can be used as a marker of the blameworthy person's overall character. As a positive motivation for change, blame shows the blamer's desire that the blameworthy person would not repeat a shameful act. While blaming seems unproductive—the blameworthy deed has already been done—it does serve as the driving force behind shaming.

Shame turns blame into social rejection or separation. Shame presumes the acceptance or administration of moral constraints. Applied equally, those moral principles guide action, continue over time, and remain inescapable. Anyone who accepts a moral principle is also committed to blaming those who violate that principle. By extension, that person is also willing to accept the blame of others. Reproach and admonishment (and some hostility) are associated with blaming and shaming.[13]

SELF-DECEPTION

One odd function of social intelligence is the brain's bias toward inaccurate self-assessment. From "honest lying" (confabulation) to consistently inaccurate memories, self-deception seems to be a hard-wired feature of all brains. Behavioral economists have noted this feature of social neuroscience in experiments that reveal the inconsistencies between people's stated values and their actual economic choices. Research has consistently pointed out how most people rate themselves "higher/better than average" on measures of performance and personal traits. Sometimes termed "the optimism bias," this thought process is a cognitive illusion—we are blinded to social realities in ways not dissimilar to our perceptions of visual illusions. Self-deception may help us avoid stress and maintain a positive approach to both the present and the future.

Our brains are consistently unreliable when it comes to the accuracy of memories. The process of recall involves the reassembly of pieces of memory into a useful shape. On the one hand, our brains need stable memories so that we can build on experience. On the other hand, memory needs to be flexible so that we can adapt to an environment that constantly changes. Because memory-making and retrieval occur as an integrated function involving many brain structures, it is difficult to pinpoint what might cause faulty memories or confabulation.

Our self-perceptions are heavily influenced by our physical surroundings, in what researchers call "embodied cognition." So we attach significance to states of mind or thought patterns because of physical sensations such as warmth, texture, or weight.[14]

From the viewpoint of social neuroscience, our skill at self-deception makes close, honest relationships even more valuable for our functioning as self-aware beings focused on fulfilling God's will for the world.

What You Might Do with Social Cognition in Your Congregation

Good news spreads into communities of people, not just individual lives. You proclaim and enact God's good news in your relationships. And many facets of what God intends—forgiveness, grace, peace, love, salvation from self-idolatry—are lived out in communities. However you practice social cognition, the truth remains: God blesses the world through your congregation!

In that spirit—and by that Spirit—here are some possible ways to put social cognition to work in your congregation:

1. Check your congregation's practice of sociality against the continuing knowledge emerging from social neuroscience. Where there seems to be disagreement, try to find the most accurate and actionable approaches to productive, pleasing relationships.

2. Think how your congregation's presence in your community might add to civility, generosity, mutuality, respect, and friendship among community members. Which of your programs or events offer these benefits?

3. How do your worship practices—a primary entry point into your congregation's life—connect visitors to the intimacy or acceptance they seek?

4. Where is loneliness still lurking in your congregation's life?

5. Consider the possibility that your congregation could be a safe place for heartfelt conversation—among people in your community who would otherwise not interact with each other.

6. Think how "healing social pains" might be part of your mission or vision statement.

7. What can you do to diminish hurtful gossip within your congregation?

8. How strongly do blaming and shaming processes motivate or control your congregation?

9. How might sermons and other teaching opportunities carve self-deception away from accurate self-perception?

Addiction

From its beginnings, neuroscience has wrestled with addiction. With the advent of sophisticated imaging technologies, brain scientists have edged closer to a full understanding of this widespread neurological phenomenon. Even as the debates continue—about the nature of addiction and pleasure—scientists have come to general agreement about addiction.

At its heart, addiction is a deficiency in the brain's reward system—or perhaps in the attention and motivation systems. The brain's "pleasure centers"—structures such as the nucleus accumbens, amygdala, and anterior cingulate gyrus—react positively to the pleasurable flooding of neurotransmitters such as dopamine, serotonin, and endorphins. The release of these feel-good brain chemicals is triggered by any of a variety of activities—not necessarily limited to substance abuse. Each chemical flooding results in a pattern of continual pleasure-seeking. Over time, the brain requires increased repetitions of a behavior to achieve the same results. And when deprived of the triggering factors—e.g., alcohol, food, sex—the brain experiences withdrawal, a term that describes complex chemical deficits.

Individuals genetically predisposed toward a dysfunctional dopamine system may also be susceptible to other difficulties—such as disinhibition, ADHD, memory impairment, or other obsessive/compulsive attributes. But the reward for dopamine-flooding behaviors is so great that the brain continues to seek it, even in the face of danger or destruction.

As health-care professionals and neurobiologists work to understand addiction, they have come to see that the triggering mechanisms for addiction might include any presenting factor. So individuals may be addicted to sex, food, shopping, love, religious ecstasy, cell phones, exercise, gambling, work, fear, anger, or pleasure itself. (The question remains whether these life-altering behaviors are chemically or behaviorally similar enough to warrant the label "addictive.") When used more metaphorically than medically, addiction continues to be a helpful descriptor of risky life patterns whose control of behaviors and attitudes seems impenetrable.

As neuroscientists unravel the biochemical elements of addiction, it seems possible that genetic and contextual markers will emerge, thus raising hope for those who are afflicted by addiction.[15]

How Addiction Might Impact Your Congregation

Given its characteristics, addiction mechanisms likely afflict the lives of most congregation members. The effects of addiction (of any kind) may interfere with the effectiveness of your congregation's message or programs. These thoughts come to mind:

- Your insistences or invitations regarding faithful spiritual practices—discipleship—may not measure up to the rewards promised by addictive behaviors.
- Your congregation's practices or programs may inadvertently or purposefully contribute to addictive behaviors.
- The incessant pleasure-seeking—self-absorption by another name—required in any addiction might be a primary barrier to joining yourself to God and God's will. ("No one can serve two masters." [Matt. 6:24].) Stewardship of any kind may not be possible for anyone controlled by addiction.
- Spiritual disciplines may help some members manage out-of-control lifestyles or expectations.

Three Big Ideas Connected to Addiction

However defined or experienced, "addiction" spreads into almost every facet of contemporary lifestyles. Three subthemes illustrate the importance of confronting the realities of addiction: the universal nature of addiction, hoarding behaviors, and recovery methods.

THE UNIVERSAL NATURE OF ADDICTION

Given the ubiquitous nature of possible triggers, it seems logical that addiction operates as a cause of many of the problems that face individuals, families, or congregations. Partner or spouse abuse among men might be evidence of withdrawal from love addiction. Acquisitive materialism might be the result of addiction to the newness of possessions or experiences. Sunday sports leagues may continue to offer more pleasure than worship services because of exercise addiction. Entertainment-based worship forms may absorb a congregation's attention because they offer addictive emotional pleasure. Economic duress in families may be caused by shopping addictions. An incapacity to love others may be connected to an addiction to pornography. Poor decision-making may relate to addictions to hurried lifestyles. Marriages can disintegrate because of alcohol and substance addictions. Life balance gets out of whack when addiction to work takes over your identity. Crimes of opportunity—robbery, burglary, fraud—can trace their connections back to addictions to dangerous drugs. The continuing epidemic of obesity—and its accompanying host of interconnected medical conditions—may be attributed to food addictions of several kinds.

A difficult question may hide inside these multiple examples: Is pleasure-seeking itself the problem? Taking a more positive view, Yale University psychology professor Paul Bloom thinks of pleasure-seeking in terms of "essentialism," a principle defined by philosopher John Locke as "the very being of anything, whereby it is what it is." Perhaps pleasure-seeking's universality is proof of its acceptability?[16]

One certainty: It's hard for your congregation to compete for attention when so many addictions are eating away at your core attitudes or goals.

HOARDING BEHAVIORS

Residing somewhere in a neurobiology that has gone awry, hoarding manifests itself as the incessant difficulty of discarding one's possessions. Hoarders experience distress at the thought (or act) of parting with items that have imagined worth or utility. Although it might be an impulse disorder or a mental illness, hoarding continues to afflict individuals and families. Invisible—except in the glaring light of "reality television"—uncontrollable hoarding is an irrational state of mind wrapped up in an attachment to possessions (or their purchasing). Although some hoarders can lead otherwise normal lives, holding jobs and engaging in friendships, hoarding can become dangerous to the hoarders and those around them. It can wreak havoc with a family's economic well-being, and threaten the safety of a living space. (Fire hazards and pest infestations are a frequent result of hoarding.) A further difficulty: Hoarders can descend into even more troubling physical or mental problems, such as frequent illness, cognitive decline, or depression.[17]

Stereotypically connected to the declining mental abilities of the frail elderly, hoarding more typically begins at a slightly younger age—as early as the preteen years. Risk factors for hoarding behaviors include an indecisive personality, a family history of hoarding, social isolation, and stressful life events such as divorce, eviction, or the death of a family member. [18]

Over two million people suffer from compulsive hoarding, with that number likely increasing as dementia continues to grow. Hoarding behaviors may comprise a self-reinforcing cycle. Societal factors—e.g., bigger homes or the increase in personal consumption expenditures—can also contribute to the progress of normal accumulation behaviors toward compulsive, perhaps psychotic activities.[19]

Diagnosis and treatment of this condition are difficult. Continuing behaviors are the most evident markers, but that diagnosis doesn't appear until later in the downward cycle, perhaps well after effective treatments could have been applied. Treatment consists of cognitive behavior therapy (CBT) or administration of selective serotonin reuptake inhibitors (SSRIs). Neither course of treatment offers assured results.[20]

ADDICTION RECOVERY METHODS

Because the neurobiology of addiction is complex, methods for diminishing its causes or effects may not offer complete cures. The most consistently effective approaches are variants of the twelve-step methodology pioneered by Alcoholics Anonymous. Based on the power of group dynamics—with some allusions to spirituality—AA's practices have evolved into treatment programs for a variety of addictive disorders. Over the past few years, an alternative program, SMART Recovery, has developed a process that relies heavily on the developing science behind addiction. Based on proven techniques of self-reliance and self-empowerment, SMART Recovery has expanded its targeted maladies to a range of addictive behaviors.[21]

Recovery programs based on talk-therapy are not always effective for those afflicted with alcohol-use disorder. In the past decade, treatment centers in Finland and the United States have reported consistent success with naltrexone, an opioid antagonist that diminishes the brain's cravings for alcohol.

Additional drugs—e.g., acamprosate and antabuse—have filled other gaps in treatment regimes.[22]

Harvard neuropsychiatrist and author John Ratey has noted the consistent results in addiction recovery programs that are based on exercise. This form of therapy replaces the neurobiological effects of addiction—the so-called "rush"—with the natural high that comes from consistent, vigorous exercise. The uptake of feel-good neurotransmitters still occurs, but with exercise there are virtually no side effects other than what some have deemed "exercise addiction."[23]

Neuroscientist and scientific writer Michel Solis reports on another route to ameliorating addiction. She cites the efforts of researchers to understand and restore the brain's ability to learn. This research is based on the possibility that, in addictive circumstances, the synapses retain a kind of rigidity that makes it difficult for an addict to change habits. The restoration of natural synapse flexibility might be accomplished by pharmaceutical means, allowing addicts to connect their desire to change with the ability to learn new habits.[24]

What You Might Do about Addiction in Your Congregation

Let me go off-script before I offer some observations about congregational life: Addiction is too important, too universal, too damaging to let it slide. You're not going to increase financial contributions if congregation members are addicted to expensive stuff. It's likely that social media addictions eat up the free time of many members; church-related activities may not provide the levels of pleasure they get from texting, surfing, chirping, and friending. Lonely hoarders are hiding—probably in shame—in their dangerously cluttered homes. Morbidly overweight members are not going to live long lives. The minds of sexual predators need exposure or healing. The lives of alcohol and substance abusers may be deteriorating under the surface of congregational life.

You can't just hope addictions will go away. They don't fade away in any other setting, and neither will they disappear in your congregation! Members' desire to fulfill God's will in their lives is being hijacked by the parts of their brains that are addicted. However you look at this matter, addictions will get in the way of every stewardshift you hope for!

You might want to consider these possible actions or directions that come from this branch of secular wisdom:

1. What would it take for you to put together a whole-congregation process of self-examination and confession about the likely addictions that afflict you? Could the coming Advent or Lenten seasons be a good time?

2. If you are privy to the inner worlds of recovering addicts, enlist their help. What do recovering substance abusers—and their caregivers—know that could be helpful for the whole congregation?

3. Take time to see the places where your congregation's programs, approach, personality, or style might be addictive and damaging to families, individuals, or the congregation itself.

4. Think about the possibility of starting a new kind of anonymous-addicts program for your community. What benefit could you offer to workaholics, sports spouses, time-starved teens, hoarders, consumers of pornography, or other addicts? Who could help you start these groups?

5. If support or caring ministries already exist in your congregation, insert addiction training into the ongoing program.

6. Start a healthy eating and exercise group—or support an already existing one.

7. Gather together mental health professionals in your community for a learning forum about multifaceted addictions. See what you know together, what are your combined assets, and what you might do together.

8. Think about this metaphor: What if you thought of your congregation as an "addiction recovery center"?

Habituation and Change

In his *Nicomachean Ethics*, Aristotle wrote that our habits show who we are at our core. Thus a knowledge of habituation and change may be integral to your congregation's flourishing.

Defined operationally, habituation occurs when your brain turns its repeated functions or responses into default actions, thus reducing the work of constantly attending to all incoming stimuli.

From a biological perspective, habituation is the outward manifestation of "long-term potentiation" (LTP). LTP denotes changes in the chemistry of individual neurons and groups of neurons so that synapse patterns assemble into easily accessed chunks. After these firing patterns are established and strengthened through repetition, neurons are more likely to prefer those arrangements in the future. Habituation mechanisms seem to involve the basal ganglia, a cluster of structures beneath the cortex that collaborate with the motor cortex and cerebellum to regulate voluntary movements, as well as memory and learning sequences.

Habits are related to the brain's autonomic functions—breathing, digesting, sensing—but are not the same. Relying on preestablished patterns of behavior requires a robust memory and assured decision-making. Addictive behaviors may be habitual, but not all habits are addictive.

According to researcher Charles Duhigg (*The Power of Habit: Why We Do What We Do in Life and Business*), more than 40 percent of our daily actions are habits, not "decisions." Habituation begins with perception of a behavioral cue, and continues with the retrieval of the routine associated with that cue—in anticipation of receiving a reward. Your brain knows which cues to attend to, and when to allow certain habits to control behaviors. Some habits can be thought of as "keystone habits," functioning as nodes or foundations for a host of related behaviors.

Habits are difficult to change or dislodge because the brain perceives that habits are useful and relies on them for the vast majority of the innumerable behaviors that occur each day. New habits can become even more durable when they include some kind of spirituality focused on God.[25]

Change theory and research engages the question, "How and why do people and groups actually change their behaviors?" The original (1947) theory of social psychologist Kurt Lewin proposed a simple three-step progression: Unfreeze (a particular behavior so that you are receptive to change), change (the behavior in question), and freeze (the new behavior in place of the old one). Lewin also proposed "force-field analysis" as a way of determining how potentials and barriers balanced each other.

In the late 1950s, social psychologist Leon Festinger and others developed "cognitive dissonance theory" as a way of explaining change. Their idea: people will seek to keep their lives in balance, and work against imbalance (dissonance), to restore homeostasis, consistency, or harmony. Perceptions about the degree of balance/imbalance are the driving force in change. Change occurs because people try to obtain more or less of a particular quality, belief, factor, possession, relationship, etc. Under some circumstances, people will instead adjust their perceptions to match their actual situation.

Both Lewin's and Festinger's work is a neurobiologically credible way to understand change. Some key concepts:

- The brain is "plastic," which means that individual brain circuits can change their functions very quickly. Like pattern recognition, this capability allows for efficiency: A limited number of neurons (one hundred billion) can enact more than 40 quadrillion possible patterns of interconnection that enable the coordinated functioning of as many as 800 identifiable brain structures. Plasticity means that your brain can handle change very well, and perhaps even seeks it.

- Human brains are conditioned within social contexts. All the mechanisms that enable or require social functioning—e.g., mirror neurons, mimicking, bonding, reciprocity, altruism—also equip the brain for changed behavior.

- The brain's capacity for memory is complex. The interplay among a variety of brain modules that form, store, analyze, and recall memories for action is still not completely understood. Your brain is capable of both short-term and long-term memory.

- Motivation for change seems to rest in the brain's emotive capabilities, the desire for self-preservation, success in relationships, the search for happiness, and genetic predispositions and malformations.

- "Learning" is sometimes used to describe the brain's capability to integrate all these functions so that your brain and body can adapt to ever-changing circumstances that surround you.

- Consciousness—the "Holy Grail" of neurobiology—may underlie all that we know about the brain, including its ability to change.

- Habituation may inhibit curiosity, creativity, or an accurate perception of your context.

- Times of personal or congregational crisis can also be fruitful opportunities for examining the habits that may have created the problem.

- Except in the case of dire circumstances, change takes place over time.

- Constant change in the world around you can call forth fear and stress-based reactivity, which may manifest itself as resistance to change.

- Change is the only constant that you can rely on.

- You can change or be changed. Both can be positive or negative experiences.

Why pay attention to change and habituation? These general observations may be helpful:

- If your congregation (as a collection of brains) lacks major neurobiological functionality—e.g., memory, learning, socializing—it may have a diminished capacity for change.

- Resistance to change could also be a matter of resisting an insistent "change agent."

- Your congregation probably operates more out of habit than from rational decision-making processes.
- The processes for changing personal habits may also work with your congregation's habits.
- Effective conflict resolution methods can rely on proven processes of rehabituation.

Three Big Ideas about Change and Habituation

As the need for change continues, habituation and other change mechanisms may deserve your attention. Among the ideas you may want to track closely are: free will, the power of suggestion, and rehabituation.

FREE WILL

In theological circles, the debate about human free will has raged for centuries. (Consider the doctrine of "original sin" as an example.) That same debate—about the nature and function of free will—has consumed neuroscientists. On the one hand, some social psychologists and neuroscientists cite the fact that much of our thinking takes place automatically, before rationality or intelligence occur. This seems to indicate a lack of willed attention or action. On the other hand, capacities for empathy, kindness, self-control, and moral judgment require more than pure automaticity in the brain.

Because scientific study about free will is substantively different than theological thinking, neuroscientists must confine themselves only to observable and replicable facts. That work is difficult: As an intricately expressed state of being, free will is hard to measure. (Consciousness research already embraces this subject and may eventually assimilate it into the larger exploration of human identity.)[26]

POWER OF SUGGESTION

Several interesting sidebars accompany free will. One of them is the truth that all of us are reliably suggestible. We respond to "suggestion"—a general term that includes but is not limited to spoken invitation—with predictable acquiescence or obedience. Sometimes we yield to temptation or trickery, but most of our responses to others' suggestions are based on willing assent. Marketers and behavioral economists have assembled a body of proof that seems unassailable: Because we are social animals, we respond favorably to prompts and recommendations from others. At times of significant life events—having a baby is the most important—consumers are more likely to change their buying habits because of suggestions from marketers, family, or colleagues.[27]

REHABITUATION

According to Duhigg, new habits—and their underlying mechanisms—can overlay old habits. He suggests "The Golden Rule of Habit Change": Alter the routine accompanying the cues that instigated the old habit and resulted in the reward of the old habit. The key to this process is knowing both the cue as well as the actual reward you seek. With a new routine in place, you can subvert the power of cravings—emotional or physical anticipation of the rewards—and help diminish the brain's automatic response to the cues. Duhigg credits Nathan Azrin, the "father of behavioral therapy," and others with developing this "habit reversal training."[28]

What You Might Do about Habituation and Change in Your Congregation

You might apply this part of neuroscientific knowledge in your setting in these ways:

1. If you think of yourself as a change agent, seriously reconsider that self-appointment. Your imagined role may rest on unproven ideas or bromides about leadership principles that might not square with the findings of neuroscience.

2. Because habits can assure both efficiency and a lack of innovation, take the time to identify your congregation's habituated programs—e.g., the annual stewardship drive or Christmas program—to see whether those habits have helped or hindered your congregation's creativity, curiosity, or self-perception.

3. If wholesale change might benefit your congregation—or if you are dealing with conflict—study the matter of organizational change carefully before embarking on even the first steps of the process. Look for authors and practitioners who acknowledge the neurobiological elements of change in their work.

4. Ask a psychologist or family therapist to help you understand cognitive behavioral therapy—a proven approach to positive change in

individuals. This methodology might have some usefulness when applied to an entire congregation.

5. Identify some of the keystone habits—those that engender or support other habits—in your congregation's life. Analyze those habits before attempting any larger change.

6. Identify the "super persuaders" in your congregation, individuals whose ability to motivate others is readily apparent. Consider how the congregation could benefit from their influences in roles other than formal leadership.

7. Include "free will" in the content of a Bible class, small group, or new-members class. Start with the scriptural/doctrinal elements of the subject, then examine the connected neurobiology.

Movement/Exercise

Movement is integral to your well-being because your brain is oriented toward movement. Movement—and by extension, exercise—is critical to physical health. But in recent years the added value of movement for healthy brain function has also been established. The findings of exercise science add weight to my invitation in the following paragraphs: Increase the amount and variety of movement in your daily life. Matters related to movement and exercise can also be critical components in the stewardship ministries of your congregation.

In 2008, renowned Harvard neuropsychiatrist John Ratey published *Spark: The Revolutionary New Science of Exercise and the Brain*, a wide-ranging synthesis of research about the benefits of movement/exercise for brains. Ratey proposed that movement of any kind—especially regular exercise—could benefit people who wanted clarity about depression, addictions, learning, dementia, stress, ongoing anxiety, and attention-related dysfunctions. One astounding finding that occurs in a number of studies: Any amount of movement or exercise benefits brains. (This could eliminate any objections to establishing an exercise regime or habit.)

Movement and exercise function as a neurobiological constant. Today the benefits of movement influence the work of educators, human resources managers, occupational and physical therapists, gerontologists, psychologists, psychotherapists, and pediatricians. The neurobiology of movement has effected changes in entire school systems, clinical practices, regimes of rehabilitation and recovery, and the daily routines of ordinary people.

The benefits of exercise to the overall health of congregation members is already well established. The neurobiological value of movement and exercise could be even more important. Consider these possibilities:

- A good share of your members may be suffering from the effects of addiction, stress, depression, PMS, OCD, ADHD, loss of memory, premature aging, or anxiety.
- Your congregation's programs and events may subtly inhibit or discourage movement and exercises. (Consider the passive physicality of a typical meeting or the absence of any significant movement in congregation programs or events.)
- All around you are societal and civic organizations that take seriously the advice of mental health professionals about the value of exercise. Your congregation's lack of attention to physical/mental health may diminish your appeal.
- If low-income or at-risk youth are part of your mission, exercise/movement programs could offer them the opportunity to free themselves from mental difficulties.
- As a stewardship leader, your example of consistent, focused exercise can encourage those who are overweight, out-of-shape, or otherwise physically diminished.

Three Big Ideas Connected to Movement and Exercise

The insights of Ratey and others can extend into any number of life-related matters—all of them part of "whole-life stewardship" and all of them influencing your ability to fulfill God's *economia* in your setting. Consider the following aspects of purposed exercise: neurogenesis among the elderly, depression, and play.

NEUROGENESIS AMONG THE ELDERLY

At one time, it was generally accepted as fact that brain cells, once created, could not regenerate; over the decades of your life, fewer neurons were available for cognition. In 1998, researchers using advanced imaging to track the spread of brain cancer noticed that thousands of new cells and their branching axons and dendrites were growing and dividing in the hippocampus.

Continuing research revealed the existence of brain growth factors—hormones implicated in neurogenesis that help increase the growth of blood flow in the brain.

Two other discoveries have been verified by research: Neurogenesis (neural growth) continues into old age, and the process is enhanced by exercise. The implications are striking: A decrease in cognitive ability among the elderly is not inevitable; and any amount of exercise seems to be beneficial.

Over the past few years, this research has resulted in significant changes in elder care, and has provided an impetus for health providers and insurers to increase the amount of exercise in programs of therapy and well-being among older age cohorts.[29]

DEPRESSION

About 17 percent of Americans confront clinical depression during their lifetimes. Some individuals attempt or commit suicide, a sadly persistent result of this condition. Most of those suffering from this illness greet each day dependent on a host of pharmacological assistance and vulnerable to a host of possibly debilitating circumstances. In his summary of depression-related research, Ratey cites studies showing how exercise increases the amounts of the "feel-good neurotransmitters" dopamine, serotonin, and norepinephrine in the brain. Perhaps the most amazing finding: The neurobiological triggers for depression—imbalances in the connectivity of brain chemicals—may themselves be regulated by brain-derived neurotrophic factor (BDNF). BDNF "turns on genes to produce new neurotransmitters, puts the brakes on self-destructive cellular activity, releases antioxidants, and provides the proteins used as material for axons and dendrites." To continue this cause-and-effect thread: The amounts of BDNF increase with exercise! Connectivity within the brain's circuitry increases and depression is diminished.[30]

PLAY

A relatively new actor in the arenas of movement and exercise, play is assuming a greater role in adult well-being. Understood as more than a necessary part of children's development, play also benefits adults. Play can be physical, intellectual, or relational. Play affords the opportunity for safe and pleasurable practice, rehearsal, or review of real-life experiences. Much of play is inherently physical, unstructured, interactive, and imaginative (inner movement), all of which involve multiple brain structures and functions. (This is sometimes referred to as "whole-brain" activity.) Play teaches resilience, cooperation, and fairness. Play requires and develops social-emotional intelligence, and may be connected with higher levels of happiness.[31]

What You Might Do about Movement and Exercise in Your Congregation

Your stewardship of the brain(s) that God has entrusted to you could improve measurably when you add exercise or movement to your stewardship ministry. Some possibilities:

1. If you engage in little or no exercise, begin reversing this unhealthy part of your lifestyle as soon as possible. Begin with small changes and work gradually toward larger goals.

2. Rate every aspect of congregational life—programs, events, goals, participants, facilities, etc.—to see how each increases or diminishes exercise or movement.

3. Pick one area of your stewardship ministry where exercise could benefit members and the wider community. After several months, see how exercise has affected the outcomes for this ministry.

4. Start and punctuate meetings or other gatherings with a few moments of simple exercise.

5. Survey the number and quality of exercise programs already available in your community—e.g., park or school districts—and encourage members to take advantage of these opportunities.

6. Host congregational events at gyms, parks, or pools.

7. Include physical therapists, coaches, personal trainers, fitness instructors, or coaches in your committees, teams, or planning groups. Ask for their special insights and recommendations about including exercise in programs or events.

8. If your congregation serves at-risk youth, low-income families, senior citizens, or other vulnerable cohorts, insert exercise routines or elements into the already existing programs or services you offer.

9. Think how movement could be integrated more fully into worship.

10. Consider how you might add some elements of play (and playfulness) into congregational life.

On the Neurobiological Horizon

By the time you read this book, a host of significant new findings about neurobiology will have appeared. Because stewardship takes place as an activity of your brain—attitudes, attention, perceptions, habituated responses, identity—it makes sense to stay tuned to brain science. What follows are quick snapshots of some areas of neuroscience that may emerge as significant or applicable to your leadership.

- *Creativity:* Research is uncovering the determinants and effects of this necessary personal attribute that undergirds hopeful, adaptable planning.
- *Exosomes:* These small packets of proteins may have the ability to repair myelin around neurons, a possible factor in addressing diseases such as multiple sclerosis.
- *The nature of sin:* As brain science tackles questions about consciousness, metaphysical matters—including sin—will likely be included in the conjecture and research.
- *Sleep:* A burst of recent studies indicates the negative effects of widespread sleep deprivation in the wider society.
- *Poly-vagal theory:* The existence of a "second brain" (or "gut-brain") involving the vagal nerve suggests important new findings about the digestive (microbiotic), respiratory, and circulatory systems, and how the vagal system joins body-wisdom to brain-wisdom.
- *Brain-training:* False and verifiable claims of self-help will continue to bedazzle and bedevil you in your search for helpful applications of brain science.
- *Endocannabinoids:* A new class of brain chemicals derived from cannabis, these substances may affect the treatment of a variety of diseases and medical conditions.

As you add to this short list the growing volume and focus of research—e.g., dementia, memory, addiction, intelligence—you can readily imagine the possibilities of newly important knowledge that you may be applying to your stewardship leadership in the future.

Returning to the Start

When we began this chapter, I invited you to consider your response to neuroscientific knowledge by answering the question, "What are you going to do with these brains?" Everything you do as a stewardship leader begins with some action or function that takes place in your brain. As the general society races to embrace the findings of neurobiology—and, perhaps too hastily, to put them to use in everyday life and commerce—it would be a shame if leaders in the church remained ignorant or distrustful of this developing science. For example, if neuromarketers are taking advantage of the brain's natural ability for self-deception, how might your congregation shrewdly counter the effects of the materialism that results? And when neuroscience starts to part the curtains on questions that the church has held to itself for centuries—e.g., the nature of belief or hope—it will make sense for you to be already conversant with the scope of those scientific inquiries.

Let me add an important aside. As you've encountered the stream of ideas I've presented here, you may have come away from the experience either awed or confused beyond your capacity to respond. You may also have begun to wonder whether truths close to the heart of religion can stand up to the discoveries of brain science. Before those attitudes encroach on your sense of ministry or leadership, let me offer these few reassuring and challenging observations:

1. The matters of faith that occupy most of your ministry are as real as the findings of brain science. Forgiveness, hope, grace, repentance, love—none of these bedrock qualities of spiritual life are going to go away. (None will escape the respectful gaze of brain scientists either.)

2. As neurobiologists begin working on matters formerly reserved for theologians and other spiritual leaders, you can expect that their findings will corroborate, complement, or sharpen what you already hold to be true. Love is a theological principle and a state of mind that can be expressed in neuroscientific terms. Forgiveness research will continue to unfold along the lines that Scripture already proposes. Grace—undeserved favor—will be described more wonderfully as research on altruism proceeds.

3. Theological knowledge about metaphysical, mystical, and essentially human matters has much to offer to neurobiology, including an ongoing sense of mystery and awe.

For these reasons, you have every reason to be glad about the work of neurobiologists who uncover and explain the wonders of God's creation inside the human skull and nervous system. And you can be assured that what neurobiology discovers about the human brain can be applied to your stewardship leadership.

Your care for the brains entrusted to you—those of individual members and of the congregation as a single entity—is a sacred task. A necessary ministry. An awe-inspiring ministry. By your stewardship of the minds—we used to say "hearts," remember?—of God's people, you ensure that God's will is done with care and respect for the incredible gifts inside the human brain.

One more nudge: This could be a fascinating shift!

Notes

1. From John Ratey, *The User's Guide to the Brain: Perception, Attention, and the Four Theaters of the Brain* (New York: Vintage Books, 2002), 114–20.

2. This system includes structures such as the amygdala, the hypothalamus, the hippocampus, and the myelin sheath. Another neuronal system, glial cells, distributes inattention functions throughout the brain. Bob Sitze, "Dancing with the Sisyphean Imperative: Clergy Well-Being with the Brain in Mind" (Unpublished conference paper, "Flourishing in Pastoral Ministry" Conference, Indiana Wesleyan University, Marion, Indiana, October 11, 2013), 2–3.

3. See University of Oxford cognitive neuroscientist Stephen M. Fleming's "The Power of Reflection," *Scientific American Mind*, September/October 2014, 31–37. *Scientific American* associate editor Ferris Jabr calls self-talk "inner speech" and notes that it can fill as much as one-quarter of your waking hours: "Speak for Yourself," *Scientific American Mind*, January/February 2014, 46–51. Also see V. S. Ramachandran's *The Tell-Tale Brain: A Neuroscientist's Question for What Makes Us Human* (New York: W. W. Norton, 2011), 118ff, 145ff, for a summary description of theory of the mind, including its relationship to autism.

4. From Jonah Berger, *Contagious: Why Things Catch On* (New York: Simon & Schuster, 2013), 22ff. The remainder of his book expands on each of these factors. Berger cautions that, although it is highly desirable in our culture, contagion is still a rare occurrence: Only .00333% of YouTube videos get more than one million views, and over 50 percent of all posted videos have fewer than 500 views (12).

5. James Danckert, "Descent of the Doldrums," *Scientific American Mind*, July/August 2013, 54–59. The author admits that defining boredom is difficult because of its highly individualized interpretations. He also centers in on the orbitofrontal cortex as a brain structure implicated in boredom.

6. Sitze, "Dancing," 9–10.

7. An example current with the writing of this book: the rise and spread of the Ebola virus. The pandemic panic that accompanied the continuing news about Ebola's course through a number of countries in Africa was evidence of how quickly small pieces of the social order—in this case, in the United States—could break off and

feed an epidemic of fear. Jeffrey Kluger, "Fear Factor." *TIME Magazine*, October 20, 2014, 30–35.

8. Brain researcher Tari Sharot offers a quick description of fear conditioning in *The Optimism Bias: A Tour of the Irrationally Positive Brain* (New York: Pantheon Books, 2011), 178–80.

9. Writing your obituary serves as a kind of preclosure on the subject, and allows you to get on with the rest of your life. Todd Etshman, "Take Your Life Into Your Own Hands: Write Your Own Obit," *The Lutheran*, November 2014, 30–32.

10. Ratey, *User's Guide*, chapter 8, "The Social Brain."

11. From UCLA professor of behavioral sciences, psychology, and psychiatry Matthew D. Lieberman's *Social: Why Our Brains Are Wired to Connect* (New York: Crown Publishers, 2013), 20, 25, 26–27, 80, 81, 92–93, 99, 133ff, 142, 144ff, 152ff, 162ff, 271–72.

12. Lieberman, *Social*, 5, 45–47, 67, 69.

13. Dr. George Sher, professor of philosophy at Rice University, "Morality and Blame" (lecture, Wheaton College, Wheaton, IL, March 19, 2014).

14. Tali Sharot explores self-deception and related perceptual problems in *The Optimism Bias*. Her further observations are targeted at learned helplessness, visual and spatial misperception, the "sweet lemons" phenomenon, and cognitive dissonance. Confabulation attracts the curious eye of German speech pathologist and researcher Maria-Dorothea Heidler in "Honest Liars: How the Brain Leads us to Believe False Truths," *Scientific American Mind*, March/April 2014, 41–44. Science writer Sarah Yager summarizes research studies in embodied cognition, noting its prevalence in many areas of life: "Your Gullible Brain: How Our Senses Influence Our Thoughts," *The Atlantic Monthly*, May 2014, 16.

15. Sitze, "Dancing," 8–9.

16. Peter Bloom, *How Pleasure Works: The New Science of Why We Like What We Like* (New York: W.W. Norton, 2010), 8–9.

17. Speaker, organizing expert, senior relocation specialist, and former gambling addict, Matt Paxton describes hoarding behaviors and treatments from his personal experiences with clients and their families in *The Secret Lives of Hoarders: True Stories of Tackling Extreme Clutter* (New York: Penguin, 2011), 54–60.

18. From "Hoarding disorder," Mayo Clinic website, *www.mayoclinic.org/diseases-conditions/hoarding-disorder* (n.d.).

19. From Lara Zielin, "In Excess: Clutter, Hoarding, and Consumption in the Modern World," *LSA Magazine* (Spring 2010): 27–31. Editor Zielin also notes the work of organizing professionals who comprise the National Study Group on Chronic Disorganization.

20. From Mayo Clinic website, "Hoarding disorder."

21. Both organizations feature group meetings, and both programs are available at no cost to participants (Alcoholics Anonymous, *www.aa.org* and *SMART* Recovery, *www.smartrecovery.org*).

22. Gabrielle Glaser, "The False Gospel of Alcoholics Anonymous," *The Atlantic*, April 2015, 50–60. Based on her research of the scientific literature, Glaser cautions against relying on recovery programs based solely on complete abstinence.

23. Ratey summarizes the positive effects of the "natural high" in chapter 7 ("Addiction: Reclaiming the Biology of Self-Control") in *Spark: The Revolutionary New Science of Exercise and the Brain* (New York: Little, Brown, 2008).

24. One fascinating side note about this effort: The effect of a doctor's empathy in placebo-oriented recoveries seems to be positive. (Michele Solis, "A Lifeline for Addicts," *Scientific American Mind*, March/April 2013, 40–44.)

25. From Charles Duhigg, *The Power of Habit: Why We Do What We Do in Life and Business* (New York: Random House, 2012), Keystone habits, xiv, 119; chunking,17; habit cycle, 19; spirituality of durable habits, 84ff; "small wins," 109–12.)

26. Yale University cognitive scientist Paul Bloom argues forcefully against any approach to free will that overlooks purposed rationality. (Paul Bloom, "The War on Reason," *The Atlantic*, March 2014, 64–70.) Georgia State University neurobiologist Eddy Nahmias questions the logic that underlies "people are only biochemical puppets" pronouncements as perhaps too quick and too shallow. (Nahmias, "Why We Have Free Will," *Scientific American*, January 2015, 77–79.) Other neurobiologists cite the critical function of the basal ganglia and anterior cingulate gyrus in volition and motivation, two likely components of free will. Duhigg, *Power of Habit*, 14, 26; Ratey, *User's Guide*, 318–19.

27. Duhigg notes the power of "predictive analysis"—a series of algorithms based on previous purchasing decisions and demographics—to extend offers to consumers, who are more likely to respond favorably. Duhigg, *Power of Habit*, 191ff. Kevin Dutton, research fellow at the Faraday Institute at the University of Cambridge, writes about "supersuasion" techniques: simplicity, perceived self-interest, incongruity (and accompanying humor), confidence, and empathy. Dutton, "The Power to Persuade: How Masters of 'Supersuasion' Can Change Your Mind," *Scientific American Mind*, March/April 2010, 24–31.

28. An eminent Skinnerian psychologist, Nathan Azrin, originated a toilet-training process that accomplished that difficult developmental milestone in one day. Duhigg, *Power of Habit*, new habits overlaid, 20; "Golden rule" of habit change, 68; Azrin citations, 74ff.

29. Exercise-enhanced neurogenesis may also be a factor in stress reduction, as well as increases in learning and memory capabilities. Ratey, *User's Guide*, 48–49, 51–53, 55, 78, 245–47. In a related matter, the continuing Memory and Aging Project of Chicago's Rush University Medical Center concludes that a higher level of total

daily physical activity is associated with a reduced risk of Alzheimer's dementia. This finding holds true even when adjusted for other factors. (A. S. Buchman, P. A. Boyle, L. Yu et al, "Total Daily Physical Activity and the Risk of AD and Cognitive Decline in Older Adults," *Neurology* 78, no. 17 (April 24, 2012): 1323–29.

30. A long-standing study of the effect of selective serotonin reuptake inhibitors (SSRIs) showed that the positive results of exercise-based therapies for depression are as strong as those obtained from traditional SSRI treatments. The effects of exercise may also last longer. Ratey, *Spark*, chapter 5 and 122–25.

31. Ratey notes that too many children come to school not knowing how to play. From John Ratey's April 17, 2012, presentation at Glenbard East High School, Lombard, Illinois. Yale psychologist Paul Bloom describes play-fighting as a necessary developmental activity and a low-cost way to learn a life skill. Bloom, *How Pleasure Works*, 193.

Chapter 9

Wild Ideals: Natural History

What's the first thing that comes to mind when you hear the words "natural history"? Something connected with "museum"? If so, your word association would fit with the experiences of most people: Visiting an impressive, perhaps venerable, edifice that houses astounding exhibits from the natural world. Lodged in those locations, collections of impressive specimens stand frozen in time, ready to receive your passing attention. You would have taken tours, listened to docents, and found the word "interesting" bouncing around your vocabulary. The experience would have inspired awe and wild imagination. The museum would have fulfilled its historic functions.

In this chapter, I hope to take you beyond those museum walls, examining natural history as a worthy source of wisdom about stewardship. I think that this collection of thought-specimens will merit your attention.

"Natural History" Parsed

Like "stewardship," this term carries any number of definitions, some very narrowly focused and others encompassing large swaths of accumulated knowledge. This is one of those places where dictionaries can capture only the bare bones of an important idea. In some cases, these definitions list the range of physical sciences that natural history gathers together under its conceptual roof. In other cases, the dictionaries describe generic activities of natural historians—also "naturalists" in this chapter. Few dictionary entries, however, do justice to the relevance of this field to human existence.

In this chapter, I'll define and use "natural history" as broadly as possible: appreciative and systematic observation, classification, and integration of any elements of the natural world for the purpose of enhancing their sustainability. This usage reflects the current understanding of the term among natural historians.

Naturalists insist that natural history is not synonymous with environmentalism or ecology. Although related to or dependent on natural history, these two fields of study explore slightly different aspects of the natural world. Natural history preceded by centuries the emergence of environmental or ecological disciplines, so both those bodies of knowledge have emerged from natural history.

Naturalists explore the natural world close-up, more often working in the field than in laboratories. Naturalists synthesize the sciences, and their field work provides the backbone of ecological and environmental study.

Natural history is unique because it unifies widely diverse areas of science and emphasizes the interaction between humans and the natural world. Naturalists integrate discoveries in sciences as diverse as botany, entomology, zoology, geology, anthropology, herpetology, and paleontology. Naturalists work as park rangers, teachers, outdoor guides and outfitters, writers and editors, social critics, government bureaucrats, poets, explorers, and environmental entrepreneurs.

As they explore human interactions with the natural world, natural historians incorporate into their work other areas of study such as law, psychology, philosophy, sociology, neurobiology, communications theory, economics, politics, and religion.

Naturalists make sense out of nature, whether it's experienced in majestic vistas, rural pastures, or in their own backyards. (The presence of nature in its common forms leads Cornell University ecologist Harry Green to remind audiences that "even cows have a natural history."[1])

Although they honor and work within scientific methods—e.g., rigorous observation and pattern-seeking—natural historians rarely engage in experimental science. When they are in the field, they face the raw power of natural processes or creatures. They ask both simple and complex questions, hoping for answers that convey wonder. They teach and write, inspiring others to regard the natural world with awe and respect. They get excited about both history and mystery.[2]

To underscore the rare qualities of natural historians, you could accurately describe them as polymaths—scholars and expert practitioners of many fields of study, who are able to apply and integrate what they learn into practical wisdom. Notable polymaths from history include Aristotle, Leonardo da Vinci, Copernicus, Hildegard of Bingen, Benjamin Franklin, Omar Khayyam, Charles Darwin, and Francis Bacon. (The term's synonym, "Renaissance man," unfortunately disregards the strong possibility that female polymaths have also permeated history.)

The Value of Natural History

Because natural history gathers together and integrates so many fields of human endeavor, it can offer you a concise vision of interrelationships within the created world. Natural history may also be important because it provides you the opportunity to reconnect to what is most essential about your humanness, about your relationship with a continuingly creating God.

"Our relationship to Nature is primal," writes E. O. Wilson, Harvard professor, biologist, environmental advocate, author, and father of sociobiology. Nature evokes some of the spirituality that scientists and religionists hold in common. In 1984, Wilson coined the term *biophilia*, his way of naming "the innate tendency (of humans) to affiliate with life and lifelike processes." Wilson saw the positive consequences of this affiliation: "The more we come to understand other life forms, the more our learning expands to include their vast diversity, and the greater the value we will place on them and, inevitably, on ourselves."[3]

Canadian naturalist and essayist Julian Hoffman speaks of the value of natural history disciplines in solidifying the sense of place that's necessary for an identity that transcends self-regard. "Place has a profound bearing on our lives, from the countries we are born into, or end up inhabiting, to the light, landscape, and weather peculiar to our home regions." He quotes environmental artist Alan Gussow, "A place is a piece of a whole environment that has been claimed by feelings." "Home" suggests a "settling-down in one location, being at ease with one's ways and surroundings." Natural history fosters and strengthens those two elements of the human spirit.[4]

Naturalist Brian Scavone thinks of his work as reinstating the skill of deep attention and inviting people into their own connections with the natural world. His summary of the lifework of natural historians: "We pay attention to the natural world—with objectivity and wonder—and then bring it back to people." Noting his reasons for entering this field of human endeavor, Scavone characterizes natural history as a way to deal with ultimate questions in life. Among those that he considers important are matters such as the place of humans in the cosmos, the qualities of a good life, humility, transcendence, and responsibility for others' well-being.[5]

Dusting Off History

As a body of thought, natural history extends thousands of years into the past. Its origins coincide with some of the same cultural influences that shaped the writers of Scripture, so it makes sense to examine the ways in which natural history developed alongside spiritual truths.

The first naturalists were probably hunters and farmers—people whose livelihood or survival depended on the accuracy of their observations about nature. Greek and Roman natural philosophers were among those who first collected and fashioned these observations into useful knowledge. Pliny the Elder and Heraclitus are examples. Their inclination to organize all useful knowledge into organized categories guided natural historians during and after the Renaissance.

Pliny was a first-century CE Roman natural philosopher and naval commander. His greatest work, *Natural Philosophy*, was a massive collection of current knowledge about the relationships of humankind to the natural world. From the knowledge of one hundred acknowledged experts, he organized twenty thousand facts about the natural world into hierarchical categories. His substantial written compilation of knowledge could be considered as the first encyclopedia.

The philosopher Heraclitus of Ephesus lived during the sixth century BCE. He was particularly interested in the dynamics of change, and considered fire to be both the ultimate source and shaping force of all matter. Attributed to him are epigrammatic ideas such as "not stepping into the same river twice," and nature "wanting to hide itself." He was particularly vocal about the importance of opposites in the natural world, as well as the failure of people to learn from nature's laws.

The themes and findings of natural history were evident throughout the development of Judaism and Christianity. The creation stories, the psalms, and allusions to the natural world throughout Scripture all attest to the importance of nature in the formation of doctrine and faith practices. Early church fathers and later theologians considered the created world to be an important element in understanding God's nature and will. Origen and Tertullian saw creation as a parallel revelation to that of Scripture. Augustine spoke about "the interrogation of creation" in his *Confessions*. Luther tilled his own garden while living under the protection of Wittenberg Castle, and showed his love of nature in his writings about the natural wonders that he experienced during his travels from his native Germany to Italy.[6]

The exquisitely detailed sciences that we know today were for centuries unified in singular bodies of knowledge. Nature was understood within an integrated, inclusive framework of exploration. (Even though newly developed sciences began to explore their own tracks, natural history retained its function as an assimilating approach to scientific inquiry.) During the eighteenth and nineteenth centuries, natural historians tried to conform their increasingly accurate observations to existing theory and theology. Sometimes that was possible; in other cases, naturalists called for new structures of scientific thought. (Charles Darwin, Alfred Russell Wallace, and Jean-Baptiste Lamarck are examples.) The fieldwork of these naturalists yielded immense collections of specimens and artifacts, resulting in the proliferation of natural history museums that exist throughout the world.

What's Going On Now?

Over the last hundred or more years, natural historians have taken on the important task of moving the general population beyond awed appreciation of nature toward actions that benefit the natural world. This major shift now defines natural history: Helping the entire populace of the world come to terms with changes in lifestyle that may be necessary to slow or stop the undeniable deterioration of the natural world because of human actions and inactions. (Here I would invoke the names and exemplary lifework of naturalists John Muir, Aldo Leopold, or Barbara Kingsolver.[7])

Organizations such as the Sierra Club, the National Geographic Society, the Wildlife Conservancy, or the National Wildlife Federation have continued their critique of environmental destruction, while now also engaging others in positive approaches to protecting and restoring the natural world.

Seeing the increased impact of civilization on almost every aspect of nature, naturalists have turned toward matters such as governmental policies and laws, sustainability of business practices, lifestyle matters, and deep questions of human existence.[8]

For decades now, naturalists around the world have been describing the urgency of matters such as global warming, species extinction, habitat destruction, or diminishing natural resources—such as clean water, clean air, forests, or arable land. The names of courageous naturalists come immediately to mind: Rachel Carson, Jane Goodall, Barry Lopez, Bill McKibben, and Wendell Berry. Because their warnings have implications in lifestyle matters, what they say may sometimes fall on deaf or insensitive ears.

Naturalists' emphases on wonder and awe continue, countering daunting or discouraging factual analyses. Natural historians continue to help people experience the natural world in all its beauty, profundity, and mystery. Their work also forms the basis for encouraging news. For example, *Atlantic* contributing editor Charles C. Mann summarizes recent books devoted to climate change, finding reasons for hope. Science writer Richard Conniff offers a fascinating description of how soil bacteria and fungi might help diminish the heavy application of fertilizers and pesticides on crops.[9]

The Future of Natural History

Naturalists, sociologists, and technology critics have noted the decline in general support for natural history. Fewer natural history courses are required for undergraduate degrees in biology, fewer PhD candidates pursue natural history emphases, and fewer higher education institutions offer natural history degrees.[10]

Nature illiteracy seems to be on the rise. Teens and children spend less time in nature, their attention co-opted by digital technologies. When students learn about the natural world, virtual experiences—games, computers, lab specimens, videos—can often substitute for direct contact with creatures and creation. Environmental education classes stress only systematic analysis of big-picture ideals, functions, relationships, or models. Wonder and awe can be co-opted by factual knowledge. As lifelong naturalist Robert Michael Pyle summarizes this matter, "As the distance grows between a tiny priesthood who know small parts of nature very well and a massive population who know next to nothing about the whole and not even the names of their neighbors, a right relationship with the world seems more and more elusive."[11]

Environmental activist, small farmer, and author Derrick Jensen speaks of the good that can come when we lose hope. Jensen sees hope as a reason for inaction and an excuse to underestimate one's personal agency. "Hope leads us away from the present," he writes, "away from who and where we are right now and toward some imaginary future state." If hope means that we are powerless, it may not be a dependable mindset if we want to preserve and protect the natural world. Waiting for rescue may not be a useful approach to natural history. For Jensen, action begins when hope dies.[12]

An increasing number of writers, entertainers, documentarians, poets, or artists offer thoughtful and hopeful critiques of a technologically overhyped world. Tech-savvy writers such as Eugeny Morozov can help us excise from our minds the beguiling notion that complex social problems can be solved by technologies awash in algorithms. An emerging folly: "Some internet-worshipers believe that its nature and descriptions are as immutable and universal as the laws of the natural world."[13]

Other positive trends, perhaps too new or diffused to be measured, seem to be emerging, especially among younger generational cohorts:

- An increased emphasis on "green living"—one way to describe ethical, responsible lifestyles that tread lightly in the natural world.
- The number of young adults who seem to be searching for careers that bring them into contact with nature. They include those who are making their living as artisans, craftspeople, or food producers.

- The broad reach of natural history museums—including their programs of outreach and education—that continue to appeal to patrons of all ages and economic levels.

Infusing Stewardship Ministries with Natural History

It seems an easy intellectual and emotional leap to see the many places where the Church could benefit from the wisdom of natural history. (And perhaps the collected influence and power of God's people could strengthen the power and influence of natural historians!) Some areas of mutual interest may bring those possibilities into focus for you.

MYSTERIES IN NATURE

As they encounter the natural world, naturalists share a sense of mystery with God's people. Where church leaders may have jumped too quickly to doctrinaire conclusions or condemnations, natural historians remain insistent about the possibility of their own ignorance, and resist rushing to judgment.

Natural history professor and author Chet Raymo cites the philosophical principle Ockham's Razor as a reminder that humility is necessary in the face of mystery. Attributed to William of Ockham, a fourteenth-century English Franciscan friar and philosopher, this incisive principle ("razor") requires philosophical parsimony in all things: "Never suppose a complex explanation when a simple explanation will suffice." Because that uncomplicated description also allows for a lack of knowledge, genuine humility can take root. Raymo scolds the Church for its sometimes reliance on "mysteries" as excuses for not approaching the natural world from a scientific mindset. He advocates instead for what he calls "religious naturalism," which he describes as "our response to the natural world (as) one of reverence and humility in the face of a mystery that transcends empirical knowing."[14]

SCRIPTURAL TRUTHS

Naturalists try to understand the natural world through the eyes of many sources of truth. Echoes of creation stewardship in the Bible can be found in the scriptures of natural history—ancient and modern classics based on the firsthand scrutiny of awed observers.

Unless they are locked into logical prisons of narrow-minded or outmoded biblical interpretation, stewardship leaders focusing on the created world don't need to fear the conclusions of naturalists. On the other hand, those who use Scripture as proof for "domination of nature" theologies, who defend a literal six-day creation process, who deny global warming, or who extol the victories of materialistic prosperity—these believers may have reason to be wary of natural history!

ECUMENICITY

In its original meaning, ecumenicity (*oikoumenikos*) denoted "the whole world." It wasn't until the sixteenth century that the term was narrowed into ecclesiastical references only. Because it brings together the work of several sciences, natural history is "ecumenical," concerned about the whole world—a goal that the Church also claims. Always tempted toward divisive sectarianism, the Church could learn from the example of natural scientists how to embrace godly wisdom, no matter its sources.

NATURAL HISTORY'S APPEAL TO YOUNG ADULTS

Natural history may approach the status of a religion in the lives of many young adults, especially those who are highly educated. As the Church attempts to reach young adults with all of God's good news, natural history may be a better crossover point than redesigning worship experiences or hiding the Church behind faddish cultural trappings. *New York Post* columnist and author Naomi Schaefer Riley speaks about misreading trends among millennials. "Young adults don't need another hip place to hang out," she writes. Instead, she reminds us about the value of bedrock connections and commitments, the intimacies and community young adults experienced in college life, experiences that can occur almost anywhere where God's people gather.[15]

CONNECTING FAITH AND LIFE

Natural historians are not content with mere descriptions of the natural world or the problems that beset it. They would agree wholeheartedly with James's injunction to early Christians disbursed into the secular world, "But be doers of the word, and not merely hearers who deceive themselves" (James 1:22). Naturalists call people to translate knowledge into actions. Because they understand change as a profound process that takes place over eons, naturalists exhibit courage as they face present-day urgencies in nature that seem to cascade over all of us.

Reaffirming Important Doctrines

Natural history confirms core beliefs of Christianity that are practical and relevant:

- Every spring the natural world shows how life once again triumphs over death, as the message of Christ's Resurrection repeats itself in the cycles of nature.
- Hope and courage are put to work by entrepreneurs looking for solutions to environmental problems.
- For naturalists as well as theologians, the sins of self-idolatry, greed, and rampant materialism deserve criticism.
- Naturalists' calls for positive societal change mirror the forgiveness cycle (repentance–confession–forgiveness–living forgiven) that extends God's grace into every phase of life.
- Pneumatology—the study of the Holy Spirit's presence—can also be understood in the neurobiology of "place" present in animal and human communities.
- "Survival of the most cooperative," a core evolutionary principle, supports the biblical truth that humans prosper best in community. This law was perhaps more important to Darwin than "survival of the fittest," which was actually proposed by his colleague Herbert Spencer.
- Care for those who are poor is inextricably intertwined with care of creation. In his encyclical letter *Laudato Si: On Care for Our Common Home*, Pope Francis reminds all Christians of "the intimate relationship between the poor and the fragility of the planet."[16]

Purpose and Meaning

Natural historians believe strongly in purposed living. Their studies bring them face-to-face with ultimate questions about the meaning of life, whose answers require the transcending of selfish individualism. Naturalists' strong sense of responsibility toward nature corresponds to the Church's cherished principles of stewardship as "awed use of God's gifts." Dying with the most toys is not a winning goal for naturalists or followers of Christ.

Relevant Witness

Infused with gratitude and mission about the natural world that it shares with naturalists, the Church might regain the attention and commitment it sometimes desperately seeks. Axiom #1: Natural history connects intimately to creation stewardship. Axiom #2: Naturalists approach the natural world with passionate commitment that appeals to people of all ages. Taken together, these two propositions suggest that the Church might integrate the wisdom of natural history into its messages about all of God's good news. The core gospel message—God's grace seen in Jesus's life, death, and resurrection—does not eliminate consideration of other aspects of God's continuing favor. They include forgiveness, healing, life-wisdom, inner peace, love, *and* the natural world.

WONDER AND AWE

Because of their continuing encounters with the natural world, naturalists speak readily of the many ways in which they experience wonder and awe. Natural historians are not content merely to observe, measure, and report what their senses take in. Ineffable experiences become part of their identities and bring them to oft-expressed gratitude about their place in the universe. Natural history writer John Tallmadge exemplifies the outpouring of wonder into words. Using a writing style similar to John Muir's, he draws readers into both his observations and his emotions. (In *Meeting the Tree of Life: A Teacher's Path*, for example, Tallmadge describes his odyssey through what others might see as the hostile environment of the Great Basin, exulting in pockets of verdant growth and little-known species of animals.[17])

In many ways, naturalists' face-to-face meetings with the world of nature mirrors and echoes the experiences of the psalmists and prophets in Scripture. Thus, both naturalists and stewardship leaders have a profound opportunity to help others find and celebrate awe and wonder in their own lives!

NAMING SKILLS

One of the first acts of humankind recorded in the Scripture is the naming of the creatures (Gen. 2:9–20). As the original naturalist, Adam had the pleasure and responsibility of assigning permanent meaning to a living creature by virtue of its name. His own name—roughly equivalent to "man of the (red) earth/dirt"—reminded him of both his origin and his destiny. For naturalists, the names of living and nonliving things are important, and so must be learned and savored in any encounter with the natural world. Without a name, any part of creation remains only a thing, relatively anonymous and indistinguishable from everything else in creation. When it has an exact name, that thing becomes more intimately known and appreciated.

Sometimes just the name itself evokes those feelings. Character, history, a specific place in the grand sweep of nature—all attach to a name. It makes sense that learning the exact names of bits and pieces of God's created world could be part of your stewardship of the natural world.

TRANSCENDENCE

Experiences with the natural world figure prominently in the history of God's interaction with humans. Thus a mystical sense of spirituality—a companion of wonder and awe—remains a strong current in the theology and practices of contemporary Christianity, increasingly among young adults.

Naturalists also experience transcendence—literally, "rising above"—as one result of their encounters with nature. They place value on matters such as quiet, flow, ineffability, and a heightened sense of presence. They name wildness as a key factor in transcendent experiences. Naturalists use that term to describe the experience of being completely immersed in the natural world, where its creatures, features, and processes are all-encompassing, overwhelming human agency or presence. It is no accident that wildness—with all its attendant emotions and self-discoveries—is best experienced in wilderness, a feature of the natural world thankfully preserved in the laws of most countries.[18]

These transcendent experiences in nature, however, can give rise to natural theologies that do not correspond well with the theism of Scripture. Animism is comprised of a set of beliefs in which soul-like consciousness is presumed to exist within natural phenomena or things. Pantheism—literally "all-in-God"—understands God to be intertwined with the natural world, so that the two entities cannot be disconnected from each other. Although animism and pantheism have been considered heretical in Christian thought, so also is a narrow theism that places God as separate from the world.[19]

In summary, your efforts to undertake creation stewardship can gain attention and power when the strengths of natural history are taken into account and applied to your pronouncements and invitations. Naturalists join God's people in sober thought about universal, eternal truths as you approach and rely on an astounding natural world.

Putting Natural History to Use

As you incorporate the wisdom of natural history and naturalists into the stewardship ministries of your congregation, you might learn better how to:

- Quiet down, chill out, and listen more carefully.
- Observe everything and everyone more carefully, insisting on detailed accuracy before coming to conclusions or taking action.
- Use the tools of natural history—e.g., journaling, field-based learning, scientific methods—in congregational life.
- Wonder and exult about both what's ordinary and extraordinary.
- Seek and strengthen humility.
- Embrace wildness, ambiguity, and mystery.
- Place programs, worship, events, and other congregational processes into the natural world.
- Absorb the history and wonder of any place you find yourself.

What Might Happen If . . .

In this final section of this chapter, I invite you to imagine that you're part of a congregation that has integrated natural science into its priorities, programs, and structure—perhaps even its core identity. In that congregation, you might find yourself engaged in some of the following situations:

- *Indoors outdoors:* You hold outdoor worship in the summer, locate meetings on the patio, use sidewalks as ground-level canvases for children's artwork, and garnish the nooks and crannies of your property with small container gardens. You've turned the church grounds over to a local gardening group that teaches high school students the rudiments of horticulture.

- *Outdoors indoors:* Because the weather doesn't always allow outdoors activities, one of the trustees came up with the idea to "bring the outdoors inside." He arranged to use part of a special memorial gift to purchase indoor trees and large plants. He started creating little pockets of greenery in surprising places—one of the restrooms, the front of the lectern, the choir loft, and both of the entryways.

- *Those vexing footprints:* A few younger members have asked for environmental audits as part of the congregation's annual report. Energy and water use are easy to assess, but you decide to think about all kinds of "footprints." You begin evaluating the congregation's trash and recycling efforts, the efficiency of the heating and cooling systems, the number of meetings that don't need to happen at church and the amount of paper products used each month.

- *A council of local naturalists:* Twice a year you bring together some of the "naturalists" in town—the high school biology teacher, county/city park people, the guy who used to be a landscaper, a few master gardeners, and the woman who started farming organically on her parents' place. You feed them a simple meal, and ask them what they've been reading and thinking about the natural world: what's important, what's new, what's exciting, and what's hopeful.

- *Searching for lifestyle wisdom:* Your church's small groups are floundering, so the education team asks group leaders to focus on this question: How can we live more simply—individually, in families, and as a congregation? You hope they'll find ways of sharing with the rest of you what they've learned. The stewardship team chooses a lifestyle-oriented theme for this year's in-gathering of pledges. The book club talks about a newly popular natural history writer. The youth group's mission trip this year includes some outdoor education experiences.

- *Beyond praise:* Taking a cue from "we worship God in nature" members, you develop worship services that include awe, silence, wonder, humility, transcendence, or mystery. You start including scenes of nature's majesty on your worship bulletins and projected images. You slow down the pace of worship services. After summer vacations, you include in temple talks some heartfelt reflections by members who've spent time in the natural world.

- *Revising the congregation's purpose statement:* Inspired by these shifts in stewardship, the church council begins work on a new purpose statement and invites several newer members to join them. Turns out these folks spend a lot of time out-of-doors, so they insist that "care of the earth" gets written into your overarching purpose.

- *Learning the natural way:* You decide to put together a summer day camp program in selected members' homes, using their yards as the laboratory. On the web you find a simple natural history curriculum for children. You sponsor community conversations about difficult environmental subjects in your locale. When there's a natural history event in town, you announce it in your newsletter.

- *The field trip church:* You have enough farmers, gardeners, and other naturalists in the congregation to fill a barn, so you start arranging nature tours for local folks and visiting church groups. The church van and members' cars provide transportation out to a farm where they're experimenting with a new technology for composting, a home garden that's in someone's basement, the new regional park, the county landfill, a small stand of hardwood trees with a fascinating history, the Army Corps of Engineers lab, and the high school botany club hothouse. The real benefit of these tours? People encourage each other to appreciate all the nature close at hand.

- *Bits and pieces:* You don't have the energy to start anything big, so you begin inserting into your newsletter a few awe-inspiring factoids about the natural world. After a while, someone volunteers to help you ferret out this information from magazines and the web. The factoids turn into a short monthly column in the newsletter, written by a variety of members, including children and youth. You still haven't started anything new. Or have you?

These possibilities illustrate how your congregation could translate its strongly felt love for the natural world into actions. Your own ideas will come from another fiercely awesome proposition: The earth is the Lord's and its fullness!

A wild ideal, indeed!

Notes

1. From Harry Green's presentation, "Tracks and Shadows: Field Biology as Art," 2014 Parsons Memorial Lodge Summer Series, Tuolumne Meadows, Yosemite National Park, CA, July 26, 2014.

2. From my interviews with Dr. John Tallmadge, natural history teacher, author, and consultant (July 15–18, 2013), and Brian Scavone, naturalist ranger and teacher in the mountains of California and Arizona (July 11, 2014).

3. Wilson wrote this book, as though a conversation with a Southern Baptist pastor, in order to help explain how natural science and religion were not necessarily at odds with each other. E. O. Wilson, *The Creation: An Appeal to Save Life on Earth* (New York: W.W. Norton & Company, 2006), 62–63.

4. Hoffman carries out his natural history work in the transboundary area of the Prespa Lakes in northern Greece. Julian Hoffmann, *The Small Heart of Things* (Athens: University of Georgia Press, 2013), xi–xiii, 7.

5. Personal interview, Brian Scavone, July 11, 2014.

6. From July 15–18, 2013, interviews with John Tallmadge; J. W. Theiss, "Luther, A Lover of Nature," in *Four Hundred Years: Commemorative Essays on the Reformation of Dr. Martin Luther and Its Blessed Results*, ed. William H.T. Dau (St. Louis: Concordia Publishing House, 1917), 228–29.

7. See Muir's *My First Summer in the Sierra* (Boston: Houghton Mifflin Company, 1911), Leopold's *Sand County Almanac* (New York: Oxford University Press, 1941), or Kingsolver's *The Poisonwood Bible* (London: Faber and Faber Unlimited, 1999) to find inspiration.

8. For an in-depth, balanced exploration of this phenomenon, see "Green Is Good" by D. T. Max, in the May 12, 2014, issue of *The New Yorker*, 54–63.

9. "How to Talk About Climate Change So People Will Listen," by Charles C. Mann, *The Atlantic Monthly*, September 2014, 86-99 and "Super Dirt," by Richard Conniff, *Scientific American*, September 2013, 76–79.

10. See "Natural Decline," an editorial in the April 3, 2014, issue of *Nature: International Journal of Science*, 7–8. The article's lead reads, "Few biology degrees still feature natural history. Is the naturalist a species in crisis?"

11. From Robert Michael Pyle, "The Rise and Fall of Natural History," in *The Future of Nature: Writing on a Human Ecology from* Orion *Magazine*, ed. Barry Lopez (Minneapolis: Milkweed Editions, 2007), 243. His terse prediction: "We are not likely to return to nature study as it once was."

12. Derrick Jensen, "Beyond Hope," in Lopez, *Future of Nature*, 28–29.

13. Eugeny Morozov, *To Save Everything, Click Here: The Folly of Technological Solutionism* (New York: Public Affairs Books, 2013), 5, 24–25.

14. Chet Raymo, *When God Is Gone, Everything Is Holy: The Making of a Religious Naturalist* (Notre Dame, IN: Sorin Books, 2008), 102, 104.

15. "It Takes More Than a Coffee Shop," an interview by Timothy C. Morgan in *Christianity Today*, July/August 2014, 52–55.

16. Pope Francis, *Laudato Si: On Care for Our Common Home* (Rome: Libreria Editrice Vaticana, 2015), sections 16, 25, 29, et al. Francis names widespread environmental migration, decreasing food supplies, and lack of potable water as examples.

17. See Tallmadge, chapter 5, "Among Shining Mountains." *Meeting the Tree of Life: A Teacher's Path* (Salt Lake City: University of Utah Press, 1997).

18. From Scavone interview, July 11, 2014.

19. For a discussion of these terms, see Gregory R. Peterson, *Minding God: Theology and the Cognitive Sciences* (Minneapolis: Fortress Press, 2003), 198–200.

Chapter 10

More Than Money: Financial Planning

In this chapter, stewardshifting takes a more prosaic direction: how to take advantage of the wisdom of financial planners. The shift here is straightforward: Your congregation could also sustain or revitalize itself by applying some of the precepts and practices of financial planning to its organizational behaviors.

Money as a Starting Point

Financial professionals usually begin any of their discussions, writings, or counseling sessions by outlining their personal observations about money. Let's do the same here.

People invented money about the time that writing and record-keeping were developed in the social systems of ancient Mesopotamia. Contrary to the long-standing ideas of financial anthropology, money did not evolve from systems of barter that were becoming too inefficient or cumbersome. This view—that money is a medium of exchange—was promoted by eminent economical theorists John Locke, Adam Smith, and John Maynard Keynes, even though little anthropological evidence backed up their theories. Instead, as British macroeconomist Felix Martin relates, money and currency emerged when the social technology of record-keeping itself—business-oriented transactions—required greater efficiency.

It's important to differentiate money from currency. To function as money, a currency must fulfill three basic conditions. Without all three of these characteristics, a currency has no value in social exchanges:

1. The capacity for abstraction in the money's various denominations or levels of value. (For example, counting can be expressed in symbols that show larger quantities.)

2. The systematized accounting of the currency, so that social interactions—trading, borrowing, investing—can be tracked accurately and with relative ease.

3. The reliability of a currency to transfer an obligation from an original creditor to a third party.[1]

Inherent in all three descriptors are several supportive characteristics of functioning societies, including trust; accountability; shared perceptions of value; governance and the rule of law; incentives and penalties; stable peace; and respectful personal relationships. Seen in this light, money—and by implication, currency—is evidence of positive human values that have undergirded civilizations for eons.

Social activist and philanthropic visionary Lynne Twist thinks carefully about the "soul of money." She uses "soul" to describe the deeper human values—many of them implicitly spiritual—that she hopes will always anchor our views and practices regarding money. With money's soul in your mind, you can include it in your stewardship.

Money-as-currency facilitates the exchange of goods and services, measures value or worth, and functions as a short-hand, symbolic expression, or evidence of basic human values. In that sense money has power. Unfortunately, the artifact (currency) may have overshadowed its embedded values. So money ends up validating greed as a legitimate human activity. Money can foment wars and other conflicts; money can give credence to the destruction of the environment; and money can facilitate the subjugation of individuals and groups. It can lose its soul.[2]

Attitudes about Money

It's fair to say that the Church holds ambivalent attitudes about money. On the one hand—because money is necessary for mission—the Church seeks the monetary donations of its stakeholders. Congregations regularly engage in sophisticated practices that encourage members to contribute generously to the congregation's work. When these donations are shared, denominations and parachurch organizations can undertake ministries that fulfill God's will around the world. Wise religious enterprises encourage both the donations and the spiritual underpinnings of financial generosity.

On the other hand, currents of unease and suspicion about financial matters may still persist among some Christians. Because it seems to be grounded in the Bible and church history, the discomfort is understandable. Let me illustrate.

It's probably accurate to characterize Jesus's parables as a direct comment on the economic abuse and oppression experienced by first-century Jewish peasants. Because of their unfamiliarity or incapacity to deal with a monetized system controlled by educated elites, those who were poor remained poor. Judas, the disciple who betrayed Jesus to his tormentors and executioners, was tainted by his love of money.

Although Paul likely didn't share all of Jesus's feelings about money, Paul's warning about "money being the root of all evil" is as old as our faulty memories about his actual statement in that regard: Evil feeds on the *love* of money. This might explain why the Church worked hard to scrub away any lusting after "filthy lucre."

Church history continued that attitude. With religious mendicants as role models, the Roman Church encouraged a lifestyle that made money—and all its trappings—disreputable. In one corner of the Protestant tradition, Martin Luther exhibited his incapability for handing money by essentially turning over the economic affairs of his household and profession to his capable spouse, Katie. In this country during the eighteenth and nineteenth centuries, members of Christian utopian communities divested themselves of money and possessions, part of their attempt to find spiritual purity. (During my growing-up years, life insurance was still considered a sign of mistrust in God's providence in some parts of my denominational heritage.)

In a lingering example of guilt by association, some Christians worry—perhaps rightfully so—that intimate encounters with money will soil their spirit. They don't want to become selfish, greedy, or otherwise idolatrous. They don't intend to be captured by the power of money, and they fear losing their spiritual core to the temptations that money parades in front of them. Instead, most Christians want to live purposefully, directed toward high goals such as integrity, generosity, courage, and commitment. They want to strengthen their trust in God, to remain fixed on the welfare of others, and to seek the greater good. They don't want money to draw their souls—their core identities—away from true abundance.[3]

The pursuit of these noble ideas can have ignoble side effects: avoiding anything but the most necessary encounters with money; excusing ignorance about financial matters; castigating those who deal with money; ceding complete responsibility of money management to others; or spiritualizing all of these attitudes with vague doctrinal nostrums. As a result of these attitudes, money can become bad or spiritually stressful. Fighting, fleeing, and freezing can characterize too many Christians' practices regarding financial matters.

Clergy Financial Illiteracy

Financial illiteracy detracts from the effectiveness of too many pastors. In some cases, they believe themselves to be faithful to their calling when they adhere to the dictates of Scripture about wealth, worry, greed, materialism, or selfishness. They want to be good examples of godliness. In that frame of mind, any skill or training in money management may seem to be antithetical to the central tenets of Christianity.

Other pastors remain relatively uneducated about financial matters because the paths of their personal development—seminary education, previous careers, interests, and passions—have trended in other directions, addressing other important life-related questions. For whatever reasons, financial matters just never attracted these pastors' attention. (The same phenomenon may explain why too many religious leaders are not conversant in scientific matters.)

This empty space in their overall competence disturbs many pastors. The lack of financial savvy can become one of the factors that creates a gulf between pastors and laypersons, whose daily vocations depend on shrewd, sophisticated skills regarding the acquisition and management of money.[4]

Understandable Confusion

Most of us can understand the basic concepts of money management. But when it comes to "high finance"—the domain of financial planners—it can be extremely difficult to navigate a maze of alphabet-soup terminology and concepts whose sophistication eludes most brains.

In his analysis of this situation, British novelist John Lanchester—who the *New York Times* has dubbed "a decoder for the financially illiterate"—describes how the language of finance may have evolved or purposely developed to the point where much of it is incomprehensible. He describes possibly deliberate linguistic antics that confuse people.

One technique is simple: ramping up arcane jargon and complex terminology. (For example, "forward-settling ETFs"; "the effect of QE2 on M3"; or "the effects of bond-yield retardation.") The obfuscation of financial matters includes a process Lanchester calls "reversification," when words take on connotations that are opposite from their supposed meaning. So credit means debt, and a hedge fund (ostensibly a way of limiting losses) can actually be a reasonable way to lose money. (Most hedge funds fail; their lifespan averages only five years.) Inflation means that money is worth less; risk means statistical probabilities; austere means budget cuts; and synergy means dumping employees.

One of reversification's most egregious historical examples—a likely cause of the recent Great Recession—is securitization, which seems to refer to safety or lowered risk. Instead, the term came to mean aggregating less-than-reliable investments (e.g., home mortgages) into bundles that could be bought and sold as though they were secure. (Profits were made from trading fees, not from interest collected on these loans.)

In a searing indictment that could apply to most of us, Lanchester writes, "When it comes to discussing money, incomprehension is a form of consent. If we allow ourselves not to understand this language, we are signing off on the way the world works today . . . the prospect of an ever-widening gap between the rich and everyone else."[5]

Why draw you into a cognitive jungle where your confusion might revert to stress? First, to assure you that you may have good reasons for being completely hornswoggled about these matters, even though you know that they have some vague relationship to your financial well-being. Perhaps more directly connected to this chapter: You probably need the assistance of someone who understands enough of these matters to help you make wise decisions about your relationships with money. Among those who can assist you in your stewardship of money are financial planners.

Financial Advice

Financial planning is part of a larger enterprise that offers wisdom about money. Lifestyle coaches, wealth managers, lawyers, real estate agents, brokers, money managers, insurance agents, and accountants—all of these professionals can offer you financial advice, much of it focused on specific aspects of the larger picture. Each is a type of financial advisor.

Specific advice can be helpful, especially if it is founded on expertise. So a family lawyer's advice is extremely valuable if you're trying to navigate the financial ramifications of a divorce. A lifestyle coach can help you analyze your money-spending habits. Or an insurance agent can help you make good decisions about the kinds of policies that will protect you from various risks.

The benefits of financial advice can be an important part of your financial stewardship. Let me tell you about two examples from my own experience.

Share Save Spend

Over twenty years ago, financial advisor Nathan Dungan saw the need for soup-and-nuts wisdom about family financial matters. He founded Share Save Spend—the name of the organization as well as its core message—to help families align their values with the day-to-day decisions they make about money. He was particularly interested in how children and teens learned the elements of financial well-being. (His popular book/DVD, *Money Sanity Solutions: Linking Money + Meaning,* remains a helpful tool for group study and resulting actions.) Dungan chose this approach because it's simple in its concepts but profound in its effects. (He cites research showing that teens who participate in Share Save Spend learning experiences make lasting changes in their financial behaviors.)

Dungan is an advisor—his particular brand of wisdom is directed at questions of values and decision-making in families. Some of that advice invites groups into essential planning: When people take his counsel to heart, they're undoubtedly more able to plan for their economic well-being over the long haul. Sharing, saving, and spending—in that order—make them wiser as well. (You can find more of Dungan's resources, advice, and availability at *www.sharesavespend.com.*)

The Financial Seminary

Possessed of a prophetic disposition and vision, Gary Moore set aside a well-regarded career in Wall Street to pursue what he believed to be a critical mission: to build bridges between the financial and moral communities. Over several decades, Gary has become a valued advisor for large nonprofit organizations and churches. He has published five books on financial well-being. And in the past few years, he has developed his own nonprofit, The Financial Seminary, as a vehicle for reintegrating ethics and financial acumen into the workings of organizations. Gary is an expert in the intricacies of "high finance" as well as a courageous interpreter of Scripture and stewardship doctrine. He has been one of Christianity's strongest detractors of the quasi-religious tenets of Ayne Rand's libertarian philosophy and economic practices. He is a prolific writer who cuts to the heart of financial/spiritual matters in plain-spoken English. An encounter with Gary Moore is like a miniature Reformation, where core concepts and practices are compacted into pithy statements and incisive questions.

Like Nathan Dungan, Gary Moore is an advisor—in his case, among movers-and-shakers in American evangelicalism, mainline denominations, and congregations. His advice starts with financial expertise, mixes in Gary's faith-filled approach to a life of stewardship, and continues into straightforward invitations and challenges for changes in attitude and actions. If you're willing to learn, Gary's your teacher! (You can find his advice—and its underlying factual/philosophical foundations—at *www.financialseminary.org.*)

Both Nathan Dungan and Gary Moore are advisors. Like many advisors, they also help people plan. Their strong suit, however, is the quality of their advice, honed over decades of study and experience. When you encounter their advice—in person is probably the best way—you come away with knowledge and wisdom that works. You know how to make financial decisions, and have a good idea of what those decisions will mean.

Both Dungan and Moore bring strong, Christ-centered faith to their work and both see stewardship as a core concept in their ministries. Their value for God's *economia* is the wealth of knowledge they are willing to share with others. They are both financial specialists: In one case, families are enriched; in the other case, large religious enterprises and congregational leaders can steer down ethical paths toward wise investment strategies.

Why Financial Planners?

Financial planners take advising to the next level: Helping you construct a strategy for achieving goals that you and the planner have developed together. Those goals are not just financially related—the size of a savings account, the safest investments, avoidance of foolish decisions—but also include matters that connect your overall well-being with financial health. Like most advisors, financial planners operate on the basis of ethical foundations. They understand how Lynne Twist's "soul of money" concept is both the starting place and the end result of financial planning.

One advantage of financial planning may rest in the quality of the plan you develop with the planner. When you finish the entire process—detailed work that takes time—you have a flexible blueprint for making money-related decisions thereafter. If the financial planner is spiritually grounded—let's assume that this is true—he or she helps you frame your life goals inside of your *economos* identity. The planner acknowledges God's sovereignty and blessings. During the planning process, you will gradually learn both core principles and a financial vocabulary.

Like financial advisors, financial planners can sell you financial products, resources, or instruments. After a plan is in place, they can help you assess its worth and help keep you in touch with developing trends. Financial planners are generalists who can connect you with the wisdom of financial specialists. Some financial planners are part of larger enterprises, where specialized knowledge and advice are available.

Choosing a Financial Planner

Not every financial advisor offers good advice. The same is true of financial planners. Just like you measure the value of financial advisors by the quality of their advice, so you can measure the worth of a financial planner by their ability to accompany you through a thorough planning process.

Chuck Jaffe, senior columnist for MarketWatch and regular contributor to public radio and television programs, offers sound advice about finding a financial planner. (He includes financial planners in the larger category, "financial advisor.") His insights in *Getting Started in Finding a Financial Advisor* can help you sort through competing claims of expertise and utility. I summarize some of them here.

Jaffe first reiterates the need to seek financial acumen. Just like you look for professional help from mechanics, plumbers, or electricians when it comes to maintaining your home or auto, so you can turn to financial advisors/planners for their expertise. Yes, you can do much of the work yourself—YouTube comes to mind here—but you also run the risk of large, costly mistakes when you get in over your head.[6]

Jaffe reminds his readers that, given the possible malfeasance of unscrupulous advisors, it makes sense to choose wisely who might best help you construct and carry out a plan for financial well-being. He lists seven "big mistakes" you can make when seeking a financial planner:

1. Interviewing just one candidate.
2. Skipping over a background or reference check.
3. Choosing primarily on the basis of style or cost.
4. Placing too much trust in professional credentials.
5. Basing "success" purely on expected returns-on-investments.
6. Turning over complete control of the plan to the planner.
7. Hiring friends or relatives.[7]

Jaffe underscores the importance of the trustworthiness of the individual you eventually hire. It makes sense that this is someone whose expertise you can establish through past performance or references. Education, experience, credentials, and certificates are important, but your personal relationship with the planner is even more important. The planner will look at the entire picture of your life, come up with a program you can follow and help you navigate that plan. That's why, in your interviewing of candidates, you should consider their personal attributes. These are the qualities of character that will bind you and the financial planner together in your shared pursuit of financial well-being. One caution from Jaffe: Don't hire a financial planner solely based on your supposed "intuition about people."[8]

A Case Study: A Financial Planner

To put all these descriptive sentences together in real-life, let's look at a financial planner whose work exemplifies the practices of this profession.

Rob Granner CFP[9] is Financial Consultant for the Chicagoland Regional Office of Thrivent Financial, a Fortune 400 financial services company. (Thrivent Financial is an ecumenical, faith-based enterprise with over 100 years of history serving people of faith across the country.) Educated originally as an engineer, Granner transitioned into financial planning as a way of connecting faith and money. As he sees it, his goal in this profession is "to help people build financial security, to help them improve their quality of life." He goes on. "People live in imagined scarcity; that's a spiritual condition that diminishes abundance."

Granner has strong views about the value of financial planning processes: "They lower stress levels, help people conquer fear, and lead them towards generosity." So he takes clients through a process that moves them from a paralyzing sense of scarcity toward the possibilities for abundance, which then opens their lives to the blessings of generosity.

Throughout the planning process—and in the following years when the plan is playing out—Granner assumes several functions: teacher, parent, truth-teller, counsellor, advisor, and friend. One role that has held his abiding interest: the kind of life coaching that occurs as he works with clients in identifying their life goals.

His long-term planning process consists of three interrelated elements:

- *Planning and projections:* Granner and clients establish life goals, analyze various statistical models for achieving those goals, and choose the most likely strategies to achieve those outcomes. Here he helps clients assess their present lifestyles, and the adjustments they may need to make—in spending, sharing, and saving practices—to reach their stated goals. He relies heavily on the technical expertise of Thrivent Financial and other financial services companies.

- *Managing money:* Granner and his staff continue due diligence: Watching the shifting values of investments and other instruments, and conferring with clients when adjustments seem advisable. In this part of Granner's work, he offers clients the security of a pair of expert eyes in the continuing management of their savings and investments.
- *Estate planning:* Granner now engages clients in long-term thinking. The shared work now focuses on ensuring a financial legacy for clients—e.g., trusts or life insurance policies—as well as providing a means for clients to share their abundance with others—becoming philanthropists!

In all three parts of his work, Granner operates with ethical and spiritual considerations tightly woven into financial matters. Along the way, he functions continually as a "professor of finance," helping clients add to their knowledge and sophistication regarding faith and money.

Because he is the member of a local church, Granner also values the contributions that he can make to the financial well-being of congregations. Granner knows that pastors and other religious leaders are not always financially astute, so he functions as an informal financial advisor for some of them. He is aware how congregations can fall into scarcity thinking, and how they may lack financial discipline or planning skills. He understands how their leaders may have difficulty talking about money. As the representative of a company that has a faith-based philosophy, Granner can offer congregations training, information, and planning opportunities that help them come to grips with their financial health.

As a financial planner, Granner values stewardship from any number of vantage points. His orientation toward generosity helps his clients understand their dependence on and gratitude to God. His views of financial security and quality of life are always instrumental: Both are blessings that you put to use for God's purposes. As part of his personal stewardship, Granner has participated in many domestic and international Habitat for Humanity projects. Because he helps his clients find balance in the larger scope of their financial lives, he sometimes thinks about his profession as a way of "having wisdom about the whole tree while pruning it." This interesting word picture might also describe the vital functions of a steward!

Financial Planning and Your Congregation

I started this chapter by naming the shift that I propose: Using the expertise of financial planners to benefit the financial health of your congregation. Let's look at that shift a little more closely.

First, and perhaps most obviously, the financial health of your congregation is dependent on the financial health of its members. It seems logical, then, to connect individual families with trusted financial planners. (If most of your members are worried or confused about money, they will not be easily persuaded to be generous or joyful as they consider contributing to the mission of God in your congregation.) A financial planner may have greater credibility and authority in financial matters than a pastor; a financial planning process may challenge congregation members to mature past fear-based avoidance of money matters toward more pragmatic attitudes and practices.

Second, if your congregation's pastor is not comfortable or facile in financial matters, a financial planner may help her or him grow more confident and capable in this part of a life of stewardship. A good place to start that shift: The pastor and a financial planner working on the pastor's own plan! From that experience will come the usual benefits of financial planning, and also the likelihood that your pastor could learn how to be a credible leader in the area of financial well-being.

Perhaps an even more interesting shift might come from the application of individual financial planning processes to the congregation's financial health. Leaders would work with financial planners to establish the congregation's long-term financial goals. They would look at models, projections, and strategies for achieving those goals, and they would covenant with the financial planner for a relationship that featured accountability, trust, and deep friendship. During the planning path, congregation leaders would learn to deal with achievable goals, to speak honestly about money, to conquer fear, to take the long view of the congregation's life, and to move toward a quality of congregational life that was sustainable.

Were you to incorporate financial planning—for individuals and the congregation itself—into your stewardship ministry, I can imagine scenarios such as the following:

- In your newsletter or written communications, your congregation would talk about money matters in realistic ways.
- Time-honored spiritual maxims would not be the only principles guiding financial decisions.
- Financially astute members would be honored and welcomed as leaders.
- The congregation's mission budget would include savings and investments.
- "Mission" and "financial health" would not be considered as opposing mindsets.

- You would not spend beyond your means.
- Your congregation would be generous—to each other, to your community, and to the world.
- Members of your congregation and community would be invited into ongoing education opportunities that honed their financial skills and sharpened the financial intelligence of participants.

The guiding metaphor here: Whatever good is available to individuals because of financial planning processes might also be available to congregations.

What You Might Do

As you and your congregation shift toward incorporating financial planning into your practice of stewardship, you might add some of these beginning steps to the scenarios above:

1. If financial planners are members of your congregation, begin an ongoing conversation with them about how their expertise might benefit the congregation.
2. Refer congregation members to these planners, especially before members are enmeshed in financial crises connected with crises such as divorce, disability, or death.
3. If you have not engaged in a formal financial planning process yourself, consider beginning it now.
4. If you need only financial advice—e.g., how to assist congregation members with long-term care insurance—find an advisor in that specific area of expertise. A financial planner can help identify that person.
5. Try sponsoring some financial wisdom seminars in your congregation, targeting them at specific needs or situations. Invite your local community.
6. Before engaging in any large changes in your budget, facilities, location, or identity, ask a financial planner to analyze them from the viewpoint of financial health.
7. If you haven't yet set up an "estate plan" for your congregation—an endowment fund or trust—ask a financial planner how that might work.
8. If your congregation is part of a faith community or denomination that is blessed by an affiliated financial services enterprise—e.g., a faith-based foundation—take advantage of the programs and services available from those mission-minded enterprises.

9. If you already have a working relationship with a financial planner, engage her or him as a partner in some creative future-thinking. Start with the question, "What if we planned the financial health of this congregation just like you plan the well-being of individual families?"

And remember: Financial planning is always about more than money.

Notes

1. From Felix Martin, *Money: The Unauthorized Biography* (New York, Alfred A. Knopf, 2014), 7–15. Martin details the fact that there is no anthropological evidence of any ancient cultures that made the transition for this reason.

2. Lynne Twist, *The Soul of Money: Reclaiming the Wealth of Our Inner Resources* (New York: W. W. Norton, 2003), 8ff.

3. Twist, *Soul of Money*, 17–18.

4. This gulf can also become a place of shame or shaming. On more than one occasion in my career, I have seen pastors' heartfelt teachings about financial matters cut short by a layperson's curt question, "Pastor, have you ever had to meet a payroll?" In those unfortunate moments, the authority of scriptural teaching was trumped by the weight of daily economic experience.

5. John Lanchester, "Money Talks," *The New Yorker*, August 4, 2014, 30–33. His most recent book is *How to Speak Money: What the Money People Say—And What It Really Means* (New York: W. W. Norton, 2014.)

6. Chuck Jaffe, *Getting Started in Finding a Financial Advisor* (Hoboken, NJ: John Wiley & Sons, 2010), 1–2. Jaffe also assures readers that the vast majority of financial advisors/planners are "honest, scrupulous, trustworthy, hard-working folks with good intentions."

7. Jaffe, *Getting Started*, 25–37.

8. Jaffe, *Getting Started*, 71–99. This chapter, "Interviewing a Financial Planner," details interview questions that you can use, as well as suggestions for establishing and strengthening the relationship with your planner.

9. From a personal interview with Rob Granner, January 6, 2015. The CFP® (certified financial planner) designation means that he has extensive experience in financial planning (three years or their equivalent), has completed rigorous training for his work (covering over one hundred topics), and passed a ten-hour qualifying test. A certificate holder further agrees to maintain professional standards with thirty hours of continuing education. The first-and-final qualification: Certified Financial Planners agree to display the highest professional ethics and to adhere to the criteria of the Certified Financial Planners Board of Standards.

Chapter 11

Love for All People:
Philanthropy

In the preceding chapter we considered the benefits that financial planners might offer to you and your congregation. In the following pages I'll continue down the financial health path by examining the possible advantages that might come from adapting the tenets and practices of philanthropy into your congregation's life. The proven elements of philanthropy—with "fundraising" as one specific element—can be fertile ground for steward leaders who want answers to practical and philosophical questions regarding generosity, giving, or congregational vitality.

Philanthropy and Stewardship

As a human endeavor rooted in "love for humankind," philanthropy shares some basic assumptions with Christianity: People want to do good with what is entrusted to them; they look for lives of meaning and purpose; they see generosity as a necessary way to live; and they want to escape the trap of self-centeredness. More to the point of this book, philanthropy may have an intimate connection with these understandings of stewardship:

1. Stewardship is about God's *economia*, God's will for the world.
2. One part of God's stewardship is God's love for the whole world, no exceptions.
3. This means that stewardship is concerned about the well-being of the whole world.
4. Philanthropy has the same large embrace: love for all of humankind.
5. At its core, philanthropy is a personal character trait that shows itself in actions of grace and charity.

6. Both stewardship and philanthropy are evident in individuals, institutions, organizations, or other enterprises.

7. Although both stewardship and philanthropy can include fund-raising for a specific institution or cause, they are never limited to those applications.

Both stewardship and philanthropy are venerable visions of how all of humankind can experience love and kindness. You could describe stewardship as God-centered and philanthropy as humanistic, but that may be an etymological misstep or a false dichotomy. Both terms have God-centered origins and both acknowledge the agency and benefits that attach to human beings. Each has a broad reach, with stewardship's perhaps just a little larger: God's *economia* includes concern for human welfare, but also encompasses God's beneficence toward creation, God's relentless love, God's faithfulness, and God's presence throughout time and space.

Parsing Philanthropy

The idea of philanthropy seems fairly straightforward—a love of all of humanity that shows itself in acts of charity that benefit all people, especially those experiencing need. If you do philanthropic things, you are a philanthropist. You are known by your generosity—usually shown in donations of money—and the strongly hopeful, positive feelings you have for others.[1]

Philanthropy—primarily a state of mind and, by derivation, an entity—shows itself in societal institutions that have formal and legal status. Foundations, trusts, repeating events, nonprofit organizations—all benefit from the fact that people of all kinds can join together in common causes that benefit others.

Those causes—and the philanthropy that lies under them—span the political spectrum. "Love of humanity" does not reside exclusively in any single political party or philosophy. Whether conservative, liberal, libertarian, or none-of-the-above—people of good will can come together under a banner that unites their voices, energy, and money. Some philanthropic efforts might tackle only part of a larger problem, and find common purpose in these smaller efforts.

Let's talk a little about "charity." Although philanthropy operates from the same attitudinal base as charity, they are not the same. Zoltan J. Acs, director of George Mason University's Center for Entrepreneurship, distinguishes them from each other:

- Charity's roots (throughout the ancient world) were in almsgiving.
- Philanthropy probably began in Greece as the patronage of the arts by those who were wealthy.
- The intent and outcomes of charity accrue to needy individuals who do not usually reciprocate or have any further relationship with a giver. Charity can be paternalistic.
- The intent and outcomes of philanthropy benefit the whole society, requiring a reciprocal relationship between the giver and the receiver—a mutual investment that continues toward the maintenance or improvement of the entire society.
- Acts of charity are essentially episodic; philanthropic actions endure in larger systems.[2]

Another important distinction: Philanthropy is not the same thing as fund-raising. Fund-raising techniques, philosophies, research, and expertise are like an engine that turns philanthropy's love of humankind into visible changes in society. Fund-raising is the means to that end, but not the end itself. The real fuel for the engine: love of humanity! Philanthropic enterprises that conflate the two ideals might raise significant amounts of money, but could lose sight of their beneficiaries—and so devote unnecessarily high percentages of their income to administration, overhead, or fund-raising expenses. To remain strong and effective, philanthropies always hold tightly to their goals and passions for the greater good.[3]

What differentiates philanthropy from other acts and attitudes of kindness is the scope of philanthropic vision and the length of its reach—the size of its hug. "Vast and ongoing" come to mind. Where a charity might confine its efforts to a local need or targeted audience, philanthropy sees the possibility that vast segments of the world might benefit from its work over the long haul. In his remarkable *Blessed Unrest: How the Largest Social Movement in History Is Restoring Grace, Justice, and Beauty to the World,* journalist Paul Hawken describes the scale of philanthropy throughout the world in terms of millions of these philanthropic organizations.[4]

Your congregation is philanthropic, sometimes fiercely so. You get what "God's love" means, what it requires of your life, your priorities, and your very souls. You believe that Jesus's example invites you to similar attitudes and behaviors. No matter the struggles you might face—keeping your congregation healthy and active—you rarely turn in on yourself as though the beneficiaries of your philanthropy lived only inside the four walls of your sanctuary.

Your congregation may also be charitable, but you are philanthropic when you refuse to be myopic about your caring, and pay attention to larger opportunities and capabilities. At wonderfully surprising moments, you shelve simple "caring" and shift toward bringing justice to the world. Your congregation can transcend fears and small-mindedness, catch or initiate a larger vision of God's calling, and get to work with a philanthropic Spirit inspiring you![5]

Philanthropy through a Statistical Lens

Let me offer a smattering of statistics to help you understand the size and scope of philanthropy in this country. These numbers—left for your interpretation— illustrate the size of philanthropic giving in the United States. Consider these examples:

- Over the past few decades in the United States, between 2 percent to 3 percent of GDP has been given away each year, amounting to about $350,000,000,000.[6]
- There are over 1.1 million charities in the United States.[7]
- As of July 2014, there were 321,839 congregations of all faith communities in the United States.[8]
- Over 83 percent of Americans claim to have donated money in 2013.[9]
- The charitable sector in this country employs over 13 million people and engages more than 64 million volunteers who contribute more than 8 billion hours of time to charities.[10]
- In 2013, the majority of charitable giving came from individuals. Specifically, individuals donated roughly $240.6 billion, which totaled about 72 percent of all giving.[11]
- Based on 2013 giving levels, the highest percentage (31 percent) of all charitable giving went to religious enterprises, including congregations.[12]
- Charities comprise about 10 percent of the country's economy.[13]

However you interpret them, these numbers suggest that the scope of philanthropic giving in the United States is huge, perhaps one reason for you to consider learning from philanthropists who carry out their part of God's *economia*.

Why Philanthropy Is Necessary

Philanthropy is a necessary part of every society in these times. David Neff, former editor-in-chief of *Christianity Today,* talks about the growing need for the world's nations to transcend individualism, and to stop ignoring their poorest citizens. He echoes Pope Francis's emphasis on economic inequality as "the root of social ills" and remembers how a strong sense of community used to characterize churches, neighborhoods, and cultural institutions. Without naming philanthropic actions as a pathway to correcting cancerous self-centeredness, Neff names the very conditions that philanthropy can abate.[14]

Let me restate the necessity for philanthropy in several different ways:

- When a society closes in on itself—usually based on fears of every kind—it gradually succumbs to individualism that can morph into mistrust or disregard for others. That loss of generalized civility can result in social upheavals or civil wars.

- Because "perfect love casts out fear" (1 John 4:18), every society needs some kind of mechanism for fostering love and caring as societal qualities. Philanthropy—love for all humanity—can fill that function.

- No matter how many small steps might be necessary to achieve its intended outcomes, philanthropic vision is always large in scope. The size of widespread philanthropic efforts begins to match the size of the problems that require attention.

- Other prosocial attitudes—e.g., respect, dignity, courteousness—can accompany and strengthen philanthropy.

Zoltan Acs adds other insights to the question, "Why philanthropy?" His basic thesis: Philanthropy—as attitude and actions—is essential for a capitalistic economic system to function. Philanthropy helps diminish the tensions between wealth creation and opportunity creation. It provides a financial foundation for innovation, distributing accumulated wealth to entrepreneurs—a good share of whom may be immigrants. Philanthropists are also entrepreneurial, finding new ways to address needs. The spirit of philanthropy can balance government-dependent philosophies about the public good. Philanthropy can dissolve institutional paralysis, as leaders set aside competition to work together on specific causes. Philanthropy builds social capital—e.g., religion, education, science, and the rule of law. As Acs summarizes the matter, "[Philanthropy] releases the concentration of wealth at the top of the society, while building institutions that support opportunity for future Americans."[15]

What Congregations Can Learn

A considerable body of philanthropic knowledge and practice has developed over many decades. As they apply to mission funding in congregations, the principles and axioms of philanthropy can be useful. Let me offer a few per-haps familiar examples that have stood the test of time.

A CASE STATEMENT ANCHORS FUND-RAISING.

Giving can be enhanced when the case is made for its outcomes. A concise written rationale informs internal and external supporters about the oppor-tunities or need(s) that will be addressed, as well as the actions that will be taken to address that situation. A case statement can attract newer cohorts of donors or volunteers—e.g., young adults, teens, granting agencies, commu-nity members. It projects competence and excellence. The case statement can collect in one place a vocabulary from which other fund-raising materials can be constructed. The statement assures leaders of the value of their commit-ments. The case is always factual, but can include personal and spiritual quali-ties. The language for a case statement already exists—in planners, donors, recipients, and other stakeholders.[16]

GIVING IS EMOTIONAL.

Any decision to contribute is basically an emotional act. Because the emo-tions that underlie giving are fairly complex, they likely involve large portions of the brain. You already know many of the emotions: love for others, love for God, sympathy, empathy, fear (and anger), hope, kinship, affinity, duty, admi-ration, joy, gratitude, generosity, surprise, delight, or humility. As with other decision-making moments in life, the decision to give occurs fairly quickly, and is ratified milliseconds later by the rational parts of the brain.

Emotion-based appeals to giving may have some downsides: Processing emotion requires a lot of brain power, making it hard for a brain to sustain an emotion for very long. Ramping up that emotion—to make it last longer—results only in a larger fall-off later. When emotions start to run roughshod over other parts of the decision-making process, the quality or resilience of a decision can suffer.

Emotion-dependent appeals can create other difficulties. In *With Charity for All: Why Charities Are Failing and a Better Way to Give*, Ken-neth Stern, nonprofit executive and former CEO of National Public Radio, describes what he calls "warm-glow donors." Here the emotions in question are questionable: These contributors may be motivated primarily by their desire to receive a tangible benefit in return for their largesse. The emotional context from which they operate is different from altruistic roots, is probably not philanthropic, and would be difficult to satisfy in a congregational setting.[17]

PEOPLE GIVE BECAUSE THEY ARE ASKED.

This truism may be obvious, but it may also be the least-practiced element of congregational mission-finding. Even a cursory look at congregational "stewardship drives" might reveal that most of us are afraid to ask other people for money. Even though we know intellectually that people will probably say "Yes," just the possibility of a (temporary) "No" can paralyze us. The quality of a mission-funding emphasis then suffers because the quality of the ask is diminished.

"The ask" is the core activity in any fund-raising relationship, and has specific qualities that are easily understood:

- Face-to-face requests or invitations are best. In our culture, brains respond favorably to eye contact, and facial recognition is strongly persuasive.
- Personal requests for contributions or pledges are simpler and more satisfying than overwrought "communications" about contributing.
- It is likely that personal requests also help forge bonds—understanding, emotions, goals, affinities, and experiences—between people. The social intelligence of a congregation increases.

RELATIONSHIPS MATTER.

"Fund-raising is friend-raising." So goes one of the enduring axioms of philanthropic giving. Positive fund-raising relationships—"friendship" is the shorthand expression—consist of "the right asker asking the right person for the right amount at the right time and for the right reasons." The rightness of each of these factors depends on strong, positive relationships among people.

Algorithms based on demographic or psychographic data can be helpful in contextualizing giving patterns or likely scenarios of response, but "I know you" is probably more effective than "I know your socioeconomic cohort's characteristics."

Anyone who is willing to give away significant portions of her or his livelihood (with little regard for possible rewards) is likely a spiritually mature person. When giving is encouraged within the context of appreciative, forthright relationships, that spirituality is encouraged, fostered, and strengthened.[18]

WORK WITHIN THE DONOR PYRAMID.

Philanthropic leaders have conceptualized the gradual development of donors with a graphic they call "the donor pyramid." This chart can help you visualize how donors to your congregation are spread over several levels of philanthropic behaviors or contributions. The pyramid suggests how you might strategize fund-raising activities to realize the full potential of contributors at all levels.

Imagine a pyramid, wide at the bottom and coming to a point at the top. At its bottom the pyramid represents the large number of giving prospects. Ideally, a fair percentage of these prospects will become donors. Because of positive relationships, some of these first-time donors will continue to contribute over time, perhaps in increasing amounts or frequencies. At its top, the pyramid narrows, showing the smaller number of donors who participate at that level of philanthropic giving.

The upper reaches of the pyramid are perhaps the most interesting. As a smaller percentage of regular donors mature in their commitment to the goals of an organization, the size of their donations increases, probably as significant one-time gifts. And at the highest levels of the pyramid a few "legacy donors" feel so strongly about the work of the organization that they are willing to commit their accumulated assets—trusts, bequests, estates, proceeds of life insurance policies—to its continuing mission.

Some observations about the usefulness of the donor pyramid:

- Every donor and every donation is valued.
- It takes effort to support a maturing relationship with donors at the beginning/lower levels of the pyramid. Some donors will remain at these levels for decades.
- Attention paid to donors at the upper reaches of the pyramid may result in fewer donations, but at higher contribution levels.
- Unless the bottom levels of the pyramid—the initial source for prospects and committed donors—are refreshed and honored, a strategy of fundraising can become imbalanced or topple.
- No single approach can appeal to donors at every level of the pyramid.

THANK DONORS OFTEN.

An often-repeated adage suggests that "a donor should be thanked seven times, in seven different ways." While the exact number of thank-yous can be debated, the factual basis remains true: Donors hope or expect to be thanked as personally as possible. The gratitude of another human being—especially the beneficiary of your generosity—is both an emotional reward and a ratification of your philanthropic disposition. In both cases, well-expressed thanks also motivate and encourage you to grow as a donor. Gratitude forges a bond between the recipient and the giver.

Pro-forma expressions of gratitude—form letters, e-mail blasts, notices in the congregation newsletter—barely qualify as thank-yous. Instead, the more personal the thanks, the more gratifying the emotional exchange. (Think face-to-face conversations, phone calls, tweets, texts, or phone calls.) One curious fact about form letters: A hand-written, signed note at the bottom of a form letter also conveys the personal emotions of the gift-recipient.[19]

Why Pay Attention to Philanthropy?

In addition to the benefits that are implicit in the preceding pages, let me offer these few observations:

- Philanthropy takes you beyond small-minded notions about the needs and opportunities your congregation could address.
- Philanthropic precepts can help you move from charity toward justice.
- The fund-raising branches of philanthropy provide knowledge and wisdom that really works. Proven practice replaces wishful thinking.
- From examining the workings of philanthropic ventures, you can learn how to organize or manage your congregation—a kind of volunteer philanthropic venture.
- In some of its newer manifestations, philanthropic work seems to have attracted the attention of younger generations.
- Your congregation can find new causes, new outreach opportunities, or new ideas how to carry God's love into the world.

What's Emerging on the Philanthropic Horizon

Partially in response to the insistence of younger donors, and the need to strengthen the place of philanthropy in the society, leaders in this field have encouraged the development of newer conceptual frameworks and methods for philanthropic thought and practice. I highlight a few major examples here:

CROWDFUNDING

A blending of philanthropic vision and digital wizardry, crowdfunding has blossomed quickly over the past decade as a preferred method for funding beneficial enterprises. Donors learn about philanthropic efforts and contribute online immediately. Originating with the venerable Kiva—the first online lending platform that enabled international microloans—crowdfunding sites have grown in number and sophistication. Two cautions: Crowdfunding may have become over-saturated with options that could dilute the meaning of "crowd." It is also possible that the relative ease and immediacy of crowd funding work against long-term philanthropic commitments.

SOCIAL ENTREPRENEURSHIP

The movement to identify, train, and fund social entrepreneurs probably began—along with the term itself—with Bill Drayton, a former management consultant and Carter-era EPA administrator. In 1980, he founded Ashoka, an organization he hoped would foster social and economic innovation. From its humble beginnings—$50,000 of Drayton's own funds— Ashoka now operates with an annual budget in excess of $30 million, and has developed more than 1,800 "fellows" (social entrepreneurs) in more than sixty countries.[20]

In his *Giving: How Each of Us Can Change the World,* former president Bill Clinton makes the case for the kind of philanthropy that moves with deliberate speed to address otherwise hidden social ills. The book is essentially a collection of stories about individuals—all of them compelled by the inner drive to "make a difference" with their lives. They find a need, analyze its dimensions (including possible solutions), and gather together the assets of likewise-committed others to take on problems that would otherwise not be noticed or addressed. These individuals do not wait for government, business, or established charities to take action. As entrepreneurs—leaders, tacticians, organizers, developers, marketers—these vision-fulfilling people lead by example, sometimes plowing their net worth into other-directed passions.[21]

PRODUCT PHILANTHROPY

Recent research from Indiana University's School of Public Policy and Environmental Affairs makes the case for "product philanthropy," a means by which businesses can benefit from donating products to charities. This practice, probably most easily seen in the vast amounts of foodstuffs donated to regional food banks, reduces waste and provides relief for people who are poor. The study examined the return on investment that businesses might realize from this philanthropic practice. The motivations for product donations extend past expected rewards: Companies understand their role as corporate citizens, accepting their responsibility to contribute to the greater good. In a sense, they may also be social entrepreneurs.

The research also determined that product donations:

- Afforded considerable savings—because of tax incentives—over cash donations to charities.
- Enhanced the image of businesses and corporations.
- Provided a superior alternative to the liquidation of merchandise.
- Did not require complicated changes or complex strategic planning.

This 2012 study also provides a framework for firms to analyze the costs, benefits, risks, and opportunities for beginning product philanthropy. It's possible that congregations shifting toward philanthropic ventures might be able to encourage these practices within the businesses in their locales.[22]

APPRECIATIVE INQUIRY

Originally developed as a positive approach to planning, appreciative inquiry was codeveloped by Dr. David Cooperrider, professor of social entrepreneurship at Case Western Reserve University. In this planning method, carefully constructed questions help individuals and groups come to fuller understandings of each other's most admirable and useful qualities.

In some places, appreciative inquiry methods have proven useful to philanthropic entrepreneurs and professional fund-raisers. In the past, those responsible for soliciting large donations have approached prospective donors with a set of exciting projects or opportunities. The process was straightforward: The donor would choose from among several possibilities and pledge a significant amount toward what was presumably an exciting goal. Appreciative inquiry methods (and their underlying philosophy) add a slight twist to that sequence: Using respectful-but-probing questions, fund-raisers first help donors identify their compelling passions or interests—what might be described as their lifework. An appreciative relationship develops between donors and the fund-raiser.

If the donors' answers coalesce in a way that matches a current need of the institution, the connection is easily made—donors' greatest yearnings for doing good are fulfilled and an institution receives a sizeable donation. But when there is not a connection, something entirely new and satisfying occurs: The fund-raiser tries to connect those donors with another recipient whose goals or mission match that of the donors! What seems to be a loss for the fund-raiser is actually the opposite: This interaction proves that the relationship with donors is stronger than the need to close a deal! The donors feel honored by the process of having their deep hopes and yearnings discovered, and so will maintain the relationship with equal appreciation. At some future time, the donors and the fund-raiser—with the relationship solidly in place—will likely find mutually satisfying projects to work on. The mutual regard between donors and fund-raiser will last, life purpose will be achieved, and philanthropic vision will grow.[23]

Case Study: 1K Churches

One example of a front-edge philanthropic venture is 1K Churches, an ecumenical Christian movement that wants to change the way congregations participate in the economic life of their communities. "1K" describes this organization's goal: to engage over one thousand congregations in a widespread effort to leverage their congregational assets to form and support microenterprises in their communities. Here a large-scale philanthropic vision—churches turning around the U.S. economy—is translated into what's actually possible: Individual congregations making microloans that start or strengthen small local businesses.[24]

The vision of 1K Churches is rooted in the principles of community organizing, and takes seriously the proven effect of microloan practices in other parts of the world. (The Grameen Bank in Bangladesh—and now in America—was one of the first examples of this kind of economic development.)

The efforts of 1K Churches are founded on the fact that an untapped pool of economic power exists among the hundreds of thousands of churches in the United States. Churches of all sizes purchase products, hire out services, borrow money, depend on local vendors, and manage endowments. Through members' participation in local economies—as customers, providers, and taxpayers—congregations support economic life around them. Some of those same members are business and governmental leaders.

After ten years of research and planning—most of it listening to experts in community development, business, and economics—the originators of 1K Churches decided to try a new strategy for local economic development: After a five-session Bible study, congregations (or groups within congregations) choose from among five investment pathways for making a small loan ($500–$5000) to a microbusiness (less than five employees) in their locality. Perhaps most importantly, the group begins and maintains a supportive relationship with the people in that business. Thus accountability, care, and other congregational assets are also made available to these small enterprises.

Former seminary president and 1K Churches volunteer Phyllis Anderson adds background details: This effort began with the realization that the economy as a whole needs to be reinvented to work for all, and that people of faith can have a distinctive voice in the matter. Anderson points out that this approach is an alternative to giving grants to good causes. "1K Churches will be partnering with profit-making businesses, not local charitable agencies," she notes. "Congregations will contribute to the well-being of businesses that are doing God's work out in the world."

The philanthropy of 1K Churches transcends charity. The churches expect a return on their investment—not only the repayment of the loan but the strengthening of their local community, one business at a time. Another obvious benefit: Congregations engage members of the community as more than needy people. Finally, because of their experiences and reflections through the eyes of faith, members of congregations will become more confident, more effective advocates for a more just economy that reflects God's hope for the world.

1K Churches fits well with the most basic tenets of philanthropy, and expands them to include investments in profit-making businesses as part of the fabric of philanthropy in a community. This approach transcends political proclivities and uses the congregation's economic assets for small-scale change within a much larger vision.[25]

What Ifs

Imagine yourself in any of these situations, thinking about how you might take advantage of the philanthropic spirit all around you:

1. What if a successful local merchant told you that she wants to deed her entire business to your congregation? How would you respond? What would "stewardship" mean now?

2. What if your congregation formed a separate nonprofit corporation to engage your entire community as partners in philanthropic ministries?

3. What if a member of your congregation became a dedicated and successful social entrepreneur? How would you support him or her in that personal ministry?

4. What if all your church buildings burned to the ground? (Your congregation would be amply insured against this loss.) How would you start over? How would you make those decisions?

5. What if your entire congregation decided to use an online platform (such as eBay) as a way of turning members' unnecessary possessions into a virtual rummage sale? Besides raising some money, what else might be the results?

6. What if a former member's estate included a one-time gift to your congregation in excess of $5 million? What would that do to your congregation's life together? To members' deeper sense of philanthropy?

7. What if you discontinued some of your congregation's charitable efforts and instead connected to existing local philanthropies?

What You Can Do

To bring the secular wisdom of philanthropy to bear on your stewardship practices—particularly in fundraising efforts—consider these steps as part of your shift toward a philanthropic mindset.

1. Using the content of this chapter, see how your current approach to congregational mission funding compares with the tenets of philanthropic fund-raising. (For example, how well do you thank donors?)

2. Make a list of congregation members or friends who have some expertise in philanthropic ventures. Engage them in appreciative inquiry—about what they know, and what they would be willing to teach you.

3. Do the same with community members who have similar expertise. Listen to the ways in which they exhibit "love for humanity" in their efforts.

4. To gain further insight about philanthropy, visit the website for *The Chronicle of Philanthropy* (*www.philanthropy.com*). As you read articles or blogs, ask yourself questions such as, "What if our congregation thought that way?" or "What's new here?"

5. If you want to try crowdfunding, select a special nonbudgeted project that emerges from congregation members. Use one of the currently available online platforms—e.g., Indiegogo, Kickstarter—to post your project and collect donations. (For a faith-based platform, see Wheat Ridge Ministries' We Raise site at *www.weraise.wheatridge.org*.)

6. Rethink how you approach congregation members who are represented by various levels of the donor pyramid. How could you tailor fundraising efforts to fit the varieties of philanthropic vision in the congregation?

7. If your congregation has already begun a shift toward philanthropy, consider the 1K Churches model as a logical next step.

From my own experience—as congregational leader and stewardship executive in a mainline Christian denomination—I am convinced that philanthropic expertise could benefit your congregation, not only as a better way to fund ministries but also as a way of thinking that can enlarge your mission vision.

Your love for all the world compels you.

Notes

1. The term is Greek in origin—*phil* (loving) + *anthropos* (mankind)—and first appears in English around 1620. The definitions of philanthropy wander through a gallery of positive attributes and actions: goodwill, charity, increase in well-being, human welfare, benevolence, general love of others. Its synonyms fall under the same umbrella of other-directedness: kindheartedness, grace, beneficence.

2. Charity is probably hard-wired in the brain's altruistic systems; philanthropy adds in equally hard-wired self-interest. Zoltan J. Acs, *Why Philanthropy Matters: How the Wealthy Give, and What It Means for Our Economic Well-Being* (Princeton, NJ: Princeton University Press, 2013), 3–4, 6.

3. You can visit The Chronicle of Philanthropy (*www.philanthropy.com*), Independent Sector (*www.independentsector.org*), Charity Navigators (*www.charitynavigators.org*), or the National Committee for Responsible Philanthropy (*www.ncrp.org*) to find guidelines for building ethical, purposed philanthropic organizations.

4. Paul Hawken, *Blessed Unrest: How the Largest Social Movement in History Is Restoring Grace, Justice, and Beauty to the World* (New York: Penguin, 2007). What is perhaps most compelling about Hawken's book is the modestly titled "Appendix," where he presents a taxonomy that contains only the *types* of organizations that

prove his thesis. There are no names of individual groups and no contact information—just a listing of the enormous variety of work that is being done. Astoundingly, this appendix lasts for 111 pages! "Blessed unrest," indeed!

5. George Johnson, author and former director for several Christian hunger-and-justice programs, also characterizes this maturing as moving beyond guilt and its connected attitudinal barriers. His newest collection, *Courage to Think Differently* (Laguna Woods, CA: Self-published, 2013), adds the blessings of radical audacity to philanthropic traits.

6. Acs, *Why Philanthropy*, 121.

7. Kenneth Stern, *With Charity for All: Why Charities Fail and a Better Way to Give* (New York: Doubleday, 2013), 2.

8. The Urban Institute, National Center for Charitable Statistics, as cited in "Time, Talent & Treasure," *Thrivent Magazine,* Summer 2014, 10.

9. *Giving USA: The Annual Report on Philanthropy, 2013*, as cited in "Time, Talent & Treasure," *Thrivent Magazine,* Summer 2014, 10.

10. Stern, *With Charity*, 2.

11. *Giving USA, 2013,* as cited in "Time, Talent & Treasure," *Thrivent Magazine,* Summer 2014, 10.

12. *Giving USA, 2013,* as cited in "Time, Talent & Treasure," *Thrivent Magazine,* Summer 2014, 10.

13. Stern, *With Charity*, 2.

14. David Neff, "Divine Economics 101," *Christianity Today,* July/August 2014, 32.

15. For Acs, philanthropy is motivated by the desire to make a difference for future generations, to express gratitude for good fortune and the feeling that wealth should not be passed on only to one's family. Acs, *Why Philanthropy,* 7, 9, 11–12, 126, 98.

16. Adapted from "Developing a Case Statement," a "stewardshop"—training workshop design for stewardship leaders—of the Evangelical Lutheran Church in America (n.d.). I wrote this workshop series as a staff member, and it's available on the ELCA website, *www.elca.org.*

17. Stern notes that these donors are motivated by an emotional reward that includes personal relationships with the charity. Thus they are not always interested in the effectiveness of an organization. Stern, *With Charity*, 132ff.

18. Personal interview, Steve Rusk, certified fund-raising executive (CFRE), Meyer Partners, Inc., October 26, 2011.

19. Most nonprofit charities establish guidelines for the timing and format of a thank-you. Rarely does the expression of that gratitude wait for more than two days. When large donations are received, some guidelines suggest that an immediate,

intensely personal expression of heartfelt thanks be communicated by a significant staff member.

20. In Sanskrit, *ashoka* means "the active absence of sorrow." From Bill Clinton, *Giving: How Each of Us Can Change the World* (New York: Alfred A. Knopf, 2007), 137–39.

21. In his postpresidency years, Clinton himself has come to exemplify this growing force within philanthropy. (The Clinton Global Initiative continues to be a gathering place for social entrepreneurs.) In the book's first chapter, "The Explosion of Private Citizens Doing Public Good," he introduces the compelling case that individuals should be responsible for social change. Clinton, *Giving*, 3–12.

22. A leader in product philanthropy for over thirty years, Good360 (formerly Gifts in Kind International) asked IU to conduct the study. From Justin Ross, lead researcher, "New Research Proves the Business Case for Product Philanthropy," news bulletin from the School of Public and Environmental Affairs, Indiana University, Bloomington, Indiana, January 24, 2012.

23. You can find out more about appreciative inquiry on the web. The most comprehensive and easily understood information can be found at Cooperrider's URL, *www.davidcooperrider.com*.

24. Personal interview with Phyllis Anderson, cofounder, January 12, 2015. Anderson characterizes 1K Churches as an example of how the "social entrepreneurship movement" can be applied to churches.

25. For more information, or to learn how you might get involved, visit *www.criterion institute.org*.

Chapter 12

When the *Ecclesia* Gets to Work: Community Organizing

This chapter presents a body of knowledge called "congregation-based (or faith-based) organizing" (CBO). In its principles and practices CBO accomplishes two major goals: strengthening outreach ministries and reinvigorating congregational well-being. In both cases, congregation-based organizing helps churches get to work.

A Little History

It might help you understand the value of organizing for congregations if you review the idea of "church" as the means by which God's work—*economia*—gets done through groups of believers.

When the early New Testament writers wanted to describe their religious gatherings, they used the secular term, *ecclesia*, which had its roots in Greek civil society. This word denoted a gathering of citizens in a city/state who were called out of their homes into a public place for the public good. These called-out people constituted the citizen assemblies that were the background of Greek democracy.[1]

Ecclesia could also be a fitting description of the form and function of your congregation. As an assembly of God's people, your church resembles the purposed gatherings of ancient Greece:

- Your congregation is composed of called-out members (citizens) who come out of their church buildings (homes) into their surrounding communities (public places) for the purpose of accomplishing godly good.
- You could think of your outreach mission as working together with others outside the church to accomplish mutually beneficial outcomes.

- Your work with others would be satisfying because all participants would have an equal stake in decision-making as well as implementation of those decisions.

What Is Community Organizing?

Congregation-based organizing derived its initial identity from community organizing, a secular body of thought and practice that emerged in the United States as early as 1939. At least four interrelated strands comprise the history of this continuing movement: the original community development work of Saul Alinksy and others; the culture of liberation theology; the civil rights movement; and the farmworker organizing efforts of César Chávez. In each case, communities of faith were integral to the development of these large-scale changes in society.

COMMUNITY DEVELOPMENT

Alinsky's efforts began on the South Side of Chicago, and included bare-knuckled approaches to issues confronting workers and community residents. (Existing labor organizations and laws extended back into the late 1800s throughout the world.) In 1941, Alinsky formed the Industrial Areas Foundation (IAF) so that training in his approaches could be available to audiences around the country. From their experiences, Alinsky and his colleagues codified the basic precepts and practices of organizing that have stood the test of time for the ensuing decades. An important consideration: from the start, Alinsky sought the buy-in of churches and their leaders, whom he knew could involve ordinary citizens in determining their well-being. Alinsky's enduring legacy includes his understanding of the positive use of power, sometimes confrontationally; his insistence on the involvement of ordinary people in their own welfare; and his trust in self-interest as a motivating force in public and political matters.

THE CULTURE OF LIBERATION THEOLOGY

As a stream of Christian doctrine and practice, liberation theology emerged in the 1960s from populist movements in Central and South America. The Second Vatican Council further inspired theological freedom and creativity. In 1971, Peruvian Catholic theologian Gustavo Gutiérrez published *Teología de la liberación*, which presented a framework of doctrine founded on the centrality of liberation. Gutiérrez also offered directions about how theology could be formulated. He emphasized the wisdom of believers who were gathered in "base communities." What developed from these gatherings was a new cultural context for "church" that included land reform, corruption, and church structure itself. These base communities were intensely spiritual at their core; they also participated in public actions—based on studied Scripture and prayer—that improved the life of ordinary people.

The Civil Rights Movement

Materializing over many decades of struggle during the last half of the twentieth century, the civil rights movement drew together strands of both secular and religious thought and practice. Strongly influenced by the religious truths of Judaism and Christianity, the early civil rights leaders—many of them pastors—also looked to the political successes of Indian activist Mohandas Gandhi and the developing practices of community organizing. Trained in organizing tactics, leaders such as the Rev. Martin Luther King used these methods to guide specific actions—e.g., voter registration drives, protests, school and business desegregation—that coalesced to form societal changes that continue today.

Organizing Migrant Farmworkers

Trained by Saul Alinsky's IAF, Mexican-American labor leader and organizer César Chávez is credited with the formation of the United Farmworkers Organizing Committee (UFOC), a union that worked against the injustices experienced by migrant laborers in California's vineyards and farms. Chávez began his organizing work in the barrios of Central California, working on bread-and-butter local issues such as voter registration, citizenship classes, education, health care, and welfare registration. Mirroring Ghandi's methods, he used hunger strikes and boycotts to attract the attention and participation of congregations and national denominations. Chávez called for churches to serve people who are poor, not only in acts of charity but also in active engagement to eliminate injustices wherever they occurred. Although his union eventually dissolved, Chávez continues today as an example of lifelong commitment to social justice, even at the cost of one's own well-being.

From its beginnings, community organizing brought together diverse community groups in order to achieve outcomes that were mutually beneficial. It was built on foundations of respect and accountability, and developed a set of practices that continue to rally people around actions that tell truth to power and affect meaningful, lasting change in local communities.

What Is Congregation-Based Organizing?

Faith-based organizations—churches, nonprofit enterprises, denominations—were part of the growth of community organizing. It seems natural that organizing would eventually become a part of the ministry of denominations and congregations.

As it has emerged more formally over the past twenty years, congregation-based organizing has added to basic organizing philosophy the strengths of faith-based motivations and outcomes, the sturdiness of congregational life, and the influence of religious leaders in a variety of faith communities. As they have joined local organizing coalitions and provided their leaders with training, congregations have incorporated into the core principles of organizing their own ethical, moral, and spiritual wisdom.

Congregation-based organizing helps congregations provide an effective way of bringing the good news of God out into the world as well as maintaining their organizational health. The following characteristics of congregation-based organizing also identify its benefits:

- CBO provides ways of thinking and acting that any group of people can access in order to get any part of God's work accomplished.
- That work starts with manageable problems or possibilities that are present in a congregation's immediate surroundings.
- Congregation-based organizing gains its strength from appreciative relationships among people, starting with focused, respectful conversations.
- CBO is strictly nonpartisan. No political parties, candidates, or platforms are ever endorsed.
- Because it enables social change, congregation-based organizing can become a powerful witness to those outside the church.
- With the Scriptures as foundation, congregation-based organizing also honors the practical wisdom that exists outside Scripture's witness.
- By its nature, CBO is nimble, honest, and realistic regarding power, decision-making, motivation, and connectivity.
- It marshals strengths (assets) for the good of God's world.
- Congregation-based organizing brings together diverse groups of people who find like-mindedness in shared goals.

- Because it is not exclusively clergy-oriented or dependent, it encourages the development of lay leaders.[2]

Does organizing help congregations as institutions? About ten years ago, Interfaith Funders, a network of secular and faith-based grantmakers working to advance the field of congregation-based community organizing, wanted to answer that question. So Interfaith Funders conducted a study of the positive effects of community organizing training on congregational life. The findings showed that congregations engaged in community organizing changed in measurable ways. A summary understanding of this research: As a result of their training and participation in community organizing, congregations were strengthened in positive relationships, leadership development, faith commitments, and reshaped self-identities.[3]

The Tools and Arts of Community Organizing

The larger work of community organizing depends on skills, activities, tactics, or methods that enable societal change at a local level. When combined in a systematic way over time, these tools comprise what organizers sometimes call "the arts" of community organizing. These art-tools include (in alphabetical order, not in the sequence of their use): agitation, effective meetings, evaluations, house meetings, listening campaigns, one-to-ones, power analysis, propositioning, research visits, team development, and turn-out. Although any single tool may seem ordinary, community organizers employ them deliberately and insistently. The tools are used in an order that yields results but is also adaptable to changes in contexts or circumstances.[4]

The Value of Community

In community organizing, "community" refers to a localized gathering of people outside of institutions or systems. The principles of community are proven by its ability to accomplish something. Community organizers understand how the practice of community strengthens and sustains organizations, neighborhoods, businesses, and entire cities. No matter how diverse they are, loosely aggregated groups coalesce and connect with each other for common purpose or the sheer joy of being together.[5]

In the minds of organizers, sustainable local communities have these characteristics:

- Community members think of everyone and everything as useful assets.
- Voluntary groups, institutions, and enterprises proliferate naturally.
- Leaders are known for their abilities to get things done.
- Physical assets are available to all.
- Interdependent economic activity flourishes.
- Shared stories portray individuals and groups at their best.
- Hope fills imaginations.
- Local organizations and their leaders resist the temptation to scale up toward inevitable unmanageability.[6]

Organizers stress the importance of manageable social groups—families, neighborhoods, or small organizations—as a principle for maintaining community. In their *The Abundant Community*, social policy professor John McKnight and cultural prophet Peter Block add "universal properties" to the list of basic ingredients for community:

- *The giving of gifts:* Community members identify, appreciate, and put to use their abundant gifts.
- *The presence of association:* When joined to others—in common interests, purpose, or crises—groups of people magnify their individual gifts.
- *The compassion of hospitality:* The depth of a welcoming view of life is carried out in actions of open kindness and valuing of all others. Where there is community, there are no strangers.[7]

The Importance of Conversation

Based on the proven capabilities of the human brain to emulate and learn from the faces and behaviors of others, natural conversation is more than surface-joviality among like-minded people. Because earnest, honest, and appreciative conversations reach to the deepest parts of our brains, conversations are the starting part for social change. (In CBO parlance, these conversations are called one-to-ones.)

In *Community: The Structure of Belonging,* Peter Block extols the value of conversation. He thinks of communities as conversations. His description of the value of conversations moves toward practicality: Mutual action occurs because of appreciative conversations. People are intimately connected with each other and a palpable sense of belonging is restored. Restorative conversations replace retributive ones. When conversations are conducted in public, they leverage the power of the group. When the focus of conversation shifts from problems to possibilities; from fear and fault to generosity and abundance; from blaming and shaming to mutual accountability; and from a focus on the leader to a focus on group members—these are the moments when community is strengthened, solidified, and prompted toward action.[8]

Although others might describe conversations only as "lost arts," the lubricant for pleasurable relationships, or the key to success in business, community organizers are far more insistent: Improved conversation skills are essential for the vitality of any group, churches included!

Self-Organization

Another basic element of community organizing methods is self-organization, the sometimes miraculous process by which groups of people intuitively agree about what to do together. Transplanted from theoretical physics into social theory, self-organization presumes that order—agreements, purpose, appreciation, and action—will emerge from what seems to be chaotic, as long as people remain in relationship. The order emerges from patterns already embedded in the complexity. Coalescence and emergence are related processes. "Communities of practice" and "informal organizations" are related terms.

You can see self-organization in the highly ordered behaviors of social insects, flocks of birds, and schools of fish. Here, simple rules of connectivity result in collective good. Community organizing presumes that the same can be true with groups of people.

Organizational dynamics professor Margaret Wheatley describes three conditions for self-organizing to take place: identity (a group's capacity to make sense); information (data with meaning assigned to it); and relationships (pathways for interpersonal connections).

According to Wheatley, self-ordering can't be planned, nor does it always occur quickly. Self-organizing groups have the ability to respond continuously to change, adjusting to their circumstances or assets. The process is less planned, directed, or controlled than it is observed, respected, and harnessed. Creativity and inquiry are necessary prerequisites as well as assured by-products of self-organization. Leadership in self-organizing social systems is less top-down; leaders work to make sure that their workers, followers, or colleagues don't become dependent on the leader's gifts, vision, or power.[9]

Unless they have settled into clergy-dependent operational dynamics, congregations are probably self-organizing. By learning the techniques of community organizing, congregational leaders can increase their effectiveness by offering ownership and accountability to all members.

Leadership with Organizing in Mind

Community organizing requires its own leadership philosophy. Those who want to take advantage of community organizing methods have to be willing to reexamine their current thinking about developing leaders:

- Leadership is less about the styles or attributes of leaders and more about their intent.
- Leadership is about convening people—to enable relatedness, to draw out possibilities, to gather assets, and to create experiences.
- Leadership is not a lost art, and leaders are not scarce.
- Leaders shape decision-making by designing gatherings of purposed people.
- The classic understandings of meetings—explaining, defending, offering opinions, persuading, goal-setting, or defining—may not be helpful.
- A primary goal of gatherings is the engagement of all participants. Gatherings create owners and leaders, not more followers.
- Leadership models that rely on extroverted charisma or expertise— inspiring, aligning, enrolling, delegating, providing oversight, or training others—may undermine the wider benefits of community organizing.
- Leaders can be effective when they let go of their need to control.[10]

In community organizing, leadership is simpler and available to all participants. This seems to fit well with the notion of "the universal priesthood of all believers," a doctrinal formula that honors the baptismal callings of all who claim to be stewards.

Case Study: Jobs in DuPage County

For about ten years, community organizing has been part of the life of Faith Lutheran Church in suburban DuPage County, Illinois. Staff and lay leaders have completed formal organizing training, and the congregation was a founding partner of DuPage United, a coalition of several dozen local congregations, mosques, and synagogues. DuPage United has initiated several formal "actions" locally, centered on justice and poverty concerns. What characterizes DuPage United and Faith Lutheran most recently has been an initiative that centers on the economic fact that healthy communities are built on living-wage jobs.

The man who initiated this still-developing project is Tom Wendorf, a retired business executive. A DuPage United member with extensive political savvy and experience, Tom embodies quietly unobtrusive charisma. Using the techniques of community organizing he learned in his training, Tom leap-frogged over the usual process of political change—e.g., putting pressure on local government officials to "do something about this problem." Instead, he spent more than a year surveying local business owners—the natural source of jobs—listening to their ideas. What he found was astounding: Thousands of well-paying, highly skilled manufacturing jobs were going unfilled in DuPage County because of the lack of qualified candidates. Tom shifted his listening ear to local school and junior college officials. He discovered that although state-of-the-art training facilities for these jobs existed in the county, a very small number of students took advantage of them. School districts were locked into "college-bound" definitions of success. They were virtually blind to the needs of businesses and the mindsets of students who were not inter-ested in a college education.

Knowing that there would be mutual advantages in this matter, Tom agi-tated for face-to-face meetings with county politicians, job-training organiza-tions, school officials, and business leaders. It soon became apparent that each group could see its self-interest in job-training efforts. And the groups could combine their assets to work together! After some negotiation, the county agreed to provide seed funding for a pilot project that would develop a path-way for the unemployed and under-employed in the county to find living wage jobs. Also included: no-cost training for midskill jobs and placement in local manufacturing firms. A new nonprofit was formed (with a board and a paid director), and it began recruiting candidates for the training. A partner-ship was forged with another nonprofit training organization with a proven record of success. The pathway was complete.

At the time of this writing, several dozen students are enrolled in courses that will qualify them for jobs requiring skills in computer-based manufactur-ing. The first graduates of the training have been hired. Next phases of the larger process—e.g., engaging school districts in identifying likely candidates for similar training—have begun.

What is noteworthy here is that Tom put to use all the principles and methods of community organizing. What emerged was not only the prospect of increased employment in DuPage County, but a new collaboration among local church leaders, nonprofit service organizations, government officials, and business leaders that will continue to address the ongoing need for a pathway to living wage jobs. Those relationships are secured by the respect and appreciation that Tom forged, one conversation at a time. Tom's leadership was effective because he worked patiently to enact the power of community organizing methods.

Where Is CBO Heading?

The principles and practices of congregation-based organizing continue to spread into the lifeblood of congregations, synagogues, and mosques. The number of coalitions is growing across the country. Other positive signs: Some seminaries now include community organizing classes or experiences in their curricula; denominations train national staff members in community organizing; faith-specific organizing resources are produced; new congregations form with community organizing at their core; and new nonprofit organizations begin operating. It seems likely that the relentless growth of successful actions will continue, as will the number of congregational leaders, pastors, and denominational leaders trained in community organizing.

Funding continues to be an issue. Community organizing is labor-intensive and so requires consistent funding sources. When congregational or denominational priorities shift, it can be difficult for CBO enterprises to maintain their viability.

The hope in all this? Eventually the sheer volume—of personal experiences and commitments, successful actions, numbers of congregations using community organizing—will reach a tipping point, tilting the entire church toward the well-being of local communities.[11]

Part of a New Model for "Church"

As a large generational shift in ecclesiology waits in the wings, other traditional approaches to congregational vitality—based on The Great Commission, clericalism, world missions, peace and justice, or caregiving—may be coming to the end of their usefulness. Congregation-based organizing may offer a new approach—even a new model—for churches to do their work.

Two streams of effort seem to exist: Congregations want to bring God's love outside the walls of their church buildings and to reclaim their institutional health. Community organizing could enable both. Let's look at each possibility a little more closely.

OUTREACH MINISTRY

Most congregations want to work on the problems of society all around them. But their efforts can be diminished or their energy dissipated because of the size and complexities of the problem they want to address. Social ministry can devolve into programs or endeavors that are shallow or saccharine. Well-intentioned church members can toil at solutions that are only token evidence of lasting change. Ministry can stop at charity. Like donor fatigue, leader burnout can emerge quickly when good-hearted people attack problems in less-than-effective ways, and experience ongoing futility.

Community organizing can help reframe congregational outreach in significant ways. As they employ community organizing principles and practices, congregations can:

- Work successfully at what really matters.
- Target and involve those who hold institutional or economic power.
- Transcend mere charity, which can become an unrelenting drain on resources or will.
- Build coalitions that connect members' daily life issues—e.g., schools, safety, corruption, pollution, job creation—with the self-interest of other citizens.
- Recognize and affirm their personal power.
- Develop followers into leaders.
- Put dearly held religious beliefs into practice.
- Strengthen the expectation that positive change is possible.
- Sidestep futility, frustration, and burnout.[12]

VITALITY OF CONGREGATIONS

Congregations also want to be healthy organizations. Some remember their vibrant relevance in previous generations and want to return to those days and those ways of thinking, in an attempt to transport themselves back to what they remember were good times.

Congregational vitality can slip away from leaders for any number of reasons, including the general culture's gradual devolution and garden-variety organizational disorders. In my observations of scores of churches throughout the country over many decades, unhealthy congregations seem to lack sufficient quantities of:

- Volition, the motivation or will to accomplish something, whether it's a continuing program or ministry.
- Capacity, the alignment of assets that can be used for any number of purposes. (Sometimes the assets are present, but just not recognized or valued.)
- Instrumentality, the intuitive savvy about how to get things done.
- Agency, a sense of personal or institutional power that may be the emotional fuel on which volition, capacity, and instrumentality depend.

Absent these essential qualities, congregations can gradually slip into disrepair and despair. They can easily become places of shaming and blaming. They can chase after fad-of-the-month transformational programs that depend on the supposed effectiveness of imitating others' best-practices. Congregational leaders may take up problem-solving planning processes—asking questions that only magnify the problems. Some congregations may continually switch out leaders—pastors—in an attempt to fine-tune leadership issues that are actually the results of their own misdirected or leader-dependent mindsets. Without anyone stating the matter directly, some congregations decide to die and spend their waning years in quiet grieving or fear of death. Organizational health may still be possible, but is discounted by congregational leaders.

Congregation-based organizing offers an alternative way of approaching the matters of congregational vitality. In addition to the benefits I've summarized elsewhere in this chapter, these outcomes may be possible:

- The number and maturity of your leaders can increase.
- More members will own more parts of your congregation's mission.
- You can prosper, even if your congregation grows smaller or divests itself of programs and staff.
- You can employ methods of change that have proven themselves in situations like yours.
- You can reinstill other disciplines of congregational life, such as accountability or respect.
- You can increase volition, capacity, instrumentality, and agency in your congregation.[13]

Research in congregational vitality seems to be consistent: Congregations whose only focus is their own health are not as likely to sustain themselves. Questions about congregational outreach and well-being are intertwined: As you strengthen one, you are making other more vigorous as well. Congregation-based organizing fits very well into the conclusions of this research.

Like any system of thought or practice, congregation-based organizing is not a cure for every difficulty in every congregation. The organizing arts or tools do not work well in places where congregations are at death's door. Organizing requires basic capacities in order to be effective. Where those capacities are minimal, congregation-based organizing may not be any more redemptive or life-restoring than any other approach to congregational health.

What Might a Shift toward Organizing Look Like?

If you decide to incorporate congregation-based organizing into your stewardship ministry, you might see changes such as these:

- *Normal skill development:* Your congregation's leaders could increase their capabilities in areas such as: appreciative inquiry, volunteer solicitation, bottom-up planning methods, or donor relationships.

- *Extraordinary skill development:* Present and emerging leaders would become proficient in matters such as agitation, active listening, persuasion, coalition-building, and conflict prevention/resolution.

- *Power analysis:* The patterns and dynamics of personal and institutional power would be known, authenticated, appreciated, and used wisely as one of the bases for visioning, program development, and member engagement.

- *Rejuvenated outreach:* Where social ministry might be stalled or subverted in your congregation, you would approach these efforts with energy and high expectations.

- *Practical approaches:* You would replace needs-based planning with the proven techniques of asset-based planning and thinking.

- *Diminished futility:* You would not spend attention, time, money, social capital, or effort on programs or directions for which you had minimal assets.

- *Ecumenical coalition-building:* Your congregation's partnerships—with other faith communities, local government, and other organizations devoted to stewardship—would be targeted, appreciative, and results-oriented.

These changes point at larger changes in your congregation's identity and spirit, including these:

- Your congregation's actions would be compelling evidence of the Spirit's work in the world!
- A can-do spirit would infuse your congregation's self-worth.
- You would talk to each other more honestly, more directly, and more insistently.
- Your leaders and pastor would not burn out because of frustration, inattention, or loneliness.
- The language of your vision, mission, or donor case statements would sparkle with specificity.

What You Can Do

Shifting toward congregation-based organizing might be a good change for you and your congregation. You can begin that long process with any of these actions:

1. Before you decide whether to embark on community organizing training, talk to leaders in other congregations who have already taken that step. Listen carefully to what they have to say. See how what they have learned also applies to you.
2. For a period of time, try out just one of the techniques of congregation-based organizing. (Two that come to mind: One-to-one appreciative inquiry and the practiced-principle "Don't do for others what they can do for themselves.") Analyze the experience for its inherent possibilities.
3. Job-shadow or interview a community organizer, preferably someone familiar with church-based organizing. Ask good questions and expect straightforward responses.
4. Compare your congregation's existing strategies for vitality with what you've read in this chapter. What do you notice? What are the emotional and physical costs of those strategies?
5. Talk with other leaders in your congregation about your present efforts at social ministry (or outreach). What's the likely future of that work? What are the congregation's levels of volition, capacity, instrumentality, and agency?
6. If you're starting to burn out or grow cynical, back off or drop out for a while. During your sabbatical from leadership, step back so that you can observe your congregation's big picture. Keep track of what you learn. (The next steps will emerge!)

7. If you're locked into a formal process or program of congregational renewal that's not going anywhere, admit it. Get out. Be still. Stop trying so hard.

Above all, remember that this shift might affect many aspects of your congregational life, including just about every assumption about what it means to be a church or an *ecclesia*. Be patient with this change, anticipating a gradual rather than immediate shift.

And when your *ecclesia* does get to work—with community organizing as your model for congregational life and purpose—be ready for surprises that no book, not even this one, could ever predict or promise!

Notes

1. Excerpted from Bob Sitze, "Dancing with the Sisyphean Imperative: Propositions and Criteria for Sustainable Ecclesiologies," *Congregations* Issue 2 (2013): 5. In its references to the gathered people of God, *ecclesia* occurs 114 times in the Septuagint and New Testament, usually denoting an assembly of people. In its secular use, *ecclesia* appears as a reference to the Ephesian silversmiths who challenged Paul's ministry. (The English word "church" is derived from *kyriakos*—another secular Greek term meaning "belonging to the lord or master"—which does not appear in Scripture.) *Strong's Concordance of the Bible* (Nashville, TN: Thomas Nelson, 1990), entry 1577.

2. Sitze, "Dancing," 5–6.

3. From Mary Ann Ford Flaherty and Richard L. Wood, *Faith and Public Life: Faith-Based Community Organizing and the Development of Congregations* (Syosset, NY: Interfaith Funders, 2004), 6–7.

4. Personal interview, the Rev. Susan Engh, director for Congregation-Based Organizing, Evangelical Lutheran Church in America, January 8, 2015.

5. Implicit in this description is the truth that communities are competent and powerful to affect change. From John McKnight and Peter Block, *The Abundant Community: Awakening the Power of Families and Neighborhoods* (San Francisco: Berrett-Koehler, 2010), 4–5.

6. From "Building Community Partnerships," a presentation by Dr. John Kretzmann, cofounder and codirector of the Asset-Based Community Development Institute (ABCD) at Northwestern University, at the Wheat Ridge Ministries Young Adults Convening, Sheboygan, WI, June 7, 2014.

7. A delightful characteristic that may easily get lost: People in community can grow in appreciation and affection for each other! McKnight and Block, *Abundant Community*, 4–5.

8. Block's description of the value of conversation supports fundamental notions of democracy and individual responsibility. See Peter Block, *Community: The Structure of Belonging* (San Francisco: Berrett-Koehler Publishers, 2009), 52–54.

9. In Wheatley's thinking, self-organization has always been an active principle in group dynamics; we've just rediscovered and renamed it for our times. See Margaret Wheatley, *Finding Our Way: Leadership for an Uncertain Time* (San Francisco: Berrett-Koehler Publishers, 2005), 33–44.

10. See Block, *Community*, 85–87.

11. "Actions" is the term community organizers use to designate targeted goals with demonstrable results. Actions are begun and completed as local victories, but also as replicable methods for change. Personal interview, the Rev. Susan Engh, January 8, 2015.

12. The likelihood of these outcomes comes from the continuing evidence of congregations successfully involved in community organizing efforts. Personal interview, the Rev. Susan Engh, January 8, 2015.

13. Personal interview, the Rev. Susan Engh, January 8, 2015.

Chapter 13

Beyond "Happy":
Positive Psychology

Most readily connected to the work of Dr. Martin Seligman, director of the Positive Psychology Center at the University of Pennsylvania, positive psychology is the scientific study of strengths/assets and virtues that enable individuals and groups to thrive. Positive psychology incorporates positive emotions and traits into individual lives and the endeavors of groups.

The original theoretical work—built on Maslow's earlier "humanistic psychology" and Diener's happiness studies—has been buttressed with continuing experimental evidence. This has led to an explosion of applications—some of them racing ahead of verifiable science—that can be useful for leaders in business, government, education, nonprofit organizations, and perhaps even churches. In its less-spectacular manifestations—resilience, grit, hope, flow, learned helplessness, self-control, perseverance, depression, or optimism/pessimism—positive psychology seems to reinforce important elements of what Scripture describes as a godly or sanctified life.

In its various forms—happiness research, studies of satisfaction and well-being, affective neurobiology—positive psychology is worth your examination. Since stewardship ministry has often been defined as "everything you do after you say that you believe," the findings of positive psychology could be incorporated into your congregation's stewardship of good news, mission, or vocation. This chapter will help you understand those possibilities.

What Positive Psychology Entails

Positive psychology is a collection of interrelated matters centering on subjective well-being. Examples of these interrelated fields of study include:

neurobiology, psychology, social psychology, philosophy, economics, social cognition, and social policy.

Several important philosophical questions hover over positive psychology. Perhaps the most important is also the simplest: What exactly is happiness? To their credit, researchers have avoided shallow, narcissistic answers. Instead, they are concerned with emotional, physical, relational, and spiritual well-being. They look at patterns of positive human traits that gather in individuals and institutions. They operate on the philosophical principle that dwelling on a positive focus may yield better results than picking apart problems. Satisfaction, emotional health, sufficiency, optimism—all serve as synonyms (or at least as descriptors) of happiness. The brain's hard-wired pleasure-seeking mechanisms may lie at the heart of this positive state of mind.

Measures of happiness might seem to legitimize the "happiness industry," whose sometimes inadequate methodologies may yield questionable conclusions. While it's important to understand our well-being, we need to be careful not to trust results that come from self-reporting surveys, extrapolations from imperfect sampling, or single-emphasis research. (For example, a true measure of a nation's "happiness index" should probably include more than just gross national product. The data could be broadened to enfold statistics such as percentages of drug use, alcoholism, and suicide rates or stress-related illnesses and economic costs.[1])

One more matter: Happiness is a good thing; "abundant living" can accompany a life of faith. God intends for us to live well, to be healthy, to flourish, or even prosper. Without falling into the self-idolatry embedded in the Prosperity Gospel, we can agree that, despite our roles as undeserving stewards in God's universal realm, we can find satisfaction, reward, and happiness in bringing God's will to bear on the world.

Searching for Happiness in the Wrong Places

Given that human nature can also show itself as greed, hedonism, selfishness, or disregard of others, our search for happiness could also send us in directions that end at eventually unhappy destinations. Two examples of these cultural pursuits come to mind: the search for happiness in materialism and the quest to tamp down harried lifestyles. Let's examine each of these before proceeding further.

Materialism

Our stuff doesn't make us happy, and may in the long run work against lasting happiness. Baylor University marketing professor James H. Roberts states the matter clearly, "We are a nation in love with shiny objects. . . . We are a nation addicted to plastic."[2]

Roberts further describes this cultural malady in these summary statements drawn from research:

- For those already infected with materialistic mindsets, the primary value of possessions rests in their ability to grant status and to present an ideal self-image. This "extended self" can become more important than your actual identity.

- There is a negative correlation between higher levels of materialism and degrees of self-esteem, happiness, quality of life, satisfaction, and self-actualization.

- People who watch more television are more materialistic.

- Fear of death—and connected terror management—is only temporarily modulated by consumption and materialism.

- Materialism is associated with other less-than-enviable personal traits such as envy, greed, nongenerosity, social anxiety, and self-criticism.

- Those who score high on measures of materialism are less satisfied with their families, friends, homes, earned income, jobs, and health.

- When held as a practiced value, materialism undermines relationships when people objectify others, become self-centered, place work over family, and assign low value to any relationships.[3]

Roberts is direct in his assessment of the probable causes for materialism. There may be a genetic predisposition to materialism, especially compulsive buying. (Social compulsion theory can be summarized in the statement, "We know ourselves by comparing ourselves to others.") But the main determinants of materialism are probably cultural. They include our tendencies to mimic and adopt the cultural values and behaviors of our contexts. Because those influences can also include church-related environments, Roberts singles out "the Prosperity Gospel" as an example of materialism gone awry.[4]

Happiness-destroying materialism is not an intractable problem. Solutions are possible, although they require attention and practice. The solutions include "environmental tweaking," Roberts's term for changing the contexts in which materialism thrives. He suggests increasing attention to personal savings, cutting up credit cards, delaying major purchases, engaging in family communication, limiting television viewing, and paying with cash or checks. These actions are signs of a person's greater concern for others than for her or his own self.[5]

Other-directedness coincides with the results of a longitudinal study conducted by Tim Kasser, psychology professor at Knox College and author of *The High Price of Materialism* and coeditor of *Psychology and Consumer Culture*. The researchers developed a program for adolescents that successfully decreased their materialism. The program helped teens understand consumer culture, clarify their core values (such as self-growth, closeness with friends and family, and contributing to the community), and make decisions based on those values. A significant ingredient of the program's success: Both adolescents and their parents participated in the program.[6]

HARRIED LIFESTYLES

Unrelenting materialism can result in hurried schedules and a sense that time is limited. In *Overwhelmed: Work, Love and Play When No One Has the Time*, Brigid Schulte, *Washington Post* journalist and fellow at the New America Foundation, offers some intriguing terminology that might help frame the near-epidemic of time-stressed lifestyles. Among the word pictures you may find useful in restocking your psychological vocabulary:

- *Frenetic families:* The market cohort of parents and children who live with unmanageable and unsustainable schedules or calendars.
- *Acedia*: A Greco/Latinate term that roughly approximates "running around while purposelessly agitated" because of existential boredom; a frantic ennui.
- *Role overload:* Trying to fill too many people's shoes at the same time.
- *Contaminated time:* Being overwhelmed by a mental tape loop that focuses mercilessly on your uncompleted tasks.
- *Time serenity:* A desirable mindset that can dispel contaminated time.
- *Gendered division of labor:* Continuing inequities in the amount of housework and child-caring responsibilities assumed by mothers as compared to fathers.
- *Episodes:* A surreal standard of measurement used to describe the progression of your daily schedule.
- *Busier-than-thou:* Framing your stuffed lifestyle as a way of gaining favor or superiority; a falsely positive rendering of the problem.

- *Time sickness:* A completely dysfunctional sense of time.
- *Skole*: A term that the ancient Greeks used to describe refreshing leisure—a time to be fully alive, deep in thought.
- *Work-and-spend life cycle:* The self-feeding circular illogic that constitutes too many lives.
- *Allostatic overload:* The debilitating burden of stress-and-recovery cycle (allostasis) that remains stubbornly hyperactive.
- *The cult of intensive motherhood:* A socially compulsive role modeling that rests on guilt, fear, and ambivalence.[7]

Having described this mindset in exquisite detail, Shulte is also helpful in her consideration of ameliorating practices or beliefs. She advocates for "grit"—the ability to stick with what you've set your mind on, especially when the going gets tough. Gratitude figures strongly in her solutions to being overwhelmed. She spends considerable time examining the virtues—and the healing power—of play, especially for women. She warns about trying to balance life and work as though both are equally valuable at all times. Like grit, "self-efficacy" can help you avoid being overwhelmed by the influence or expectations of others. And she advocates for a more mindful view about time, describing the transcendent serenity of *kairos* time (knowing and valuing "just the right moment") over *chronos* time (a clock-bound view of time's marching on).[8]

Because of your spiritual core, God's revelation in the Scriptures and the examples of other time pilgrims in your congregation, you may already know how to avoid fruitless meandering in search of happiness. You could be satisfied about that!

Significant Theories and Research

Positive psychology work continues in the nooks and crannies of social science. Several strands of theory and research stand out as particularly notable for your shifting stewardship ministry. Let's look at several of them now.

HAPPINESS AS THE PURSUIT OF VIRTUES

An intriguing framework for positive psychology centers on the possibility that happiness, well-being, or positive emotions are themselves derived from a deeper set of virtues.

With his colleagues, Everett Worthington, licensed clinical psychologist and director of the Psychology Counselling Program at Virginia Commonwealth University, has proposed that the classic virtues of Greek culture and Christian doctrine—e.g., mercy, forgiveness, and humility—may be clearer evidences of happiness. In Worthington's research and resources, virtues correlate strongly with many of the elements of positive psychology.

Virtues are both the cause and result of strong character traits. For example, mercy may underlie and be strengthened by empathy, compassion, and love. Humility may describe a quiet factor in prosocial behaviors of humor, self-forgiveness, or gratitude. Forgiveness—different than forebearing or forgetting—reinforces strong mental and physical health. Virtuous persons are happy because they behave according to an established hierarchy of rewarded actions.[9]

EMOTIONAL STYLES OF HAPPINESS

Psychologist, lecturer, and stand-up comic Brian King speaks about "emotional styles" as another way to describe the deeper aspects of positive psychology. Here happiness is a special emotional or personality style—a collection of interrelated emotions that characterizes your approach to life. The ideas of "dispositions" (patterns of preferred response) or "temperaments" (large patterns of feelings) might also capture the idea of emotional styles. Most emotional styles involve the regulatory interplay among the prefrontal cortex—directing the brain's logical/sequential functions—and the amygdala—the center of the brain's affective operations.

These emotional styles are associated with happiness:

- *Resilience:* The time it takes for you to recover from negative circumstances or events so that you can endure emotional duress without collapsing. Resilience engages your memory of past successes and applies it to present difficulties.
- *Positive outlook:* The preference for optimism over pessimism. (This is the classic choice that names the allegedly half-full glass as preferable.)
- *Social intuition:* Your capacity to interpret interpersonal cues accurately, and to put them to use in relational settings.
- *Self-awareness:* The degree to which you are able to combine your body and mind signals into a meaningful picture of well-being.
- *Focus:* The ability to gather attention mechanisms for a singular purpose or direction. Happiness is difficult when your thinking is distracted or diffused into attentional shards.[10]

HAPPINESS AND GENEROSITY

The findings of positive psychology suggest that generosity correlates strongly with happiness. The relationship is particularly strong when generosity is enacted, not just sought as a preferred personality trait. To state the matter directly: People who live generously live happily.

In a sweeping survey of more than 200,000 adults in 136 countries, researchers found that there was a positive link between donations and measures of happiness in 120 of those countries. This was true in both poor and rich countries. The researchers tested for causality, and found that donating to charities resulted in a "happiness boost." This increase in satisfaction held true across various cultures, leading investigators to wonder whether the connections between generosity and well-being might be a universal human trait. (In a separate study, other social scientists found that giving is more spontaneous than greed, which requires more thought and therefore more time.)

Generosity can be seen in behaviors other than donating money. Volunteerism—a generosity of time, expertise, and energy given for the benefit of others—is perhaps an even stronger evidence of satisfying liberality. In a small study of high school students in British Columbia, investigators found that students who volunteered had lower levels of cholesterol and inflammation—markers of heart health.[11]

ARTICULATING YOUR FUTURE SELF

"People who wonder about their future exhibit an especially healthy form of curiosity, one that augurs greater well-being over time." So writes John D. Mayer, psychology professor at the University of New Hampshire. Citing continuing studies, Mayer finds evidence for what he terms "personal intelligence," the ability to name and integrate information about our personalities—our capacities to read faces, judge intentions, understand ourselves, and construct credible self-images for the future. Somewhat analogous to theory of mind, Mayer's framework suggests that people with greater personal intelligence are able to put together more accurate and realistic pictures of their future selves. These self-pictures can help them be more content with the trajectories of their lives. Detailed images of our future selves can help keep our present behaviors in line with the requirements of those future selves. Personal intelligence also helps people avoid the disabling effects of fantasy or fanciful imagination. (Implausible or wishful views about one's future self may be connected to risky behaviors such as drug use.)[12]

Although Mayer's research summary doesn't yet suggest concrete steps for attaining this skill set, his "personal intelligence" model fits well with research regarding wisdom and cognition.

WEALTH AND HAPPINESS

"Money can't buy you happiness." Research consistently affirms this truism from pop psychology. More accurately, there is little or no correlation between levels of income and levels of happiness. Wealthy people are neither more nor less happy than less wealthy people. (One notable exception: Money brings happiness only when it alleviates extreme poverty or financial distress.)

Investigations of the relationships between wealth and happiness yield consistent findings. They include the following:

- The relational, emotional, and physical costs of attaining wealth may outweigh its positive outcomes.
- Higher-paying jobs may produce higher levels of stressors that result in more anger, anxiety, and excitement.
- Within a year, lottery winners experience levels of life satisfaction at about the same levels as before they won millions of dollars.
- Britain's rising gross domestic product—one measure of general wealth—has not appreciably changed the levels of citizens' reported happiness.
- Even though the U.S. standard of living has risen dramatically over the last sixty years, Americans are not any happier now than they were back then.
- Other life factors—e.g., health, relationships, respect, purpose, and meaning—may be more important markers of well-being.[13]

Although the general tenor of these findings has remained consistent over decades, wealth-seeking remains a curiously durable phenomenon in individual and societal behaviors. The fear of poverty or death may continue to drive the desire for increased income. More ominously, the worldwide scandal of income disparities between the super rich and the rest of the citizenry may soon come to a head. Sullen discontent among the world's poorest peoples may turn into violent social movements that seek to correct the futile happiness-seeking of the most wealthy.

Smaller Strands of Positive Psychology

In matters of happiness and well-being, social science research continues to sow seeds. Let me summarize just a few of some intriguing kernels here:

HUMOR

Stand-up comic and psychologist Brian King reports on theories of humor and the effects of laughter. Among his learnings: Laughter can lower blood pressure, reduce stress-induced hormones, and increase the response of tumor-fighting and disease-killing cellular mechanisms. Laughter also improves memory, alertness, creativity, and learning.[14]

HAPPINESS AND MIDLIFE

One strand of positive psychology looks at relationships between satisfaction and a long life. An emerging body of research seems to indicate that people grow happier after their forties. Following the general shape of the U-curve, high life satisfaction occurs in the second and third decades of life, followed by a marked slump during one's fourth decade. The happiness curve edges upward again during a person's fifties, continuing until the inevitable decline of physical and mental capabilities late in life.[15]

MINDFULNESS AND NEGATIVITY

The applications of mindfulness training now extend into positive psychology. Amishi P. Jha, associate professor of psychology at the University of Miami, reports on research in this matter. When cognitive therapies are based in mindfulness practices, they can help alleviate negative emotional and physical conditions such as sadness, depression, other mood disorders, and stress-related ailments. Mindfulness may increase a patient's ability to deprive negative thoughts of their holding power.[16]

BURNOUT

Professors of psychology Michael P. Leiter (Acadia University in Nova Scotia) and Christina Maslach (University of California at Berkeley) describe the cycle of burnout and its amelioration. From their research, they extrapolate three main components of breakdown: exhaustion, cynicism, and inefficacy. Workplace unfairness seems to be a major trigger. The solutions center on improving workplace civility, and establishing respectful patterns of social interaction.[17]

The Stewardship Significance of Positive Psychology

Given the widening and deepening scope of happiness research—and a perhaps growing yearning for what it promises—it seems wise that you should continue to pay attention to this field of inquiry, as well as its applications to daily life stewardship. The possible impact of positive psychology on your congregation's stewardship ministry could have two possible directions, one perhaps filled with questions and cautions and the other overflowing with practicality. Let's take them in order.

A CAUTIONARY VIEW

Happiness can remain essentially shallow, evidence of immature narcissism or worse. In a culture whose economy is partially dependent on pleasure-seeking, happiness can be an eventually destructive force. Greek history and mythology tell the stories of the Sybarites and Odysseus's "lotus-eaters." In both cases, the results of hedonistic pleasure-seeking were not pleasurable. The enemies of the city of Sybaris—perhaps because of their envy of its extravagant opulence—destroyed the city many times over, leaving it in ruins that are barely distinguishable today. The mythological lotus-eaters—drugged into apathy and inactivity by their incessant consumption of a narcotic plant—served as an example of a pleasurably pathetic society doomed to failure.

Perhaps the Greeks were on to something. Research shows that the amount of leisure does not correlate positively with levels of happiness. The accumulation of wealth and possessions does not mark happy people. The pursuit of perpetual happiness is probably self-defeating, if only because that search flies in the face of reality: Overcoming adversity can also be deeply satisfying.

Although researchers have maintained the focus of positive psychology on measures of well-being and satisfaction, the term "happiness" has also invited into our culture easily achieved positive emotional states—and the savvy marketers who offer pleasure at every turn. Whatever hat or costume it wears, though, hedonism doesn't pass muster as a desired framework for measuring a life of stewardship.

AN APPRECIATIVE VIEWPOINT

Still, positive psychology could authenticate how a life of faith offers valuable assets for well-being such as empathy, forgiveness, generosity, or humility.

The rewards for spiritual attributes can be named in the language of positive psychology. Continuing research into the sources of emotional well-being will likely correlate with the teachings and lives of Jesus and other biblical figures. Where positive psychology warns about false happiness, those findings will add specificity to the age-old wisdom of the Scriptures. The body of research connecting faith and well-being may eventually offer scientific proof of what we already know to be true about contentment, happiness, and joy.

With both caution and appreciation in mind, you can assign stewardship-related significance to positive psychology. These observations:

1. Positive psychology might provide you with new frames of reference, new vocabulary, or new entry points into most of the life-related aspects of whole-life stewardship.

2. As hedonism and narcissism work their way into congregational life, your questions can bring both Scripture and science to bear on what are ultimately destructive ways of thinking.

3. Positive psychology and faith-based stewardship part ways in their answers to the question, "What's the purpose of being happy?" Positive psychology may not be able to include God-directed service in its answers; stewardship always does so.

4. Positive psychology can shift the entire direction of your congregation away from problems and difficulties. (For example, the question, "How can we fix what's wrong with this church?" can change to "What are the emotional strengths of this group of believers?")

5. The qualities of emotional well-being can also serve as standards you can use in the selection of congregational leaders, pastors, or other staff members.

6. As "the pursuit of happiness" continues to grow into a near-obsession in our culture, a spiritually oriented version might be an appealing part of your congregation's witness to the world, especially among young adults looking for purpose, meaning, or intimacy.

Just between You and Me

It has occurred to me that nowhere in this chapter have I considered the question, "What's rewarding or emotionally satisfying about being a steward?" Even if you're not expecting a reward for remaining a steward leader, perhaps that question deserves some comments:

- "Duty" language is not implicit in stewardship theology and practice. Being dutiful can invite a dour, sour outlook on life. (The older son in the Parable of the Prodigal Son comes to mind.)
- Happiness is not a reward for faithful stewardship. Instead, satisfaction and emotional well-being occur *at the same time* you exercise your roles as faithful stewards.
- The role of steward is always filled with privilege and opportunity, which probably function as unnamed qualities of happiness.
- As you have read about sources or results of happiness, I hope you've seen yourself reflected positively in some of these descriptions.

To be even more personal, here's how I experience satisfaction in my identity as a steward:

- I always feel blessed, even when life is difficult. (I live with cancer and I've been through some crushing emotional wringers in my life.)
- When I compare the challenges of being purpose-driven with the personal assets God has given me—I'm happy to be able to make a difference in the world! My lifework is fun!
- I'm surrounded by mature, contented, and happy people. I'm always glad to know that so many of us are working on this "God's will" thing!
- For any number of reasons, stewards can laugh. My sense of humor correlates positively with my happiness!
- When I'm thinking like a steward, I'm less able to think of myself as a minor god come to earth. That takes off a lot of the pressure of carrying the entire world on my shoulders!

Does any of this make sense to you? Good! Then let's go on to finish this chapter in a positive way.

What You Can Do

1. If you are responsible for teen or adult spiritual development, you might construct some learning experiences where positive psychology and godly virtues are placed side-by-side for comparison and contrast.
2. Engage in conversation with those congregation members who work in psychologically oriented professions. See where you have mutual

questions, mutual appreciation, and mutual hopes for this field of human inquiry.

3. If your congregation—or your personal leadership—has slipped into negativity, think of this attitude as a call to change.

4. If you participate in daily devotions, shift their focus over to joyful Psalms, some of the exquisite encouragements in the Wisdom literature, or the places in Jesus's and Paul's teachings where they gush with gladness.

5. Find and complete some "emotional well-being" survey instruments on the web. Even though they are not likely scientifically reliable or valid, see what the completed surveys tell you about your emotional style. How positive, contented, or satisfied are you?

6. Redirect the attention of people who look up to you—you are a leader, right?—when they start to follow the advice of self-help gurus.

As you consider how positive psychology might imbue your congregation's stewardship ministry with fresh or comforting content, remember that God's will always includes real and lasting abundance. As you serve the *economia* of God, be assured that God's continued blessings will leave you satisfied, content, and happy.

It's the joyful part of your work!

Notes

1. Another simple standard to consider: The average number of hours of sleep that people get each night. See Arianna Huffington, *Thrive: The Third Metric to Redefining Success and Creating a Life of Well-being, Wisdom and Wonder* (New York: Harmony Books, 2014), 108–11.

2. See James A. Roberts, *Shiny Objects: Why We Spend Money We Don't Have in Search of Happiness We Can't Buy* (New York: HarperCollins, 2011), 2.

3. Roberts, *Shiny Objects,* 5, 6, 15–16, 86–87, 159.

4. Roberts, *Shiny Objects,* 172, 175, 177ff, 188, 202ff.

5. Roberts, *Shiny Objects,* 262ff.

6. As reported in Tori Rodriguez, "How to Let Go of Materialism," *Scientific American*, July 2014, 17. The rest of Kasser's extensive explorations of materialism deserves your investigation at *https://www.knox.edu/academics/majors-and-minors/psychology/kasser-tim.*

7. See Brigid Shulte, *Overwhelmed: Work, Love and Play When No One Has the Time* (New York: Farrar, Straus, and Giroux, 2014), 7, 11, 22, 27, 28, 32, 34, 45, 48, 51, 53, 54, 179.

8. See Schulte, *Overwhelmed*, 208, 210, 243, 259–60.

9. From Everett Worthington, "Positive Psychology," the keynote presentation at the "Flourishing in Pastoral Ministry" Conference at Indiana Wesleyan University, Marion, IN, September 2013.

10. Excerpted from "Developing Positive Emotional Habits," presentation by Brian King (Institute for Brain Potential), Glen Ellyn, Illinois, May 17, 2013.

11. See Marina Krakovsky, "Generosity Is Its Own Reward," *Scientific American Mind*, September/October 2013, 9.

12. Mayer is also one of the authors of the internationally regarded Mayer-Solovey-Caruso Emotional Intelligence Test. See John D. Mayer, "Thinking about Tomorrow," *Scientific American Mind*, March/April 2014, 34–39. (The article is an adapted summary of Mayer's *Personal Intelligence: The Power of Personality and How It Shapes Our Lives* (New York: Scientific American/Farrar, Straus and Giroux, 2014.)

13. See Tali Sharot, *The Optimism Bias: A Tour of the Irrationally Positive Brain* (New York: Pantheon Books, 2011), 79–81, and King, "Developing Positive Emotional Habits" presentation.

14. King, "Developing Positive Emotional Habits" presentation.

15. See Jonathan Rauch, "The Real Roots of Midlife Crisis," *The Atlantic*, December 2014, 88–95.

16. Amishi P. Jha, "Being in the Now," *Scientific American Mind*, March/April 2013, 26–33.

17. See Michael P. Leiter and Christina Maslach, "Conquering Burnout," *Scientific American Mind*, January/February 2015, 30–35.

Chapter 14

Just Enough: Lifestyle

This chapter is about the way you live. More to the point, how you might live as a steward. It's a subject that could have filled this entire book. In fact, lifestyle-related thoughts currently fill entire issues of magazines, shelves full of books, and innumerable hosts of blogs. (More than enough about "just enough"?) I saved this subject until now for several reasons:

1. "Simple living" wraps into a single concept the core foundations of this book. Simplicity-seeking most completely answers the "So what?" questions that have arisen in each chapter.

2. Protestant Christianity may have enabled consumerism. Religion columnist and editor Rodney Clapp outlines the gradual absorption of consumeristic thought into the lifestyle principles of post-Reformation Christianity. Sentimentalism, revivalism, the sanctification of choice, the vaunted "Protestant work-ethic," elements of prosperity theology—each of these small seeds of pleasure-seeking have been fertile soil for the growth of continuing strains of Protestant theology. It's fair to ask ourselves whether we are called to remove the resulting weeds from our theology and our lifestyles.[1]

3. "Secular spirituality" can be found in simplicity seeking. Those who claim no faith—or at least no religion—sometimes see simple living as their expression of spirituality. Simple living is one of those places where secular-minded stewards can meet stewards-of-faith and find common spiritual stirrings.

4. The whole world is watching. The economy of the United States— embodied in the lifestyle of its citizens—is being watched throughout the world. Because of its promises of freedom, safety, comfort, and prosperity, "the American way of life" can be both mimicked and despised. Our lifestyles use a disproportionate amount of the planet's resources. As

they duplicate themselves around the world, our lifestyles help multiply environmental, political, and economic catastrophes.

5. God's *economia* extends to the whole world, and because we are stewards of that plan (or arrangement) we have a special responsibility to shift our entire way of living so that God's will for the entire world can be fulfilled.

6. We can't avoid this subject. The ecological, economic, and relational problems that have emerged because of hedonistic lifestyles are not going away by themselves. Still, God's Spirit equips us to extricate ourselves from the mess we've made of our God-given blessings.

The Tone and Direction of This Chapter

It would be easy to frame "simple living" as only a collection of lifestyle problems. I could load up your brain with descriptions of misguided time management. I could trot out statistics about how your children are being manipulated into early consumerism. I could rail against the brain-deadening effects of digital toys. Or I might list all the physical and mental ailments that correlate with frenetic, futile, or faithless lifestyles. That would be a juicy way to fill this chapter with content.

I've learned over the years, though, that this approach has some major problems. It contributes to information overload, which can clog your brain to the point of confusion, anger, or frustration. That kind of stress easily motivates you to freeze. (Along with fighting and fleeing, freezing is one of the ways we all respond to stress.) By describing lifestyle problems in detail, I would give them more power to overwhelm you, paralyzing you from taking action on any possible solutions.

Instead, I'm opting to focus on the question that has characterized the rest of this book: Where in the secular world is there wisdom that might help you and your congregation live out your stewardship?

I presume that simple living is something you've thought about before. The scriptural wisdom here is deep and broad, and already well known to those of us who follow Jesus. So the shift I'm proposing in this chapter is itself simple: Settle back into what you already know to be true, but with assurance and conviction.

Why Think about Lifestyle

This subject—how we live together on this planet—carries great significance for all the world's peoples. The following answers to "Why lifestyle steward-ship?" may illustrate the magnitude of this matter.

The Future of the World Hangs in the Balance.

It doesn't take too much probing to unearth general unease or anxiety about the ebbing of humanity's well-being. Evidence of impending collapses—economic, environmental, sociological, or political—cannot be easily ignored or dismissed.

The lifestyles of American consumers seem to be a primary cause for the ills of the world. For example, although the secondary reasons for worldwide hunger include war, destruction of arable land, pestilence, political instability, and unsustainable economies, under these contributing causes is usually a common source: the consumptive consumerism of American households.

In my years as a denominational hunger education executive, I learned about examples like these: Central American forestland is cleared to provide pastureland for cattle that supply North American appetites for fast food. Rural Mexican villages disintegrate as drug lords coopt entire regions for the production and northward distribution of illicit drugs. Chinese factories belch out pollution trying to keep up with the demand for inexpensive goods destined for use by American families. In each case, the well-being of others— usually people who are poor—is severely compromised so that lifestyles in the United States can be maintained.

Duane Elgin, consultant and author of the classic *Voluntary Simplicity: Toward a Way of Life That Is Outwardly Simple, Inwardly Rich*, talks about "our entry into a stage of civilizational crisis." He sees this as part of the cycle of human existence, which in our day has circled back to "a winter of civilizational breakdown." Elgin observes that our times are already characterized by cynicism, skepticism, and the dissolution of social consensus. Trust in leaders to solve problems? Rapidly declining. The "social glue" between people? Coming undone. His assessment at the time of the book's writing (1981) may be even truer today: If our lifestyles continue as they are, the gradual trajectory of societal collapse will demand wholesale changes no later than the 2020s![2]

Members' Lifestyles Determine Your Congregation's Life.

This truth is so obvious that it can hide in the open. Think about these possibilities:

- People whose daily schedules are rushed, hectic, or stuffed probably don't have the time to participate in the congregation's life.
- Families living at the edge of overconsumption may not have excess income from which to contribute generously to your congregation's mission.

- Members used to thinking of pleasure as the major determinant in their well-being may not accept easily a "theology of the cross."
- Individuals living with constant stress, worry, or anxiety seek love, intimacy, and understanding—not necessarily the added work of congregational committees or task forces.
- People devoted to purposed careers that also accomplish godly good may find it difficult to see your congregation as worthy of their time or effort.
- Members who are insatiable consumers may not be satisfied with programs that "don't meet our needs."
- Members immersed in overstimulated interactivity may need your congregation to be a place of quiet rest, not more activity.

In each case, your congregation might suffer a lack of attention, involvement, attendance, or contributions that is directly connected to lifestyles that are not manageable or sustainable. Instead of blaming yourself, your policies, or your style, consider how these lifestyle-related matters are actually the root cause of congregational malaise or decline. None of us likes to have our idols torn down, but ultimately our garden-variety idolatries stand in the way of our congregations' health.

VOLUNTARY SIMPLICITY IS STILL POSSIBLE.

"Pay now or pay later." So goes one of the maxims of business philosophy. For Elgin and other social critics, there is still time for simple lifestyles to have an effect on the world's downward slide. If involuntary simplicity eventually becomes a requirement for staying alive, it seems prudent to learn and practice the precepts of voluntary simple living now.

Elgin describes voluntary simplicity as "outwardly simple and inwardly rich." He defines the term as "a way of being in which our most authentic and alive self is brought into direct and conscious contact with living." According to Elgin, people who seek voluntary simplicity are joyful, deliberate, and purposeful; dependent on their awareness of themselves, others, and the world around them; adverse to distractions and open to possibilities.

Simplicity is *not* simple, according to Elgin. Finding balance among complex priorities is a continuing struggle. Although simplicity weighs less than complexity, it still requires effort to shoulder its responsibilities. Thankfully, living with less (noise, worry, possessions, hectic schedules) may result in living with more (fulfilment, satisfaction, relationships).

Voluntary simplicity can be easily misconstrued. Countering stereotypical ideas, Elgin maintains that a voluntarily simple life is not impoverished, confined to rural contexts, progress-adverse, or lacking in beauty, pleasure, or happiness. He is certain about this truth: Except for those among us who live with poverty, voluntary simplicity is attainable by all of us.[3]

MOST PEOPLE OF FAITH KNOW ABOUT THESE THINGS.

The most difficult part of your stewardship ministry may be addressing the sacred cows in congregation members' lives. ("Taking the bull by its horns" seems to fit here.) The opposite may in fact be true: Most of the members of your congregation know intuitively that this matter—how we live every day—is the elephant in the room. To further mix the metaphors, they know that it has to be tackled or shooed out.

Most members of your congregation feel some discomfort about the way the world is devolving. For some of them, this fact is painfully real—they have lost their jobs or faced medical emergencies—and are forced to live extremely Spartan lives. Others are coming to grips with lifestyle matters in their workplaces. Still others deal with the relational or societal effects of materialistic mindsets.

As you shift toward lifestyle matters as part of your stewardship ministry, remember the hopeful fact that the members of your congregation are ready, willing, and able to take up these questions!

Parsing Simple Living

Lifestyle stewardship elicits questions such as these: Why are so many of us chasing our existential tails in circles? How can we settle into the places where we want to be truly Christ-like? How can simple living become something real enough to seek, to hold onto, and to live out?

Simplicity is a complex phenomenon. In his *Simplexity: Why Simple Things Become Complex (and How Complex Things Can Be Made Simple),* Jeffrey Kluger, senior editor at *TIME Magazine*, writes about the interplay of simplicity and complexity. Kluger shows how confusion—about everyone else, our instincts, the social structure, the scale of things, fear, death, speed, success, our goals, flexibility, and even loveliness—can prevent us from finding a vantage point from which we can determine what's simple and what's complex. He suggests this "decidedly unscientific question" that can determine complexity or simplicity: "How difficult is it to describe the thing you are trying to understand?"[4]

My answers look like this: A lifestyle that is simple is first manageable. That means you can handle the size, speed, and scope of your lifestyle with joy. "Manageable" means that you can integrate the various pieces of your life within your larger goals and your deeper spiritual yearnings. When your lifestyle is manageable, it implies that you can plan enough of its features, or adapt nimbly enough to its changes. Manageability allows brain space for beauty, surprise, and delight. Manageable means that your brain's stress-chemicals don't stay at high-octane marks permanently. The term signifies that the levels of your agency, instrumentality, volition, and capacity in daily life match the demands of your chosen lifestyle.

When your lifestyle is manageable, it can also be sustainable—manageability continues over time. Just getting through every day is not a good sign that you're managing your life. Your simple living can be constructed around your answer to this question: How long can you keep on living this way?

Simple living may not be a state of being or frame of mind that can be measured as a whole. Instead, it's frangible, breaking up into tiny particles of behaviors and attitudes that may or may not coalesce into something that can be observed with assurance. If you confine simplicity to the cubic footage of your possessions, the speed or volume of your day's activities, the number of neurons you devote to a thought or act, or the decibel levels of ambient sound during your dinner time, you may have measured without finding meaning. If, on the other hand, you notice the ways in which continuing stress debilitates your physical and mental health—then you're getting a rough estimate of how manageable your lifestyle is. Continuing stress levels—strictly speaking, the number of cortisol-laced neuronal firings in your brain—might be a good measure of whether your lifestyle is simple or not.

Simple living may function in your life like all metaphors—a guiding concept that attracts other precepts, yearnings, curiosities, or ideals. "Simplicity-seeking" may be a better term to portray how Christians can approach their lives: always on a journey, never quite arriving at a destination we can only partially describe. A direction rather than a place.

Seeking Simplicity throughout Life

One frustrating aspect of simple living is its seemingly whack-a-mole character: You get your closets cleaned and organized, then realize that you're spending too much time following blogs written by other earnest declutterers. You say NO to several down-at-church volunteer opportunities and soon notice that spiritual loneliness has crept into your soul. You get so caught up in the details of living simply that you forget how to find pleasure overall. (The "Law of Unintended Consequences" comes to mind.)

In order to spread simplicity seeking into your entire life, it might be helpful to sharpen your awareness of the multiple places in your life where it's possible. Let me spend a few moments reminding you about these lifestyle niches. I'll include some questions to help you stay vigilant but not worried.

- *Attention:* The first and most essential quality of living. Who or what deserves your attention? Which attention-getters distract you, and which enrich your life? Who pays attention to you, and for what reasons? To what/whom would you like to give more attention?
- *Presence:* Your place at a single moment in a single space. What pulls you into the myth of multitasking? How do you remain appreciatively present anywhere and anytime? How might "time away" benefit your simplicity seeking? What or who slows you down into a manageable pace or place?
- *Possessions:* The useful material things that surround you. How can you find satisfaction in having fewer, less complex possessions? How might you compare the benefits of your possessions with their costs to your well-being? What keeps you from becoming trapped by consumerism?
- *Relationships:* The people who bring meaning to your life. Which relationships are key to your identity? Who loves you dearly, and whom do you love? What helps you initiate, strengthen, repair, or deepen relationships?
- *Noise:* Unwanted sound. Where/how do you find time and space for quiet? Who most respects your need for silence? For whom are you "noisy?" What noise-polluters could you avoid or eliminate?
- *Priorities:* Purposed choices that determine your lifestyle. What's your mission in life? What or who strengthens your priorities? How or when do you evaluate your choices and make necessary changes? How well do others know what's important to you?
- *Identity:* The core of your being, your ability to self-differentiate. How well do you know yourself? What do others name as your essential qualities? Who are your role models? Who learns from your lived-out identity?
- *Inner satisfaction:* The pleasure of enough. Who or what fills your life to overflowing? How do you resist "more"? When are you most content with your lifestyle?

- *Joy:* Unbound pleasure that reaches into your entire life and infects others. What or who makes you smile? Besides your possessions and your relationships, what else brings you joy? What are you grateful for? Who experiences joy because of you?
- *Hope:* A courageously positive attitude about the future. Where do you find hope? How do you sidestep hopelessness? What actions do you take to bring your hopes to fruition? In what ways is your lifestyle filled with hope?
- *Courage:* Persistently purposeful activity in the face of difficulties. How do you remain committed to living simply? How willing and able are you to stand out or stand up for what's right? To hold onto your authentic self?

Secular Lifestyle Wisdom

You might already know enough about simple living to make it part of your congregation's stewardship ministry. Scriptural wisdom—about self-idolatry, greed, materialism, other-mindedness, life purpose, humility, gratitude, and generosity—has provided you with highly useful information and motivation to live simply.

Secular sources for that wisdom are also available for your adoption or adaptation. In the following paragraphs I'll try to characterize some of that wisdom and where you might find it.

First, these few introductory observations:

1. What you might name as "secular" is frequently based on spiritual qualities or experiences. For example, some of the most insistent secular simplicity leaders have also experienced transcendent moments in the natural world, been motivated toward simplicity by shame and guilt about their own lifestyles, want to find redemption or forgiveness, or are willing to give away their lives for the sake of the whole world. Their spiritual insights are humbling.
2. Much of the secular wisdom about lifestyle is filled with scientific expertise—replicable experiences or theoretical constructs that fit together well. Leading a simple life, and inviting others to do the same, is perceived as a reasoned approach to living. Combined with metaphysical, mystical, or spiritual motivations, this wisdom seems rich and complete.
3. Secular simplicity seekers can be examples of both admirable and questionable lifestyles. Some are worth emulating and others serve as warnings.

4. Secular wisdom gets down to specifics—tactics, how-tos, new information—that fill in the blanks where wishful thinking or religious pronouncements end. Practicality augments broad principles.

Let's look now at some elements of secular lifestyle wisdom. I'll characterize each of these broad bands of thought, and provide you with some ways to follow up what you read here.

THE BIG PICTURE

Lifestyle stewards in the secular realm have done excellent conceptual work in describing how lifestyles affect almost every aspect of human existence. I've already cited Duane Elgin's *Voluntary Simplicity,* but can also recommend anything written by Bill McKibben, Frances Moore Lappé, Wendell Berry, Bill Moyers, Barbara Kingsolver, or Jared Diamond. The key value of their insights: They see how the smallest details of daily life can coalesce into large-scale problems for the world and its peoples. They also see how solutions could take the same developmental path.[5]

LIVING WITH LESS

One strand of secular (and religious) simplicity revolves around the principled necessity of consuming less. This tenet seems inescapable, if only because of the diminishing capacities of the planet to care for an increasing population. One of the original and most enduring resources for this kind of thinking remains: *Small Is Beautiful: Economics as if People Mattered,* written in 1973 by British economist E. F. Schumacher. Over the decades, other simple living adherents have added heft to Schumacher's broad strokes, providing specific suggestions for living joyfully and frugally, but with lowered expectations about what that might mean. A newer designation for this lifestyle: LBYM (Living Below Your Means).

Perhaps easily stereotyped for their insistent specificity about lifestyle matters, those who seek simplicity in this way are also the most admired—for their prophetic vision and for their willingness to practice what they preach.[6]

DEALING WITH MONEY

One cohort within the larger group of financial advisors specializes in money management that keeps simple living in mind. Among the most highly respected and longest lasting resources is *Your Money or Your Life,* by Vicki

Robin and Joe Dominguez. Hundreds of thousands of people have taken the course derived from this book, and many times that number have read it. What emerges from these experiences seem to be universal: changed attitudes and habits about money.[7]

FINDING LIKE-MINDED OTHERS

Those who have taken on simplicity-seeking as the core of their personal transformation sometimes speak of an existential loneliness. They can become strangers (or just strange) to their extended families or their friends. They can find themselves at odds with prevailing attitudes or ways of living. And they can't always find a sense of community—even in their churches. In the secular world, communal support can be carried out by informal relationships (social media, blogs-with-followers) and in more formal group memberships.

Over the years, several of these kinds of associations, cohorts, or guilds have emerged. The most recent example is The Center for the New American Dream (*www.newdream.org*). Founded in 1997, this group has taken an additional step beyond disseminating information. Among their programs is "Collaborative Communities"—groups of simple living "New Dreamers" form around the country. This effort seems to be well-supported with resources, staff, and volunteers.[8]

THE SHARING ECONOMY

In the past ten years, a significant change in consumerism has emerged. In the "sharing" economy, buyers and sellers transact the purchase of goods and services directly with each other. These transactions bypass traditional forms of exchange. Some of the purposes of the sharing economy seem to be consonant with the ideals of simple living. At the time of this writing, smartphone apps can now connect you with services that enable the sharing of cars and transportation services, homes, meals, garden plots, clothing, home goods, and parking spots.

This growing segment of the worldwide economy also attracts justifiable criticism—e.g., those most in need of sharing may not be able to take advantage of it, and these services may be displacing service-economy workers. Over time, this shift in the economy may disrupt large sectors of traditional business cultures. As its pros and cons shake out—e.g., how could "sharing" take place without being monetized?—the sharing economy may offer some larger good to society.[9]

QUESTIONABLE EXAMPLES

Strangely enough, one of the most important sources of secular lifestyle wisdom may exist between the covers of glossy journals with "Simple" on their masthead. Here the wisdom comes not from what the magazine proposes as helpful, but from readers' critique. Simplicity chic rarely provides useful hints or insights. Still, under the blatant consumerism of these publications, there are occasional flashes of lifestyle wisdom, even if it's only "Don't do this."

MOTIVATING EXAMPLES

The blogosphere is filled with the helpful observations of people living simply. Along with social media twitterings, these blogs may not seem to add much to the body of knowledge about living simply, but their contributions may be even more valuable. Each of these intense practitioners opens a window on the feelings—the soul—of simple living. Their writing exposes their most sincere desires, most difficult problems, and most instructive experiences. Their testimony can be inspiring.[10]

LIFE COACHING

Life coaches provide for individuals with out-of-control lives the benefit of an outside observer, advisor, counselor, or partner. Life coaches help restore order, sanity, or enjoyment into lifestyles that may be overburdened by possessions, debts, responsibilities, failure, or soured relationships.[11]

DECLUTTERERS

Emerging from the field of life coaching is another source of secular wisdom about lifestyle: "Declutterers"—courageous individuals who will come into your life and detoxify your home, office, car, garage, or other personal space. The wisdom here is both practical and personal. These individuals, also known as "professional organizers," can help you change the attitudes that might have caused disabling disorder. Declutterers can be especially helpful in places where hoarding has gotten out of control.[12]

OCCUPATIONAL THERAPY

Early in its history, this unique form of therapy focused on those who were mentally ill. Over several decades, occupational therapists have expanded the original vision of their profession's usefulness to include physical as well as mental dysfunctions—so that patients might function well in any of their roles or "occupations." (For occupational therapists, this term denotes all aspects of a full, productive life.)

As a source for stewardship wisdom, occupational therapists—not to be confused with physical therapists—can address some of the psychosocial elements of simplicity-seeking. They can help their clients examine and establish healthy routines and habits. They can assist those they serve to reframe their identities and work toward achievable goals. They can guide their patients away from depression. They can help their patients revive a sense of personal power and willingness to affect change. Although simple living is not usually the primary focus of their work, occupational therapists are skilled at bringing sustainable well-being into people's lives. It makes sense that this kind of wisdom could cross over into simplicity-seeking.[13]

SIMPLE PARENTING

One of the more hopeful streams of simplicity-seeking is directed at family life. Why hopeful? Because long-lasting lifestyle attitudes and skills are formed in families. Parents can be equipped to deal with the vagaries of peer pressure—a subtle form of lifestyle bullying—and default cultural presumptions. With training, parents are more likely to help their children resist temptations to adopt consumerist lifestyles.[14]

What You Can Do

If you've decided to absorb this focus in your congregation's stewardship ministry, you might try some of these ideas:

1. Begin a simple living conversation with someone you trust. (Remember that heartfelt conversation is a primary source and motivation for any change.) Any conversation about simplicity becomes earnest, personal, and emotional fairly quickly!

2. f you've decided to undertake any of the shifts promoted in previous chapters, see how simplicity-seeking might be a first step. Conceptually and pragmatically, simple living connects to any of the subjects in this book.

3. Think how "simple living" might also apply to the workings of your congregation—its programs, levels of staffing, organizational structure, sense of purpose, or vision.

4. To be even more insistent about this shift, evaluate the ways in which your congregation might deter members—especially committed leaders—from their own simplicity-seeking.

5. If your congregation already encourages simple living, double-check the tone of that encouragement to be sure that it remains positive, hopeful, and joyful. You want to foster change, not shame and guilt.

6. If your congregation's committee structure has shrunk down to only a few active committees, combine their mission into a "lifestyle enrichment task force."

7. Offer community-wide workshops or seminars that improve skills or wisdom in simplicity-related topics such as recycling, stress reduction, preparation for retirement, or frugality. Make the events celebratory.

8. See where your cycle of sermon texts already includes simplicity-related matters. Remember to proclaim both Law and Gospel.

9. Consider recasting your congregation's identity as a place where simplicity is welcomed. "We're the people who keep it simple" could be the tag line on your publicity.

10. Institute more sharing practices within your congregation. People might come together for shared meals; borrow each other's equipment or tools; cooperate in childcare or eldercare; collect and redistribute food coupons; or group-tutor each other's children.

11. Start a cooperative blog, social media page, newspaper column, or website that collects simple living insights for your whole community. Feature local residents who understand and practice some elements of simplicity.

12. Assemble a cadre of "simplicity experts" whose wisdom you can tap. Think of people on fixed incomes, trash collectors, grocery store workers, long-term unemployed people, young parents, social studies teachers, marriage counselors, mental health professionals, recent retirees, handymen, and other trade-workers. Gather them together periodically for a potluck breakfast or dessert hour. Hold the gatherings somewhere other than your church basement.

However you begin or continue simple living, rest assured that this wisdom can benefit the people of your congregation and help bring more than enough of God's blessings to the whole world.

Notes

1. The article is even more specific: Calvinist understandings of lifestyle may have inadvertently created a theological atmosphere that allowed consumerism, at the same time decrying it. Rodney Clapp, "Why the Devil Takes VISA," *Christianity Today*, October 7, 1996, 4–6.

2. Duane Elgin, *Voluntary Simplicity: Toward a Way of Life That Is Outwardly Simple, Inwardly Rich*, rev. ed. (New York: William Morrow, 1993), 163–75.

3. Elgin, *Voluntary Simplicity*, 24, 25, 26–31.

4. In each of his chapters, Kluger relates how axioms, algorithms, formulas, predictive analysis, statistical probabilities, and theories can add to both the simplicity and complexity of any matter. Perhaps the same is true of simple living? Jeffrey Kluger, *Simplexity: Why Simple Things Become Complex (and How Complex Things Can Be Made Simple)* (New York: Hyperion, 2008), 26, 304.

5. Among my favorites: McKibben's *Eaarth: Making a Life on a Tough New Planet* (New York: Henry Holt and Company, 2010); Lappé's *Hope's Edge* (New York: Jeremy P. Tarcher/Putnam, 2003); Diamond's *Collapse* (New York: Viking, 2005); and Berry's *Selected Poems* (New York: Counterpoint, 1998).

6. Among the examples I am familiar with: *Mary Hunt's Cheapskate Monthly* (*www.everydaycheapskate.com*); Doris Janzen Longacres's *The More-With-Less Cookbook* (Scottdale, PA: Herald Press, 1976); and Jim Merkel's *Radical Simplicity: Small Footprints on a Finite Earth* (Gabriola Island, BC: New Society Publishers, 2003). (This is his first-person account of how to measure ecological "footprints" as a way to assess your lifestyle).

7. Lynne Twist's *The Soul of Money: Reclaiming the Wealth of Our Inner Resources* (New York: W. W. Norton, 2003) approaches simplicity with attention to inner tranquility and satisfaction. *Your Money or Your Life,* by Vicki Robin and Joe Dominguez (New York: Viking, 1992) remains a classic, practical resource for acting your way into thinking. The no-nonsense advice of Suze Orman frequently alludes to lifestyle-related matters. Hosts of details-rich websites dedicated to personal finance (e.g., *www.simplethriftyliving.com*) also offer insights about money matters with simple living in mind.

8. Communal support is one of the functions of congregations. Similar secular groups can be important sources of wisdom—about organizing and supporting local communities of practice—for your simplicity-shifted congregation.

9. Joel Stein, "On-Demand Economy," *TIME Magazine*, February 9, 2015, 32–40. Stein notes that "the sharing economy is really the experience economy, and more specifically the experience-it-right-now economy."

10. One long-lived blog that caught my attention recently: Happy Simple Living (*www.happysimpleliving.com*).

11. Should you want to avail yourself of the services of a life coach, inquire about the person's training or experience. Membership in the International Coaching Federation (ICF) indicates that the coach has been trained and accredited under rigorous standards of ethics. (See *www.coachfederation.org* for further information.) Among the many books that help form life coaches is one I consider my personal bible in this field: *A Generous Presence: Spiritual Leadership and the Art of Coaching,* by life and writing coach Rochelle Melander (Herndon, Virginia: The Alban Institute, 2006).

12. In the United Kingdom, the Association for Professional Declutterers and Organizers (APDO) makes a distinction between those who merely clean up a messy living space (declutterers) and those who leave behind a system of tidiness that can be continued (organizers). Point well-taken. These folks have more wisdom to offer at *www.apdo-uk.co.uk.*

13. My inklings about the possible stewardship wisdom of occupational therapists come from descriptions of this profession's historical and therapeutic inclinations in Gary Kielhofner, ed., *A Model of Human Occupation: Theory and Application,* 1st ed. (Baltimore: Williams & Wilkins, 1985), vii, ix, 248ff.

14. Among the secular sources for this kind of day-to-day approach to simple living, you might want to read—and discuss—*Simplicity Parenting: Using the Extraordinary Power of Less to Raise Calmer, Happier and More Secure Kids* (New York: Ballantine Books, 2009). The authors are Kim John Payne (family counselor, educator, and parenting coach) and Lisa M. Ross (writer and editor). An accompanying blog and newsletter grace the book's website. (*www.simplicityparenting.com*).

Chapter 15

The Gallimaufry Chapter: Miscellany

In the world of gastronomy—another part of stewardship?—one question always remains after any meal is cooked, served, and eaten: What shall we do with the leftovers? In most cultures, that question is answered by shrewd chefs in a simple way: create a tasty concoction, comprised solely of what remains. For the French, that motley mixture of foodstuffs is called a gallimaufry—literally "a hash made from leftovers." The etymology of the term suggests pleasurable eating.

This concept, this term, and this etymology describe what I hope you find in this chapter of the book: a tasty collection of the conceptual bits and pieces of content that didn't quite make their way into the rest of the book. I hope that what you consume here will give you pleasure.

In the pages of this chapter, I'll include summaries of several other fields of human endeavor that might also offer secular stewardship wisdom. I'll trust that your curiosity about any of these subjects will compel you to search further for deeper applications of these matters to your stewardship ministry.

Where Good Ideas Come From

It might be important for you to remember how useful ideas emerge. To that end, let me summarize the insights of prolific science writer Steven Johnson, whose volume, *Where Good Ideas Come From,*[1] unfolds this subject with fascinating details and stories. Johnson suggests seven answers to the implied question of the book's title.

- *The adjacent possible:* Ideas come from what's next to them. Here "adjacent" is more than physical proximity, suggesting that the doors of every idea open into the rooms of other ideas. (Mental health professionals consider answers to questions that wisdom researchers might also ask.)

- *Liquid networks:* The richness, flow, and plasticity of an idea enable it to form networks of other ideas that affect what occurs next. (Gerontology might eventually move or morph its way into the exploration of a congregation's "stewardship of death and dying.")

- *The slow hunch:* Good ideas can take a long time to hatch. Sometimes the incubation period might involve decades of pursuing a subject—or leaving it alone—before a *kairos* moment arrives. The key to this source of good ideas: The hunch has to stay alive during those years. (The early simple living prophets exemplify this matter.)

- *Serendipity:* Good ideas seize order out of chaos, or at least recognize the shape of a possible pattern. The formation of good ideas is nearly accidental and perpetually unpredictable. (A seemingly obscure scriptural term may suddenly materialize as the key insight connecting the effects of altruism with the doctrine of the Holy Spirit.)

- *Error:* What seems to be a mistake or fault can become a good idea. A miscalculation or blunder can be seen in a different light or put to use for different purposes. By definition, a few good ideas are dependent on the presence of many "bad ideas." (Our culture's infatuation with digital toys may turn out to be the source for new forms of interconnectivity, influence, or inspiration within congregations.)

- *Exaptation:* This term—using something for a different purpose than its originally intended function—applies to ideas that are borrowed from one field, perhaps accidentally, and given greater utility in another. (The findings of behavioral economists might form the core of a series of stewardship Bible studies.)

- *Platforms:* Good ideas live inside of the contexts that surround and enliven them. The broader the conceptual platform, the more likely its capability to house and nurture good ideas. (Neurobiology's search for "consciousness" may be the best platform for understanding the self-identity of an *economos*.)

The purpose for this side trip? To suggest that the "lesser ideas" in this chapter might be major sources of wisdom for your stewardship ministry. Especially if you remember how good ideas can form!

A Collection of Miscellaneous Secular Wisdom

In the following paragraphs I outline several subject areas or fields of study that you might consider investigating.

LEADERSHIP DEVELOPMENT AND ORGANIZATIONAL DEVELOPMENT

Leadership seems important to almost every human enterprise, so almost every leader looks for the elusive qualities that might distill order from what seems to be chaotic, complex, or unsatisfying. Several sources for leadership wisdom deserve your attention:

- Trailblazers who apply recent research in social science.
- Writers with years of successful experience as consultants or organizational mentors.
- Strategic thinkers who are ferreting out qualities of exemplary organizations.
- Leaders who have constructed successful and long-lived training programs.

Among the stewardship-related questions that these organizational development professionals and leadership experts can answer are the following:

- How can I develop other leaders, not just accumulate followers?
- What parts of organizational development practices can apply to congregations?
- What's central to effective leadership?
- How can congregations lower their expectations and yet prosper?
- What can be done about perpetually ineffective leaders?

POLITICAL SCIENCE AND ELECTIONS

At its core, political science can explain noble sentiments that coincide with stewardship principles: freedom, personal responsibility, liberality, pursuit of the common good, individual rights, love of country, peace, or the elimination of poverty. Political scientists also frame critiques of government or political processes—e.g., elections—that are being coopted by oligarchs or leaders who have only their own self-interest in mind.

Stewardship leaders can learn important lessons from political science. The art of persuading and mobilizing citizens can be a model for soliciting congregational energy. Critiques of political or governance processes can also be applied to congregational dynamics. "The greatest good" could be compared to "God's will." The dimensions and uses of power—a staple of political theory—might inform your leadership. As you learn to approach politics and politicians with civility, clarity, and respect, you can learn to speak of stewardship (lifestyle/money/goals) in the same ways. The subtleties of political or election-cycle research can help you frame your congregation's approaches to stewardship-related subjects—e.g., preferences, goals, priorities.

From political science and the dynamics of elections, you might find answers to stewardship-related matters such as these:

- Why do people vote or make decisions that are clearly not in their economic self-interest?
- How are decisions actually made in a large group?
- How might mass hysteria affect a group's assumption or pursuit of noble goals?
- How does humility help or hinder effective congregational leadership?
- How might the dynamics of elections instruct your congregation's anointing of leaders?

SOCIAL JUSTICE ENTERPRISES

The vast worldwide movement toward social justice has continued to grow larger over several decades. Although they are sometimes invisible, proponents of justice continue to form coalitions of like-minded leaders, adherents, and organizations.

Christians are not the sole claimants in owning this historic moment, nor are we necessarily the most effective force in bringing justice to bear on the world God loves. You can align yourself with secular leaders and organizations in areas such as racial justice, hunger/poverty, politics, gender equality, tax reform, refugee and immigration policy, job training, housing, education, or advocacy focused on corporate responsibility—all possible elements of stewardship ministry focused on God's *economia* for the whole world.

Leaders and resources from these organizations might help you in any number of ways. Smaller nonprofit organizations and for-profit companies target specific needs or niche opportunities. Accurate data regarding social justice matters—as well as careful analysis of that data—is readily available. These organizations can create flashpoints that call for concerted attention, energy, and expertise among church members. Some of these groups have proven that they are attractive to emerging generations. These organizations produce notable publications or events worthy of congregation members' attention. Social justice heroes, stars, or spokespersons—some of whom operate from a spiritual core—work within these groups. These enterprises can attract socially responsible investing, which also makes them sources for grants, expertise, or partnerships.

As social justice efforts spread across the world, stewardship leaders may find willing teachers among a growing cadre of highly committed social justice activists. Social justice enterprises can answer compelling questions about stewardship, such as:

- How do these organizations attract attention in the society?
- What compels participants in these organizations to contribute their energy, time, and money?
- How have these enterprises learned from their mistakes?
- To what do their leaders pay attention?
- Which of these organizations could be partners in your congregation's ministries?

BEHAVIORAL ECONOMICS

Just a few years ago, the "dismal science" of economics was rocked by the research and conclusions of a seemingly renegade group who came to be called "behavioral economists." Their basic working premise: The study of economics should be based less on time-honored theories—rooted in the presumptions of enlightened self-interest—and more on the actual behaviors of people. The findings of these economists now serve as the bedrock for the axioms, algorithms, and approaches of effective marketing and advertising. At the center of the research is the startling reality that people make economic decisions that they know are not in their best interest. Another proven fact: We are easily persuaded. Still another: Our skill at fooling ourselves is sometimes stronger than our ability to discern truth.

Given that most memories and self-perceptions are tilted toward inaccuracy or self-delusion, it is always important to sharpen what we hold to be true about stewardship. The costs of ministry that congregation members are willing to bear might be explained better by behavioral economics than by fond hopes. As it continues to develop, social reciprocity theory may offer proven methods by which to increase funding of congregational ministries.

Some questions that behavioral economics might shed light on:

- How do church members measure the (economic) value of their congregations?

- Which parts of behavioral economics also apply to members' donations of attention, time, and expertise to congregational programs?
- Is self-delusion a phenomenon you simply name, or one you try to correct?
- How strongly are (behavioral) economic considerations the key factor in your congregation's decision-making, purpose or identity?
- Which parts of accepted behavioral economics coincide with stewardship?

Although this field of inquiry is presently oriented toward explanations of economic behavior in commercial spheres, its findings can become increasingly useful in the day-to-day operation of congregations. Steward leaders might want to seek out congregation members who apply behavioral economic theories in their daily work. (These members might work as sales professionals, professors of economics, recent MBA graduates, marketing gurus, agronomists, or advertising professionals.)

GERONTOLOGY

Research into the processes of aging has increased our knowledge of both the problems and the opportunities in growing older. Congregational stewardship ministry can certainly focus on the problematic aspects of aging— decreased capabilities, dysfunction, chronic and life-ending maladies, or poverty. From that viewpoint, care-giving aspects of stewardship ministry might continue to be a helpful part of congregational life.

Perhaps more forward-looking are the capabilities and assets of older adults whose lives remain full, whose hopes are strong, and whose inclinations to follow Christ remain undiminished by time or circumstance. Rather than seeing the presence of "seniors" in your congregation as a sign of its slow death, you might think of them as "elders"—respected, cherished, and useful guides, truth-tellers and active leaders. Gerontology and its related fields could be helpful in that shift.

The front edges of gerontology include newer findings about neurogenesis (revitalization of neuronal circuits); the impact of technologies in enhancing the well-being of older adults; early diagnosis and treatment of life-altering physical conditions; pharmacological discoveries; retirement preparation for Baby Boomers; and lifestyle factors that correlate with late-life health and vitality.

Research into the quality of life that members might experience in their later years could help your congregation answer questions such as these:

- What inheritances—of faith, knowledge, expertise, wisdom, or financial resources—exist within the cohort of older congregational members, and how can these legacies be passed on?
- In what ways can intergenerational relationships benefit both elders and younger members?
- How could stewardship ministry include awareness training related to death and dying?
- How best does a congregation engage its older members as attention-worthy leaders?
- How does your congregation get over "millennials anxiety"—worry about the real or imagined absence of young adults—and celebrate the assets of its older members?

TECHNOLOGY CRITIQUE

Unless economic collapse, cataclysms in the natural world or political conflict increase rapidly, the flood of technological change will not likely diminish. As a stewardship leader, you are left with vexing questions that help you determine whether technological change enables or disables stewardship ministries:

- Which aspects of stewardship theology or practice are thwarted by digital inventions? (How do social media platforms steal time from other worthwhile activities?)
- Which technological marvels enable God's *economia*? (How has world hunger been reduced measurably because of new technologies?)
- Among the subtle presumptions guiding the development of new technologies, which of them violate the most basic tenets of steward-ship? (How might self-idolatry prosper because of the utopian promises of technology?)

A small and insistent group of social critics has continued to raise questions about the effect of technology on the human condition. Perhaps not as easily noticed as the technologies they criticize, these lifestyle prophets might be especially helpful when some parts of the technology bubble burst. Because your congregation's stewardship ministry is directly affected by members' purchase, use, or dependence on various technologies, you might benefit from expert criticism about technology's reach.

The still-forming field of technology critique might help your discern-ment in matters such as these:

- What's the difference between a toy and a tool?
- What are the net effects—the entire range of costs—for technological dependence?
- How can a congregation be both wary of and inventive with technology?
- Which addictions can technology feed? Which can it break?
- How might various kinds of technology increase or diminish your sense of living purposefully for God's will?

PHYSICAL/MENTAL HEALTH

The care and maintenance of our bodies and minds seems a natural focus for stewardship ministry. Available to all congregations are current findings about mental and physical health conditions such as obesity, bullying, diabetes, exercise, dieting, autism, depression, vaccinations, pharmacology, epidemics, addiction, or health assessment. Health-oriented journals, blogs, social media sites, films, and videos proliferate. The most reputable of these resources provide scientifically verified knowledge. Congregations that promote parish health can find expertise as close as their local school district, health department, insurance agent, or medical practice.

Among the stewardship-related questions answered by health professionals are these:

- What practices, events, or programs in our congregation might increase or inhibit health?
- How do we strengthen each other's resolve to be healthy?
- How well does our congregation accept and minister to people with mental illness?
- What is our responsibility for correcting false or harmful information about health?

EPIGENETICS

This multidisciplinary body of knowledge and experimentation examines the ways in which the genetic material in our cells can be changed by lifestyles and diet. Perhaps even more startling: Epigeneticists are finding that some of those genetic changes can be inherited by our offspring. It seems possible that our stewardship of God's will right now might affect the genetic material that effects the future development of God's plan for the world. Some examples:

Curbing the worldwide epidemic of obesity now might result in inherited dispositions that decrease rates of diabetes, heart problems, or cancer. Attention to the diets of people in developing countries now might strengthen genetic armaments that ward off diseases for generations to come.

Among the questions that this emerging field of study might address are these:

- Besides purely physical traits, which inherited dispositions or temperaments might be strengthened by attention to lifestyle and diet?
- Which stewardship choices are most important for the future of our offspring? For the world in which they will live?
- How might congregations be sources or sites for experimentation or study in this field?
- In what ways does epigenetics encourage stewardship as a response to God's goodness?

EXPERTISE STUDIES

This field first emerged a few decades back as a small blip on social science radar screens. Expertise studies look at high levels of know-how that endure over time. Interest in expertise seems especially strong in business, industry, government, and education. The field continues to offer important approaches to training, learning theory and technology, employee compensation, management style, and organizational development. Some basic presumptions of expertise studies: Expertise is a desired quality in all human enterprises. Expertise is available to all people and lasting expertise can be achieved through careful application of techniques.

Congregations interested in this variety of secular wisdom might find answers to questions such as these:

- How can members become proficient in church-related skills such as personal witnessing, prayer, or care for others?
- Where in a congregation's life do the people of God find opportunities to practice life-related skills—e.g., forgiveness, listening, or conflict resolution?
- How might a congregation evaluate the existing expertise of prospective professional or lay leaders?
- What aspects of "pastoral expertise" are always going to be elusive or unmeasurable?

- What expertise is already available within the membership of your congregation?

What You Can Do

Permit me these general observations about further investigation of any of these miscellaneous sources of secular wisdom:

1. Don't chase every rainbow that appears in the sky. The pace and scope of streams of secular wisdom are too quick and too substantial for you to absorb completely.
2. Not everything that's new is necessarily better.
3. Anchor your search and discernment in a trusted concept or mindset. Most likely you can find that mooring in the Scriptures, your fervent desire to serve God's will, or the wisdom of others.
4. When you are searching for secular wisdom, ask yourself questions such as these: What's missing here? Where does this wisdom work and where does it fall short? What details are left out and which unintended consequence are likely? Who benefits from the adoption or adaptation of this wisdom?

Above all, continue to be on the lookout for the next wise thing—an important development that has survived fad-of-the-month status. With the assurance that God continues to reveal God's will in both sacred and secular wellsprings, you can find sources for wisdom right under your nose, on the distant horizon, or even in the motley mixtures of daily life.

In the gallimaufries.

Notes

1. Steve Johnson, *Where Good Ideas Come From: The Natural History of Innovation* (New York: Riverhead Books, 2010), chapters 1–7.

Chapter 16

Shifting into "Next": Continuing Thoughts

These final pages bring to its end a book that will likely continue to be written—in your mind and in your actions. I'll use these final pages to offer some observations that I hope will help you continue your stewardshifting.

Revisiting "So What"

One of the important questions that we've considered in every chapter is "So what?" (What good will come of this?) When answered with honesty and hope, "so what" can also become a strange motivator. (As in, "If this idea survives tough scrutiny, perhaps it merits some tough work.")

A New Kind of Congregation

If you required me to answer this book's "So what?" as an elevator speech, I'd say this: When stewardship shifts, so will congregations. In a longer version, I'd expand my answer to include the following thoughts.

The functional value of Christian congregations remains strong. We (God's people) have been given what the world needs. We've also been presented with more possibilities and challenges than what we imagine now. Our stewardship of God's will—it's what we do well—extends past any desperation about institutional survival. As our congregations disperse into daily life, members' behaviors transform the context in which members live. God's *economia* is layered onto daily life by God's *economos*.

The shifting trends in our culture are not going to support the present format of congregations for very much longer. Primary among those trends is the gradual movement of financial support away from congregations and denominations. Another, perhaps more significant change: The relevance of the institutional church may also diminish. Not good.

What can be good, though, is the ability of congregations to change shape. They have the capability to ask bigger questions—about identity, structure, purpose, staffing—and to answer forthrightly. (The "emerging church" movement is one current example.) Equally exciting is the growing ferment for change that makes most congregations emergent entities as well. They are discarding unusable or untenable assumptions, rerooting themselves in Scripture—especially the witness of Jesus—and taking big risks in order to comprehend how best to serve God in these times. An elevator exultation: Churches are already shifting!

Continuing the Shifting

I have purposely saved one understanding of "shift" until now: the idea of changing gears. In order to get the greatest results out of an automobile's engine, you have to drive in the right gear. If you want to torque your way out of a ditch, you use one gear. If you want to cruise along a highway with high fuel efficiency, you use another one. You don't go forward in Reverse, and Neutral gets you nowhere while still slurping up fuel. If you shift into Park while moving along, you may destroy the transmission. And think what a useless invention an automobile would be if it had only one gear!

This analogy might fit your thinking about how to change stewardship ministry in your congregation: Going backward—to the imagined "glory days" of congregational vitality thirty years ago—will get you nowhere fast. Parking or idling in stewardship Neutral renders your congregation basically useless. Using a lower gear, you might be able to move quickly, making changes in your stewardship ministry that get you out of the ditches, quagmires, or snowbanks in which you are mired. But if you stay in those lower gears—reliance on quick-fix tactics, splashy programs, or charismatic leadership—you'll expend a lot of energy and probably burn up the engine. On the other hand, if you try to begin any changes in stewardship ministry in a higher gear—a heavy-duty evaluation, planning, or transformation process—your congregational motor will stall. Too much of a load for too high a gear. What's best? Using all the gears, shifting them wisely.

How might you shift the gears of your congregation's stewardship ministry? Some additional observations:

- *One shift at a time:* You can't make all the changes that I've outlined in this book. There are too many possibilities—even inside of one area of secular wisdom. Trying to do everything all at once immediately every time—that's probably another way to describe foolishness.

- *One action to start with:* It's better to pick one body of secular wisdom as a place to start. (Or perhaps choose a few concepts that seem to cluster together.) Consider any chapter's explicit and implicit invitations to action. Pick a first step, and complete it as soon as possible.

- *One area of expertise:* As you think about which of these sets of wisdom you might use as another basis for your stewardship ministry, you might want to choose a field of study that you're already familiar with, where some expertise already exists in your congregation, or where you've already begun shifting.

- *One multitude of possibilities:* Think "what-if." Do some dreaming, some emergent thinking, looking past the obvious. This doesn't involve wild-eyed creativity. Do the kind of thinking that combines two and two and comes up with twenty-two instead of only four!

- *One reason:* Keep focused on the major reason for all this shifting: equipping your members to be effective stewards of God's will out there in their worlds of influence, relationships, or power.

Back to Emergent Thinking

Some shifting can't be planned—it just happens! That kind of thinking might help you shift your congregation's stewardship ministry more toward members' total lives. How might that happen? Consider these possibilities.

- *Spot word patterns:* With your congregation's stewardship ministry in mind—and a possible content area dangling in front of you—go back through a relevant chapter, circling words and phrases that strike your eye. When that task is complete, look for patterns, connections, if/then relationships, or a possible flow between the circled items. What does all of this suggest for what's next in your thinking or acting?

- *Revisit Scripture and theology:* Spend time with the scriptural or theological sections of this book. Pray or meditate about questions such as these: Where do you sense God's tuggings? God's assurances? God's challenges? Write out your tentative responses. What thought shapes reoccur? Which ideas land closest to your personal identity as a steward?

Which match your congregation's yearnings—including those that are unspoken?

- *Trace idea paths:* Follow a single train of thought as far as it leads. (For example, you could track generosity-related themes throughout this book, and note their appearance in other resources, other connections, other actions.) When you get to the end of a trail, give the destination and the trail a name. Now retrace your steps to the start of your thinking. What do you notice? What did you miss the first time through? What seem to be the strongest possibilities for changed thinking and changed actions?

- *Celebrate:* You can find joy in stewardshifts that are already underway. Mark all the places in this book where your congregation has already begun absorbing new wisdom from scriptural or secular sources, and where you're already taking action on what you know. How will you speak gratefully about these developments, and build on what you've accomplished so far?

- *Start a conversation:* Talk with someone else about what you've read. Conversation helps your brain organize previously unconnected thoughts into logical sequences, hierarchies, or collections of ideas. Better yet, include food or libation with the conversations, and continue them over time. Soon enough, a new idea or organizing thought will arise from the dialogue. And a shift will have begun!

Shifting Away from Only Piety

Your love of God, the church, or the Bible can be summed up as "piety." In any spiritual lexicon, piety (pious thought) is a good thing. Piety inoculates you from self-idolatry. Your devotion to God helps you make sense out of matters that logic alone cannot fathom—e.g., forgiveness, hope, grace, faith itself. Piety provides its own rewards: The more you examine or proclaim your devout feelings about God, the stronger they become. That strengthened piety then engenders further acts of devotion. This self-reinforcing cycle of spiritual motivation can be effective and long-lasting.

When it comes to living as a steward, though, piety by itself may not be enough. Devout feelings can mask or pass over objective realities that also require attention. Framing congregational ministries—stewardship included—with only pious reverence can short-circuit other spiritually valuable thought processes—e.g., discernment, wariness, causality, calculation, or planning. When piety trumps or overwhelms logic and reason, stewardship decisions might be made solely on the basis of piety-focused emotions.

Without piety, stewardship could become merely transactional. Without reason, stewardship might not accomplish its goals. Because stewards also depend on wisdom, skill, and reason, a balance of devotional and cognitive mindfulness seems necessary.

Not Rocket Science

As you approach your chosen focus and process for stewardshifting, keep in mind its essential simplicity. No complex formulas are necessary. There is no need for arcane scriptural algorithms or complicated step-by-step tactics. You don't have to learn a special vocabulary or alphabet-soup acronyms. As wonderful and life-changing as it is, the wisdom of God—in Scripture and in the secular world—is not rocket science.

A Book without an End

In a very real sense, this book won't end when you close its cover. When it comes to God's revelation, the "book of stewardship wisdom" is still being written. New scribes and editors are working on new language, new niches, new possibilities. Your congregation's actions will become part of the continuing journal of enacted stewardship.

God's wisdom grows daily. As you continue to seek that wisdom, you will learn about stewardship from educators, theologians, anthropologists, farmers, archaeologists, historians, tradespersons, artisans, and poets. In fields of study that we've seen in this book, new discoveries will bloom everywhere. More insistent scholarship and more approachable translations will freshen and deepen scriptural wisdom. New theories will be proposed and proven; new sciences will be crafted; new truths will be proclaimed. God's Spirit will always move on the face of the waters that could characterize the continuing chaos of contemporary life. More areas of God's revelation still await your exploration and understanding.

It stands to reason, then, that God has led you to this moment in your life of stewardship. It's time you started your stewardshifting. As soon as you close this book, you're ready to. . . .

Acknowledgments

As I have worked on this book, I have been aware of how strongly supported I am, how well-advised and invisibly motivated by the people around me. The list that follows is not exhaustive, nor do my short descriptions of these writing-collaborators express enough of my gratitude. To all who I note here—and those whose contributions did not break through the limitations of my memory—my deepest thanks!

Chris Sitze: I begin my recognition where the book began—with my spouse and partner in so many of these ventures. For the constancy of your listening, your willingness to absorb my fulminations, and your encouragement to keep at this subject.

Beth Gaede: For the years you have accompanied me in this book's development, from its first hesitant stages through the proposal writing, and for being an insistent first-draft reader and gosh-darn positive cheerleader.

Richard Bass: For your churchmanship, embodied in constant reassurances about coming ecclesiastical matters. You told me that this book was worth working on; your editorial craft has helped me remain focused on a positive approach.

Liz Hunter: For giving me the place to expand my thinking about simplicity into an ongoing blog, and for your continuingly appreciative chuckles at my writing style.

The soul sisters and brothers of A WORKING GROUP (Faith Lutheran Church, Glen Ellyn, IL): For regularly opening windows into the refreshing secular world in which most Christians live and work.

Former stewardship colleagues Nancy Snell, Laurel Hensel, Michael Meyer, and Steve Rusk: For the years we shared, radically reforming stewardship and hoping that Betty Nyhus's legacy would grow in us and in those who followed us.

Sally Simmel: For your partnership in ideals that we hoped would wring renewal out of tired ecclesiology, and for inspiring by your quiet example what's truly important about the mission of the church.

Jim Honig: For your on-the-ground and over-the-horizon pastoring of a congregation that exemplifies so many of the hopes I have for the church.

Steve Rusk: For your expert, no-nonsense connections to the worlds of nonprofit fund-raising and philanthropy.

Sue Engh: For your wide-ranging insights into the promise of church-based community organizing—its theology, practice, and connections to stewardship.

Brian Angelo Scavone: For your wisdom as a practicing naturalist who inspires awe and wonder in all who meet you.

Rob Granner: For your witness as a financial planner who can integrate faith and values into numbers that make sense.

Phyllis Anderson: For your energetic entrepreneurship in helping congregations exert economic power where it can make a difference.

John Talmadge: For your honest self-examinations as a naturalist, teacher, and author who exults in God's created world, creating word pictures that honor what's truly wild.

Tom Wendorf: For allowing me to summarize your creation of an economic development engine that works justice in the right places.

To the content reviewers who checked my ideas and sources with objective clarity and emotional honesty: Cindy Crosby, Gary Moore, Mike Bennethum, Mark Vincent, Lynn Miller, Phyllis Anderson, and Julie Frakes.

To all the friends, colleagues, fellow conspirators, and raconteurs who have waited for me to come out of book writing's relational cave: Thanks! Now we can get back to our rabble-rousing, plot-hatching, and joyful partnerships.

Bibliography

Acs, Zoltan J. *Why Philanthropy Matters: How the Wealthy Give, and What It Means for Our Economic Well-Being.* Princeton, NJ: Princeton University Press, 2013.

Anderson, Gary A. *Charity: The Place of the Poor in the Biblical Tradition.* New Haven, CT: Yale University Press, 2013.

Anderson, Phyllis, personal interview, January 12, 2015.

Beckwith, Robert T. "Sacrifice in the World of the New Testament"." In *Sacrifice in the Bible*, ed. Roger T. Beckwith and Martin J. Selman. Grand Rapids: Baker Book House, 1995, 105–10.

Berger, Jonah. *Contagious: Why Things Catch On.* New York: Simon & Schuster, 2013.

Betz, Hans Dieter. *2 Corinthians 8 and 9: A Commentary on Two Administrative Letters of the Apostle Paul.* Philadelphia: Fortress Press, 1985.

Block, Peter. *Community: The Structure of Belonging.* San Francisco: Berrett-Koehler, 2009.

———. *Stewardship: Choosing Service Over Self-Interest.* San Francisco: Berrett-Koehler, 1993.

Bloom, Paul. "The War on Reason," *The Atlantic,* March 2014, 64–70.

Bloom, Peter. *How Pleasure Works: The New Science of Why We Like What We Like.* New York: W.W. Norton, 2010.

Bolt, Peter. *Jesus' Defeat of Death: Persuading Mark's Early Readers.* Cambridge: Cambridge University Press, 2003.

Buchman, A. S., P. A. Boyle, and L. Yu, et al. "Total Daily Physical Activity and the Risk of AD and Cognitive Decline in Older Adults," *Neurology* 78, no. 17 (April 24, 2012): 1323–29.

Clapp, Rodney. "Why the Devil Takes VISA." *Christianity Today,* October 7, 1996, 4–6.

Clinton, Bill *Giving: How Each of Us Can Change the World.* New York: Alfred A. Knopf, 2007.

Conniff, Richard. "Super Dirt." *Scientific American,* September 2013, 76–79.

Danckert, James. "Descent of the Doldrums." *Scientific American Mind,* July/August 2014, 54–59.

Dau, William H. T., ed. *Four Hundred Years: Commemorative Essays on the Reformation of Dr. Martin Luther and Its Blessed Results.* St. Louis: Concordia, 1917.

Donahue, John R., SJ, and Daniel Harrington, SJ. *The Gospel of Mark.* Collegeville, MN: Liturgical Press, 2002.

Duhigg, Charles. *The Power of Habit: Why We Do What We Do in Life and Business.* New York: Random House, 2012.

Dutton, Kevin, "The Power to Persuade: How Masters of 'Supersuasion' Can Change Your Mind." *Scientific American Mind,* March/April 2010, 24–31.

Evangelical Lutheran Church in America, "Stewardshop Design: Developing a Case Statement," *www.elca.org,* n.d.

Elgin, Duane. *Voluntary Simplicity: Toward A Way of Life That Is Outwardly Simple, Inwardly Rich.* Rev. ed. New York: William Morrow, 1993.

Engh, Susan, personal interview, January 8, 2015.

Etshman, Todd. "Take Your Life Into Your Own Hands: Write Your Own Obit." *The Lutheran,* November 2014, 30–32.

Flaherty, Mary Ann Ford, and Richard L. Wood. *Faith and Public Life: Faith-Based Community Organizing and the Development of Congregations.* Syosset, NY: Interfaith Funders, 2004.

Fleming, Stephen M. "The Power of Reflection." *Scientific American Mind,* September/October 2014, 31–37.

Fritschel, Ann L. and Steve Oelschlager, Steve. "Financial Stewardship." *The Lutheran,* August 2014, 14–15.

Gillman, John. *Possessions and the Life of Faith: A Reading of Luke-Acts.* Collegeville, MN: Liturgical Press, 1991.

Glaser, Gabriell. "The False Gospel of Alcoholics Anonymous." *The Atlantic,* April 2015, 50–60.

Gloer, W. Hulitt. *Smyth & Helwys Bible Commentary: 1 & 2 Timothy-Titus.* Macon, GA: Smyth & Helwys, 2010.

Goodman, Cindy Krische. "Stress-Busting Tactic Catches on at Work as Firms Cite Results." *Chicago Tribune,* February 10, 2014, business section, 4–5.

Granner, Rob, personal interview, January 6, 2015.

Green, Harry. "Tracks and Shadows: Field Biology as Art." Lecture as part of 2014 Parsons Memorial Lodge Summer Series, Tuolumne Meadows, Yosemite National Park, July 26, 2014.

Haanen, Jeff, and Chris Horst. "The Work of Their Hands." *Christianity Today,* July/August 2014, 66–71.

Hagberg, Janet O., and Robert Guelich. *The Critical Journey: Stages in the Life of Faith.* 2nd ed. Salem, WI: Sheffield, 2005.

Hall, Stephen S. *Wisdom: From Philosophy to Neuroscience.* New York: Vintage Books, 2010.

Hartman, Tova, and Charlie Buckholtz. *Are You Not a Man of God?: Devotion, Betrayal, and Social Criticism in Jewish Tradition.* New York: Oxford University Press, 2014.

Hawken, Paul. *Blessed Unrest: How the Largest Social Movement in History Is Restoring Grace, Justice and Beauty to the World.* New York: Penguin Books, 2007.

Heidler, Maria-Dorothea. "Honest Liars: How the Brain Leads Us to Believe False Truths." *Scientific American Mind,* March/April 2014, 41–44.

Herzog, William R. *Parables as Subversive Speech: Jesus as Pedagogue of the Oppressed.* Louisville, KY: Westminster/John Knox Press, 1994.

"Hoarding Disorder," Mayo Clinic, accessed September 2, 2015, *http://www.mayoclinic.org/diseases-conditions/hoarding-disorder/basics/definition/con-20031337.*

Hoffman, Julian. *The Small Heart of Things.* Athens: University of Georgia Press, 2013.

Huffington, Arianna. *Thrive: The Third Metric to Redefining Success and Creating a Life of Well-being, Wisdom and Wonder.* New York: Harmony Books, 2014.

Jabr, Ferris. "Speak for Yourself." *Scientific American Mind,* January/February 2014, 46–51.

Jaffe, Chuck. *Getting Started in Finding a Financial Advisor.* Hoboken, NJ: John Wiley & Sons, 2010.

Jensen, Derrick. "Beyond Hope." In *The Future of Nature: Writing on a Human Ecology from* Orion *Magazine,* ed. Barry Lopez. Minneapolis: Milkweed Editions, 2007, 28–29.

Jha, Amishi P. "Being in the Now." *Scientific American Mind,* March/April 2013, 26–33.

Johnson, George. *Courage to Think Differently.* Laguna Hills, CA: Self-published, 2013.

Johnson, Robert K. "Meeting God at the Movies." *Christian Century* 131, no. 17 (August 20, 2014), 24–27.

Johnson, Steve. *Where Good Ideas Come From: The Natural History of Innovation.* New York: Riverhead Books, 2010.

Kasser, Tim, and Allen D. Kanner, eds. *Psychology and Consumer Culture: The Struggle for a Good Life in a Materialistic World.* Washington, DC: American Psychological Association, 2004.

Keener, Craig S. *1–2 Corinthians.* New York: Cambridge University Press, 2005.

Kielhofner, Gary, ed. *A Model of Human Occupation: Theory and Application.* 1st ed. Baltimore: Williams & Wilkins, 1985.

King, Brian. "Developing Positive Emotional Habit." Presentation at Institute for Brain Potential Seminar, Glen Ellyn, IL, May 17, 2013.

Kluger, Jeffrey, "Fear Factor," *TIME Magazine,* October 20, 2014, 30–35.

———. "The Art of Living," *TIME Magazine,* September 13, 2013, 44–50.

————. *Simplexity: Why Simple Things Become Complex (and How Complex Things Can Be Made Simple).* New York: Hyperion, 2008.

Köstenberger, Andreas J., and David A. Croteau. *Reconstructing a Biblical Model for Giving: A Discussion of Relevant Systematic Issues and New Testament Principles.* Wake Forest, NC: Southeastern Baptist Theological Seminary, web-published paper, 2006.

————. *"Will a Man Rob God?" (Malachi 3:8): A Study of Tithing in the Old and New Testaments.* Wake Forest, NC: Southeastern Baptist Theological Seminary, web-published paper, ca. 2006.

Krakovsky, Marina. "Generosity Is Its Own Reward." *Scientific American Mind,* September/October 2013, 9.

Kretzmann, John. "Building Community Partnerships." Presentation at the Wheat Ridge Ministries Young Adults Convening, Sheboygan, WI, June 7, 2014.

Lamott, Anne. *Help, Thanks, Wow: The Three Essential Prayers.* New York: Riverhead Books, 2012.

Lanchester, John. "Money Talks." *The New Yorker,* August 4, 2014, 30–33.

Leiter, Michael P., and Christina Maslach. "Conquering Burnout." *Scientific American Mind,* January/February 2015, 30–35.

Lieberman, Matthew D. *Social: Why Our Brains Are Wired to Connect.* New York: Crown Publishers, 2013.

Lohfink, Gerhard. *Jesus of Nazareth: What He Wanted, Who He Was.* Collegeville, MN: Liturgical Press, 2012.

Mann, Charles C. "How to Talk About Climate Change So People Will Listen." *The Atlantic Monthly,* September 2014, 86–99 .

Martin, Felix. *Money: The Unauthorized Biography.* New York, Alfred A. Knopf, 2014.

Mayer, John. "Thinking About Tomorrow." *Scientific American Mind,* March/April 2014, 34–39.

McKnight, John, and Peter Block. *The Abundant Community: Awakening the Power of Families and Neighborhoods.* San Francisco: Berrett-Koehler, 2010.

Minor, Mitzi. *The Spirituality of Mark: Responding to God.* Louisville: Westminster John Knox Press, 1996.

Montague, George T., S. M. *First Corinthians.* Grand Rapids, MI: Baker Academic, 2011.

Morgan, Timothy C. "It Takes More Than a Coffee Shop." *Christianity Today,* July/August 2014, 52–55.

Morozov, Evgeny. *To Save Everything, Click Here: The Folly of Technological Solutionism.* New York: Public Affairs Books, 2013.

Nahmias, Eddy. "Why We Have Free Will." *Scientific American,* January 2015 , 77–79.

"Natural Decline." Editorial. *Nature: International Journal of Science* April 3, 2014, 7–8.

Neff, David. "Divine Economics 101." *Christianity Today*, July/August 2014.

Newberg, Andres, Eugene d'Aquili, and Vince Rause. *Why God Won't Go Away: Brain Science & the Biology of Belief.* New York: Ballantine Books, 2001.

Niebuhr, H. Richard. *The Meaning of Revelation.* New York: Macmillan, 1941.

Oakes, Pete., *Reading Romans in Pompeii: Paul's Letter at Ground Level.* Minneapolis: Fortress Press, 2009.

O'Brien, Peter T. *The Letter to the Ephesians.* Grand Rapids, MI: William B. Eerdmans, 1999.

O'Toole, Robert, S.J. *Reading Ecclesiastes: Old Testament Exegesis and Hermeneutical Theory.* Rome: Editrice Pontificio Instituto Biblico, 1988.

Paxton, Matt, with Phaedra Hise. *The Secret Lives of Hoarders: True Stories of Tackling Extreme Clutter.* New York: Penguin, 2011.

Peterson, Gregory. *Minding God: Theology and the Cognitive Sciences.* Minneapolis: Fortress Press, 2003.

Plymale, Steven F. *The Prayer Texts of Luke-Acts.* New York: Peter Lang, 1991.

Pope Francis. *Laudato Si: On Care for Our Common Home.* Rome: Libreria Editrice Vaticana, 2015.

Powell, Mark Allan. *Giving to God: The Bible's Good News About Living a Generous Life.* Grand Rapids, MI: William B. Eerdmans, 2006.

"Pulpit Disappointment: Interview with J. R. Riggs." *Christianity Today,* July/August 2014, 87.

Pyle, Robert Michael. "The Rise and Fall of Natural History." In Lopez, *Future of Nature,* 243.

Ramachandran, V. S. *The Tell-Tale Brain: A Neuroscientist's Quest for What Makes Us Human.* New York: W. W. Norton, 2011.

Ratey, John. Presentation at Glenbard East High School, Lombard, IL April 17, 2012.

———. *Spark: The Revolutionary New Science of Exercise and the Brain.* New York: Little, Brown, 2008.

———. *The User's Guide to the Brain: Perception, Attention and the Four Theaters of the Brain.* New York: Vintage Books, 2002.

Rauch, Jonathan. "The Great Recession." *The Atlantic* July/August 2014, 19–20.

———. "The Real Roots of Midlife Crisis." *The Atlantic,* December 2014, 88–95.

Raymo, Chet. *When God Is Gone, Everything Is Holy: The Making of a Religious Naturalist.* Notre Dame, IN: Sorin Books, 2008.

Reumann, John. *Stewardship and the Economy of God.* Grand Rapids, MI: Eerdmans, 1992.

Roberts, James A. *Shiny Objects: Why We Spend Money We Don't Have in Search of Happiness We Can't Buy.* New York: HarperCollins, 2011.

Rodriguez, Tori. "How to Let Go of Materialism." *Scientific American*, July 2014, 17.

Ross, Justin, lead researcher. "New Research Proves the Business Case for Product Philanthropy." News bulletin from the School of Public and Environmental Affairs, Indiana University, Bloomington, Indiana, January 24, 2012.

Rusk, Steven, personal interview, October 26, 2011.

Salstrand, George A. E. *The Story of Stewardship in the United States in America.* Grand Rapids, MI: Baker Book House, 1956.

Scavone, Brian, personal interview, July 11, 2014.

Schulte, Brigid. *Overwhelmed: Work, Love and Play When No One Has the Time.* New York: Farrar, Straus and Giroux, 2014.

Selman, Martin J. "Sacrifice for Christians Today." In Beckwith and Selman, *Sacrifice in the Bible*, 157–69.

Sharot, Tali. *The Optimism Bias: A Tour of the Irrationally Positive Brain.* New York: Pantheon Books, 2011.

Sher, George. "Morality and Blame." Lecture at Wheaton College, Wheaton, IL, March 19, 2014.

Sitze, Bob, "Dancing with the Sisyphean Imperative: Clergy Well-Being with the Brain in Mind." Paper presented at "Flourishing in Pastoral Ministry" Conference, Indiana Wesleyan University, Marion, IN, October 11, 2013.

———. "Dancing with the Sisyphean Imperative: Propositions and Criteria for Sustainable Ecclesiologies." *Congregations* Issue 2 (2013).

———. *It's NOT Too Late: A Field Guide to Hope.* Herndon, VA: Alban Institute, 2010, 4–7.

Solis, Michele. "A Lifeline for Addicts." *Scientific American Mind,* March/April 2013, 40–44.

Stern, Kenneth. *With Charity for All: Why Charities Fail and a Better Way to Give.* New York: Doubleday, 2013.

Stevens, Marty. "Stewardship: Biblical Perspective," *The Lutheran Magazine,* September 2014, 14–15.

Strong, James. *Strong's Concordance of the Bible,* Nashville, TN: Thomas Nelson, 1990.

Sweet, Leonard. "Freely You Have Received, Freely Give: Toward a Post-Tithing, Post-Stewardship, Postmodern Theology of Receiving." *http://www.leonardsweet.com.*

Tallmadge, John. *Meeting the Tree of Life: A Teacher's Path.* Salt Lake City: University of Utah Press, 1997.

————. Personal interviews, July 15–18, 2013.

Taylor, Shelley B. *The Tending Instinct: How Nurturing Is Essential to Who We Are and How We Live.* New York: Times Books, 2002.

Thrivent Magazine, "Time, Talent & Treasure," Summer 2014, 10–11.

Twist, Lynne. *The Soul of Money: Reclaiming the Wealth of Our Inner Resources.* New York: W. W. Norton, 2003.

Verhey, Allen, and Jospeh S. Harvard. *Ephesians.* Louisville: Westminster John Knox Press, 2011.

Ward, David. "The Missing Ingredient in Clergy Wellness." Workshop presentation at "Flourishing in Pastoral Ministry" Conference, Indiana Wesleyan University, Marion, IN, October 11, 2013.

Weidmann, Frederick. *Philippians, First and Second Thessalonians and Philemon.* Louisville: Westminster John Knox Press, 2013.

Wengert, Timothy J. *A Contemporary Translation of Luther's Small Catechism: Study Edition.* Minneapolis: Augsburg Fortress, 1994.

Wenham, Gordon J. "The Theology of Old Testament Sacrifice." In Beckwith and Selman, *Sacrifice in the Bible,* 75–85.

Wheatley, Margaret. *Finding Our Way: Leadership in Uncertain Times.* San Francisco: Berrett-Koehler, 2005.

Whitehead, Evelyn Eaton and James. *Seasons of Strength: New Visions of Adult Christian Maturing.* Winona, MN: Saint Mary's Press, 1995.

Wilson, Edward O. *The Creation: An Appeal to Save Life on Earth.* New York: W. W. Norton, 2006.

Wisdom Research: The University of Chicago, *www.wisdomresearch.org.*

Worthington, Everett. "Positive Psychology." Keynote presentation at "Flourishing in Pastoral Ministry" Conference, Indiana Wesleyan University, Marion, IN, October 12, 2013.

Yager, Sarah. "Your Gullible Brain: How Our Senses Influence Our Thoughts." *The Atlantic Monthly,* May 2014, 16.

Yoder, Christine Roy. *Proverbs.* Nashville: Abingdon Press, 2009.

Zielin, Lara. "In Excess: Clutter, Hoarding, and Consumption in the Modern World." *LSA Magazine,* Spring 2010, 26–31 (Ann Arbor, MI: College of Literature, Science and the Arts, University of Michigan).